# *Good Morning, All:*

## *Musings of a Nonagenarian*

By

**Dr. Juanita Patience Moss**

**Heritage Books**
**2025**

**HERITAGE BOOKS**
*AN IMPRINT OF HERITAGE BOOKS, INC.*

**Books, CDs, and more—Worldwide**

For our listing of thousands of titles see our website
at
www.HeritageBooks.com

Published 2025 by
HERITAGE BOOKS, INC.
Publishing Division
5810 Ruatan Street
Berwyn Heights, MD 20740

Copyright © 2025 Juanita Patience Moss

Heritage Books by the author:
*Anthracite Coal Art of Charles Edgar Patience*
*Battle of Plymouth, North Carolina (April 17–20, 1864): The Last Confederate Victory*
*Created to Be Free: A Historical Novel about One American Family*
*Deeply Rooted in North Carolina: Two Runaway Slave Brothers Forever Separated After Joining the Union Army*
*The Forgotten Black Soldiers in White Regiments During the Civil War, Revised Edition*
*The Forgotten Black Soldiers in White Regiments During the Civil War, Volume II*
*Good Morning, All: Musings of a Nonagenarian*
*Tell Me Why Dear Bennett: Memoirs of Bennett College Belles, Volumes I-III*

*Edited by: Dr. Ruth L. Baskerville*
*www.wwexcellence.org*

*Cover Design by: Dr. Juanita Patience Moss*

All rights reserved. No part of this book may be reproduced or transmitted in any form or by any means, electronic or mechanical, including photocopying, recording or by any information storage and retrieval system without written permission from the author, except for the inclusion of brief quotations in a review.

International Standard Book Number
Paperbound: 978-0-7884-4966-6

# Dedication

This book is dedicated to all who have encouraged me to write it:
Friends and Family Members.

I offer special acknowledgements to publicist Reba Burruss Barnes; editor Dr. Ruth Baskerville; assistant Ashlyn Mejer; publisher Craig Scott; daughter Brenda Moss Green, J.D.; and friend Joan Bonfonti Shannon.

I want to thank all of you 303 persons who have read my musings for the past two and a half years. Hopefully, they have been a blessing. May you be so inspired to write your own memoirs.

### Books by Dr. Juanita Patience Moss

*Created to Be Free*

*Battle of Plymouth: April 17-20, 1964: The Last Confederate Victory*

*Forgotten Black Soldiers Who Served in White Regiments, Volumes I & 2*

*Anthracite Coal Art by Charles Edgar Patience*

*Tell Me Why Dear Bennett Volumes I, II, III*

*Deeply Rooted in N.C.*

# TABLE OF CONTENTS

| | |
|---|---|
| Foreword | vii |
| Introduction | xi |
| Good Morning, All | 1 |
| 2022 Musings | 3 |
|     Christmases Past | 7 |
| 2023 Musings | 11 |
| Response- A Merry Christmas Eve | 48 |
| 2024 Musings | 51 |
| Response from a Cousin | 58 |
| Response About Handwriting | 60 |
| Crows in Minnesota | 60 |
| 2025 Musings | 175 |
| Post Script | 177 |

# ILLUSTRATIONS

| | |
|---|---|
| Juanita Bernice Patience Moss at 6 Months of Age | viii |
| Eric, Juanita, Brenda, and Edward Moss | viii |
| Juanita Moss at home | ix |
| Juanita and Reba at book signing | ix |
| Juanita Bernice Patience at 93 Years of Age | 1 |
| Lillian Mariah Patience Cuff at 85 Years of Age | 9 |
| Patience Clan | 23 |
| Sgt. Harold Lee Patience Sr. During World War II | 36 |
| Juanita Patience Moss Receiving Honorary Doctorate | 42 |
| Smithsonian Display | 64 |
| Charles Edgar Patience Carving the George Washington Bust | 76 |
| Plaques | |
|     Mother Moss | 100 |
|     Boss Moss | 101 |
| Anthracite Coal Heart | 102 |
| Mother Cora Richley Johnson | 105 |
| Sgt. Alice Patterson WAC During World War II | 111 |
| Crowder Patience Civil War Soldier | 112 |
| Actor Danny Glover and Juanita Moss at Bennett College | 126 |

# FOREWORD

For the last two and a half years I have been sending daily *"Good morning"* messages to friends and family members. The following is the explanation for why I began. A *Bennett College* sister called me one morning to ask if I had heard from a mutual friend of ours whom she had been trying to contact for several days. I had not and suggested she contact the manager where our friend lived. Several days later I got the bad news that she had been found dead in her bed. She was living alone. Shocked, I asked my Bennett sister who lived alone, too, "Who knows you are awake in the morning?" She replied, *"No one."* "Well, someone should," I said.

So, I told her that we would send a message to each other every morning. *"Up"* would be all that was needed. I then told my daughter who lives in Connecticut what I was doing, and I added her name to my list. Then I added her two sons and my son in California and his daughter. When I told some friends that I was e-mailing daily messages, they wanted to be on my list, which has now grown to 303!

The list consists of friends and family members who are males and females; Black, White, Hispanic; Catholic. Protestant, Jewish, and Jehovah Witness; very young, middle-aged and very old; from the North, middle-America, South, and West; goddaughters; Bennett College sisters; *Delta Sigma Theta, Inc.* Sorors; church members; former work colleagues; former students; friends; neighbors; a daughter; a son; grandchildren; a sister; nieces; great nieces; a nephew; a great nephew; cousins of different generations; sisters-in-law; a bridesmaid; a flower-girl; and *St. Mark's United Methodist Church* choir members from New Jersey. Some of you are in more than one category and each one is beloved. I hope I did not miss anyone. If so, please forgive.

My varied musings have covered a myriad of topics because I have many interests. When I go to bed at night, I don't necessarily know what I am going to write about the next morning, except to let people know that I am "up and at it" for one more blessed day. I check my computer first to see if there is any mention of why that day may be a special one. Then I check the *Washington Post* to see if there is some uplifting news. I will not send any that is not.

If I cannot find any good news to muse over, I can always find something to write about from my 93 years of life. So much has changed in this world since I was a child. I am grateful for my mind being sharp enough to be able to share much with many younger folks, including telephone party lines and rumble seats that were all the rage in my father's generation in the 1930s.

My daughter has suggested that I publish what I have written since I began in March 2022 because some people may want to read all of my trips down Memory Lane. This book is not an autobiography. It simply includes many thoughts about my life in the past and present. My intention is to share memories of a time not possibly imagined by the generations following me, of which there are four in 2025. I learned much about my ancestors from my Great Aunt Lillian three generations before me. I know she would want me to share our family history with others younger than myself. Now due to *ancestry.com* and *23and Me* I have discovered a fifth generation.

How to read my book is up to you. Perhaps, you'll read one or several musings a day, not paying attention to the date or the length, which can vary. Just read for pleasure. On the "Notes" pages you might want to jot down a date or a particular topic such as a song or a poem for a future remembrance.

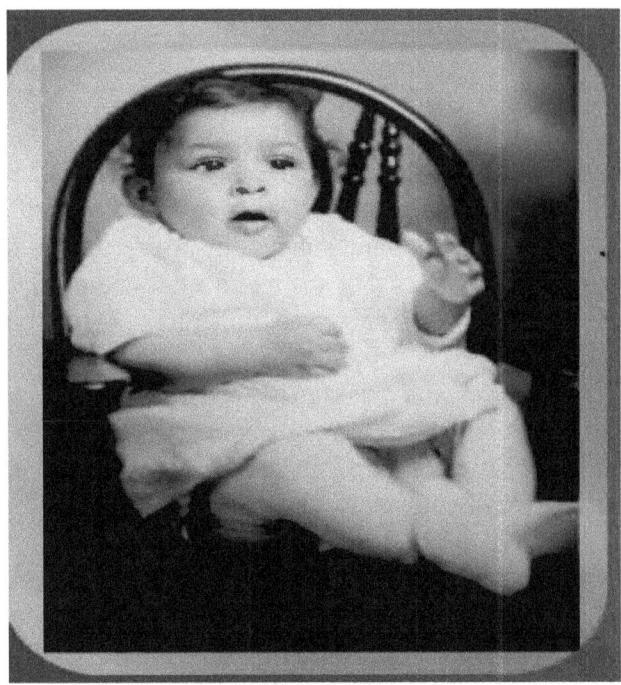

**Juanita Bernice Patience Moss at Six Months of Age saying "Hi!" to All**

**Eric, Juanita, Brenda, and Edward Moss**

# INTRODUCTION

### From a Friend, Joan Bonfanti Shannon
### (A Former West Pittstonian)

*A few weeks ago, I borrowed an audio book from the library so my husband and I could listen as we traveled. It began by describing an old woman, bent over, walking slowly as she mopped the floor. On and on, setting her up as decrepit.*

*It turned out that she was 70 -- my age! Wait, what?? "Oh, come ON," I yelled more than once as I listened. I learned that the author set it up so that there was an "awakening" in her later on and a purpose for exaggerating her description. But I say again, "Come ON!" I think I'm young. I feel young most of the time. I remember asking my mom on her 80th birthday how it felt to be 80. She said, "I feel like I'm perpetually 16 inside!"*

*Thinking of this reminded me of how you have been a wonderful example to me. You seem ageless, and I think of you as my example for how to live life fully. There are people my age who I wish could know about you when I see them giving up, aging mentally, and letting themselves go physically. I know it takes some luck to get older, and some people aren't fortunate. Some develop serious illnesses and disabilities, but others just give up.*

*So, I love to read your emails every morning and to see you curious about the world, informed, reaching out to others, staying active, planting your garden, treating yourself to lunches with friends, and getting manicures. You're strong in faith, always praying for others and asking for others' prayers. Well, I just want to tell you I want to be like you when I grow up.* 😁

*Thank you for being my role model in so many ways, Dr J.*

*May God bless you.* 💕

*Dr. Juanita Moss*

PS. The book was *Remarkably Bright Creatures* by Shelby Van Pelt.

# GOOD MORNING, ALL

## The Musings of a Nonagenarian

Griot Juanita Bernice Patience Moss at 93 Years Old

**March 1, 2022**

Good morning, Dear Friend. Here I am "up and at it" again. I hope you are, too. Have a wonderful day.

**March 27, 2022**

Good day, all 10 friends and family members on my musing list. "*It's a beautiful day in the neighborhood,*" as I recall Mr. Rogers' greeting while attired in his signature cardigan sweater that he wore on his television show for children that ran from 1968 to 2001.

**September 7, 2022**

Good day, all 12. I remember that in my youth in West Pittston, Pennsylvania, I was concerned about what I was going to wear on the first day back to school. I had to have something brand new, of course. Last year's school shoes would become this year's play shoes. That is, unless my feet had grown too big for them. I always wore comfortable brown and white saddle shoes to grade and high school, and even to college. Other girls wore penny loafers, but they were uncomfortable on my feet. Why were they called "penny loafers?" Because there was a little insert on the top of the shoe where a shiny, bright copper penny might be placed.

Our schoolteachers had to report on the Wednesday following Labor Day, but we students didn't report until Thursday. My other concern was which homeroom I would be in, since it changed every year. What I remember is that the high school homerooms were assigned by gender. Why I was so concerned is that I played intramural basketball. Imagine that! Me on the court in my green gym suit!

It was called "girls' basketball" or "half-court" back in the day because we played by the following rules: six players on a team consisting of three guards who did not shoot and three forwards who did. No one could ever cross the center line. Since we were considered too fragile to play "boys' basketball," some of us girls would go after school to the YMCA in Pittston across the Susquehanna River where we could run up and down the court as we pleased.

Consider the gender differences in "Ys" in the late 1940s. YMCAs were for men's activities and YWCAs for women's. Pittston had the former, but not the latter, whereas Wilkes-Barre, located ten miles away, had both. Also, there were two YMCAs there, one for White men and one for Black men. The YWCA there was also segregated.

In Montclair, New Jersey, where my two children were reared, there were two YMCAs, too, both racially segregated until the late 60s. There was one YWCA that was only for Black women who needed safe housing.

Back to my high school. By the 10th grade, we girls knew who the best basketball players were. Juanita Patience was one of the best guards. My friends and I hoped that one year we would all be in the same homeroom and become champions, but we never were. There was a girl in the class below ours who was tall, skinny and very fast. The competition was between grade levels, so, my homeroom always wanted to beat hers, but I don't remember if we ever did. It was just a lot of after-school fun in the gym.

I played on the *Wilkes College* basketball team during my freshman year in 1950, still with girls' "half-court" rules, which did not change until 1971, long past my college ball playing days.

**October 20, 2022**

Good day, all 18 from chilly Connecticut. The ride north was quite beautiful yesterday. The leaf coloration is at its peak here. The gold, amber and rust shades are very bright. Not so much red yet. Tomorrow, my daughter and I will be taking a train down to NYC to meet my son, his wife and their daughter, who are visiting from California.

I plan to consume two of my favorite foods while in the "Big Apple." One will be a corned beef sandwich on rye, and the other will be lox and bagels. Yummy!

**October 27, 2022**

Good day, all 19. I'm home and "back in the saddle again." I had a lovely time in New York yesterday. The scenery was spectacular in both Connecticut and N.Y. I was praising God for His creativity, while thinking about my annual photosynthesis lesson that I taught for 33 years at *Bloomfield High School* when my captive students learned the answer to this question: *"Why do leaves turn color in the fall?"*

I wonder if any of them remember collecting leaves for my class. I also wonder if any of my students on this musing list remember the answer to my question, and if they do not, they would like to know the answer because they know I'd love to remind them. Yes, I am aware that everyone is not interested in everything that I am, but just in case you might be.

**October 31, 2022**

**Happy Halloween**, all 20. I'm sure you have some very happy memories of "trick or treating" from your youth.

Mine differed from my children's, who dressed up and then expected neighbors to fill their bags with candy. Same goes for today, but back in my day, we school children were taught poems to recite and songs to sing when we rang bells or knocked on doors. We had to perform, or no treat. Imagine that! We also wore our Halloween costumes throughout the school day. I think during my daughter's era they were still allowed, but by the time my son came along eight years later, I believe they had stopped. Remembering this little ditty from my childhood:

*"Oh, out in my garden some pumpkins I found.*
*They were big, yellow pumpkins that lay on the ground, ....."*

For you who answered my query, the reason leaves turn color is that green chlorophyll is no longer being manufactured by photosynthesis due to less sun and cooler temperatures. And so, whatever other color (red, orange, or yellow) that has been in the leaves all the while will show. The Gingko, tulip tree, and Norway maple will always be bright yellow. Red maples and red oaks will always be red. Each year the same. It's a wonder! It's a sign of God's faithfulness.

**November 1, 2022**

Good day, all 20. Today is my 70th wedding anniversary. It was a beautiful Fall Day in Pennsylvania in 1952. I was only 20 and Ed, a mature 25. Thanks, my Dear Husband, for all the wonderful memories we made together.

**November 2, 2022**

Good day, all 20. Seventy years ago today, Ed and I were honeymooning in New York City. It was my first time in the "Big Apple," and my first time attending a Broadway play, which was *Guys and Dolls*. Two second row seats were given to us for a wedding present. We had to stay at the famed *Hotel Theresa* in Harlem because Blacks could not stay in any of the Manhattan hotels in 1952. It would be some years later when the *Dixie Hotel* opened to us near Broadway.

Election Day 1952 was on the Tuesday after our wedding. Gen. Dwight D. Eisenhower became President of the U.S. Since I was only 20 years old, I could not vote because the voting age at that time was 21. I would have voted Republican because my father was one whose father had been one, and also because Abraham Lincoln had been one. As you know, he freed our ancestors from slavery in 1863, even though not in all states such as Maryland, Delaware,

Missouri, and Kansas had remained in the Union. Lincoln did not want to lose them. Many Black homes had his photo hanging in a prominent spot. We did when I was very young.

Interestingly, my father had to go to the Luzerne County Courthouse with Ed and me to sign me away to get married because I was not yet 21, the marrying age in 1952.

Lots of things have changed since then. For instance, we had radios but no televisions yet in our homes. We got our first one in 1955. Jackie Gleason on Saturday nights was popular. Ed Sullivan was on Sunday evenings and "Tennessee" Ernie Ford was at noon on weekdays. Television-watching began as a family thing, with only three stations that had to be changed manually by kids who watched with their parents. No such thing as a remote!

**November 5, 2022**

Good morning, all 20. 'Tis the first Saturday of *noviembre* 2022. We will rejoice and be glad in it. Looks like a beautiful fall day again in Virginia. Don't forget to turn your clock back tonight since Daylight Savings Time will cease. Ugh! I'll be physically and mentally off for at least three days. I hate the change.

**November 6, 2022**

Good morning, all 20. I'm "up and at it" early on this dreary rainy morning. I'm trying not to think about having gained an hour overnight. What will that mean to my body today? Since I do not have to go anywhere, I will just nap as need be.

**November 8, 2022**

Good morning, all 20. I rose early today to do my duty to my country. That is, to **VOTE!** Our democracy is in peril. History books tell us that good has always battled evil in every place where humans have existed. The *Bible* tells us the story of Cain, who killed his brother Abel because he was jealous of him. I think that's why we love movies so much, albeit much is propaganda. We all like a happy ending where the good folks ride off into the sunset. Not necessarily so in real life. I've lived through too many wars. Now every other country's war is on our televisions and in our newspapers, too. We cannot avoid seeing the continuous fight between good and evil on our planet.

Our country's Constitution was created to keep despots from taking over. Seemed to have worked well in the past. Now democracy in the USA is in real peril. While reciting *The Lord's Prayer,* we plead to Our Father, *"Thy will be done on earth as it is in heaven."* As I vote this morning, that prayer will be in my mind.

**November 9, 2022**

Good morning, all 20. We remember our favorite veterans on this **Veterans Day**. Included is my husband, Edward Irving Moss, whom I did not know when he joined the Army at age 18 in 1946 right after graduating from high school. He was a man; I was still a kid. I knew his younger sister, though. She adored her brother, "Buddy." It was a good decision to join the Army during peacetime because he was trained to be a laboratory technician, which became his life's employment. A banner with his photo is hanging on a pole in Wilkes-Barre, Pennsylvania, his hometown. The city honored many veterans in a similar manner. Ed's name was submitted by his youngest sister, and Ed is on this list.

**November 14, 2022**

Good morning, all 20. The garbage trucks and the loud blowers of the lawn company woke me before I was ready to rise. Oh, well. Such is life in 2022. In the olden days people in my hometown disposed of their garbage daily by burning it outside in an incinerator of some sort. They also burned piles of fallen dead leaves along street curbs in the fall.

Disallowing those activities has long been the law because it was considered dangerous to people who could get burned, especially playful children, and to people who were allergic to the chemicals found in dead leaves. In Wilkes-Barre lived a young boy whose trousers caught fire when his father was burning a pile of leaves. The boy was burned badly. Fortunately, he lived but always walked with a limp.

**November 19, 2022**

Good morning, all 20. Have a lovely day, especially those of you getting ready to prepare your delicious Thanksgiving meal. It is interesting learning what foods different cultures prepare along with the requisite turkey. It is a day for serving their ethnic foods. My Italian friends serve pasta dishes, my Jewish friends a cheese noodle pudding, the Polish have pierogies, and Blacks sweet potatoes. I think cranberry jelly/sauce may be a universal dish now. I prefer the whole berry version. How about you?

Many Black families prepare what is typically known as "soul food" in our culture. The requisite collard greens and macaroni and cheese are placed on the table alongside other favorite dishes. For dessert, I prefer sweet potato pie to pumpkin pie. My grandson likes corn pudding and my son an oyster dressing. Dressing used to be called "stuffing," but no one stuffs any more due to the fear of salmonella from a turkey not roasted long enough.

**November 25, 2022**

Good morning, all 20. Going to purchase a Christmas wreath today so it will be the first one up in my neighborhood. When I moved here in 1993, I went all out with lights and red bows on my railings, in addition to a decorated Christmas tree in my front window. However, through the years without my Ed, I have done less and less. My decoration is now just a joyful wreath on my front door. I will keep it up for several dreary winter weeks. Should my daughter ever move back to Virginia, my house will be festive again, I know, with a live, decorated Christmas tree.

**November 29, 2022**

Good morning, all 20. 'Tis the 5th and last Tuesday of *noviembre* 2022. Here is another little ditty from my childhood:

*"Christmas is coming.*
*The goose is getting fat.*
*Please put a penny in the old man's hat....."*

The month is going to fly by quickly, and I will not be dreaming of a white Christmas. I don't like snow much anymore. Not like when I was a kid and prayed for it so my pals and I could go sledding for days at a time. After school we'd drag our sleds to a hill on the *Fox Hill Country Club* grounds for an hour or so and stay there until almost dusk. Had to be safely home before the streetlights came on, or else. Oh! It was such fun sledding down the hills with my friends.

**December 8, 2022**

Good morning, all 20. The rain has ceased here, and the sun is shining brightly. I will run errands at midday when the temperatures rise. Mother Hubbard's cupboard is getting low again. Good thing I don't have a doggie to feed a bone. Have a great day doing whatever you are doing.

A friend told me yesterday that she is bored with her life. I don't think I've ever said that about mine. I always have lots of things to do and if I'm not doing them, then I'm thinking about them. For instance, I've got piles of books all over my house just waiting to be read.

In my hometown, Monday was always laundry day. Friends I've asked said that it was not necessarily so in their neighborhoods. I grew up with Monday always being wash day and Tuesday ironing day. Every household was responsible for getting rid of its own garbage, and so people would burn it in their backyard. There was an unwritten rule that no one burned on Mondays, allowing women to hang their laundry outside without fear of it smelling like smoke. I thought that was the custom everywhere, but some of you on this list have told me otherwise.

**December 10, 2022**

Good morning, all 20. 'Tis time for me to bake *Toll House* cookies for my son in California and mail Christmas cards to folks who do not have e-mails. Yes, there are some of those in my life. Many of you will receive a Jacquie Lawson card from me nearer to Christmas.

When considering how much a stamp costs nowadays, I can e-mail many greetings for just the cost of maintaining the account which I love to use for other occasions, too. I know there are additional e-cards, but I love the animations on the English Jacquie Lawson ones.

In the olden days the cost of a stamp was 3 cents and that lasted for many years when I was growing up. Then the price went to 5 cents, then to 7 cents until now 58 cents! I don't want to put the Post Office out of business. However, to say "*Merry Christmas*" to all the people I am blessed to have in my life, I am very happy with the e-cards.

**December 12, 2022**

Good morning, all 20. Just in case you don't know this about my favorite Christmas shrub, the poinsettia, I am sending info to you today. What looks like red flowers are not flowers but red leaves. The flowers of the shrubs are yellow and quite small. Why do I call the poinsettia a shrub? Because its stems are woody. It's a perennial that blooms in winter and can grow to 15 feet high. I saw them growing quite tall in the Caribbean on the island of St. Lucia. Indigenous to Mexico and Central America, the poinsettia was named after the first U.S. Minister to Mexico, Joel Roberts Poinsett. He introduced the beautiful red plant to the U.S. in the 1820s.

**December 15, 2022**

Good morning, all 20. 'Tis the Ides of *deciembre*. Six more days 'til the winter solstice and ten more 'til Christmas day. My Jewish friends will begin Hanukkah on Sunday, and Kwanzaa for African Americans starts on the 26th.

Here you will find a Christmas letter I mailed to family and friends back in 2012. When my Ed was still living, I used to enjoy composing Christmas letters, and I still do enjoy receiving them. Since he passed away, I have not written anything. I pulled the following out of my autobiography folder today because I thought some of you might enjoy reading it.

## CHRISTMASES PAST

*One afternoon back in the 70s when I was driving with my Great Aunt Lillie and was about to make a left turn, I engaged the indicator and waited patiently for the red light to turn green. Aunt Lillie surprisingly remarked, "Oh! I think I hear a horse coming." Even though Aunt Lillie was in her 90s at the time, she was definitely in her right mind, so I didn't tune her out. Instead, I was wondering what it was that she was hearing.*

*I discovered it was the staccato of the indicator, which to her sounded like the hoof beats of horses in her past. Back in the 1890s my great grandfather would take his children for rides in a wagon driven by the team of horses that he worked on his employer's farm. So that clicking of the indicator brought back a memory to her that certainly I did not have.*

*Just like the remembrance of that sound was to Aunt Lillie, some of my family and friends share some similar memories with me from our Christmases past. But what do I share with my "seasoned family and friends" that my children and, certainly their children, do not? Many changes in lifestyles. The reason I enjoy Grandma Moses' paintings so much is that they preserve long-ago scenes when streets were empty, and kids could sled for hours down hilly slopes. Those scenes were from Aunt Lillie's childhood and probably my father's, too.*

*In later years Norman Rockwell painted everyday scenes from my early days in northeastern Pennsylvania where the same snow lasted for weeks, and we children loved it. When lakes and ponds were frozen solid, we would skate on them all Saturday afternoon, even though our toes felt like they were frozen. A welcome cup of hot chocolate would warm us from head to toe after we had walked home.*

*In my home Christmas decorations were not put up until the weekend before the holiday and taken down the day after New Year's Day. Bright red velvet poinsettias hung in each window of our house. Not until Christmas Eve would many parents decorate their live tree. Such was our custom. Of course, the children had to be cajoled to go to bed with, "Or else Santa Claus will not come to this house." In my hometown children wrote their letters to Santa and then threw them in the coal stove for them to fly to the North Pole. That is, of course, after their parents read them first.* ☺

*Then the same children would sit by the radio for the next several days until they heard Mrs. Santa read their letter. For instance, "Now, little Juanita Patience would like a new bicycle under her tree." Oh! The wonderful imagination of children! I got a two-wheeler at age ten, as well as the first book of my very own, Heidi. By that time, I knew exactly who gave them to me, and it wasn't Santa.*

*When many of us became parents, we carried on some of the same traditions with our children, both religious and secular. However, to the chagrin of my daughter and son who must have live trees, I prefer an artificial one that I can put up on the day after Thanksgiving and take down in February. I like the colorful lights in windows during the early dark winter evenings. Besides, I don't like vacuuming dried prickly evergreen needles for weeks.*

*Through the years I have seen family traditions come and go. Aunt Lillie loved roasting chestnuts in the oven. She had to have some each Christmas, which was the only time they could be found in grocery stores. I thought one year I would roast chestnuts as a remembrance of her. I didn't realize, however, that they had to be punctured first, and since I missed that vital step, they exploded all over my oven. What a mess it was to clean! Never again!*

**Great Aunt Lillian Mariah Patience Cuff at Age 85**

**December 21, 2022**

    **Happy Winter Solstice**, all 20. Today will have the shortest hours of sunlight. Tomorrow will be just like yesterday. as the earth has tilted on its axis as far as the Creator ordained. Ancient people worried that tomorrow would be shorter than today and that the days would keep getting shorter until the sun was never seen again. So, when "tomorrow" came, they were joyous. The Smorgasbord in Scandinavia was one such celebration. Food, fun and fellowship! Romans celebrated the Feast of Saturnalia during this time.

    Early Christians in Rome were afraid to acknowledge their faith in Jesus Christ, lest they be captured and fed to lions for Roman sport. The Christians wanted to celebrate the birth of Jesus and so chose to do so during the time when the pagans were celebrating Saturnalia. Hence came the Christ Mass in December which eventually became Christmas.

    Only three more months 'til spring. I will just "grin and bear" winter. The flower buds are waiting to pop open on my forsythia bush. I have so much on my plate 'til spring in Edenton, N.C. and our Patience/Lawrence monument dedication in April. Don't have a moment to waste.

**December 24, 2022**

    Good morning, all 20. I'm up! 'Tis only 12 degrees in Alexandria today. I turned my heat up a bit before retiring last night and I slept very well. The sun is shining for anyone who must brave the weather today. Dress with several layers. In the olden days the first layer would have been a thermal undergarment. I still have one among my ancient belongings, should I need one, which I hope I will not.

    Enjoy getting ready for the big day tomorrow. I will be streaming church today and listening to a CD of the *Hallelujah Chorus*. Several of you former Choralaires will remember how everyone's breath was held at the end when you sang it during your Christmas concert. Over the 17 years of the choir's existence, no one ever messed up!

**December 25, 2022**

Good morning, all 20 on **Christmas Day**. I remember Christmas pasts when my Ed and I would be up until 4 o'clock in the morning setting the scene to show that Santa had been to our house for the good children who lived there. Santa always ate the chocolate chip cookies they had set out for him. Ed and I would retire for a very short "winter's nap" because soon the kiddies were up and pleading to tumble down the stairs to see what Santa had left for them. What joy 'twas!

When Christmas was on a Sunday, as it is today, we attended church at 11:00 a.m. I don't know how I could have stayed awake, but I had to go. I don't remember if Sunday School classes were held, but I would have been there, too, because I was a teacher for years and Superintendent for a while, too. The things we will do for our children and for our grandchildren! Someone on this musing list was in my first Sunday School class around 1960. It was a sixth-grade class of exceptionally precocious children. I remember you sitting in your pews in the back of the church.

I've been invited to Christmas dinner at the home of a former Choralaire who attends the same church as I. Her mother and I were dear friends for years back in N.J., and her daughter is such a joy to me. She drives me "hither and yon," since I no longer drive distances. *"Count your blessings. Name them one by one."* Each of you on my list is my blessing.

**December 26, 2022**

Good morning, all 20. Today is **Boxing Day** in many countries that are or once were under British rule. I first heard of Boxing Day when I was in England one Christmas. Anyone interested can Google it. Clue**:** It has nothing to do with the sport of boxing. I had a delightful time with old and new friends yesterday. Thank you, Lord, for the blessing of good friends.

**December 30, 2022**

Good morning all 20. This is the 5th day of **Kwanzaa**, the theme being "purpose." President of *Bennett College*, Dr. David D. Jones, when I was a student in 1951, would go up to any student and ask, "*What is your purpose, young lady?*" And we were supposed to always be ready to answer him. Ask yourself that question today. Seems it may be for me to ask that of you today.

**December 31, 2022**

Good morning, all 20. 'Tis the last day of *deciembre* 2022, the 5th Saturday as well as **New Year's Eve**. I'm going to the noon New Year's Eve Service at church. FYI, in many African American churches, "Watch Night" services have been held on New Year's Eve since 1862 because President Abraham Lincoln had promised to sign the *Emancipation Proclamation* on January 1, 1863. If only he would, then many slaves would become free -- only in states that were in rebellion with the Union. It would not include the slave-holding Maryland, Delaware, Kansas, or Missouri because they had not separated from the Union.

So, on New Year's Eve in 1862, Black churches were filled with folks on their knees praying for President Lincoln to sign the *Emancipation Proclamation*, which he did on January 1, 1863. Of course, it took much longer for the word to spread, but in 1865 the news reached Texas. Since we don't know the specific day, we celebrate "Juneteenth" each June 19th. Watch Night services are still held on New Year's Eve at midnight in many Black churches, always followed by a feast. My church here in Virginia has a noon service. Sadly, the origin of that service is being lost, but I wanted you to know about New Year's Eve being called Watch Night in case you didn't already.

**January 7, 2023**

Good morning, all 23. I was awakened by the sound of a bird chirping away. It sounded like a robin, but it seems too early for him to be back here if he had migrated in the fall. There are robins that have sufficient food to never leave this area. I spied a horsefly on my deck last week. Seems that the temperatures have not been cold enough to kill their eggs. Also, it may not have been cold enough to send earthworms deeper in the ground, or else the robins would have their favorite meal available.

Every new day has its surprises as spring approaches. Just a few warm days could cause my forsythia to bloom early. I have not seen any daffodil leaves poking up yet on the south side of my house. Have you seen any, yet?

In 1891 Zora Neal Hurston was born in Notasulga, Alabama. An African American author, anthropologist and documentary filmmaker, she wrote about racial struggles in the 20$^{th}$ Century American South. Her most popular novel is "Their Eyes Were Watching God," published in 1937. In 1957, she interviewed Oluale Kossola (Cudjo Lewis), who had been on the last slave ship, the *Clotilde*, which arrived in Mobile, Alabama, in 1859. Even though U.S. involvement in the Atlantic Slave Trade had been banned by Congress in 1807, the practice illegally continued for years. Cudjo Lewis would live until 1935, and his story is in Neal's non-fiction book *Baracoom: The Story of the Last 'Black Cargo.*

**January 17, 2023**

Good morning, all 23. I'm up early because a piano tuner is coming this morning to tune my piano. My Pastor's favorite hymn is *Come Ye Disconsolate*. I love it, too, but I have other favorites such as *Amazing Grace*, and Richard Smallwood's *Total Praise* which is very difficult for me to play.

Have you heard Whitley Phipps singing *Amazing Grace?* The author had been the captain of a British slave ship, but God called him out of it. Phipps discussion on *YouTube* will bless you. On my piano I have several favorite classics to relearn, like *Clair de Lune*. I still have my lesson books from when I was a teenager, as well as several hymnals and sheet music of songs that were popular many years ago including *Bridge Over Troubled Water.*

I grew up with a piano in my home, when most kids took piano lessons. I took lessons from ages 10-16. My teacher, Sister Mercia, a nun at *Immaculate Conception Church* in my hometown, told me that I could become an accomplished pianist if only I would practice my lessons more. But like most kids who are not piano prodigies, I would practice only on the day before the lesson. Now I play for my own pleasure. I have new computer glasses to be able to see the music better. I am not gifted to play by ear like Stevie Wonder, Ray Charles or the Minister of Music at my church, an accomplished *Bennett College* sister who is on this list.

**January 27, 2023**

Good morning, all 23. Three days from now Punxsutawney Phil will be in the news again. Whatever he predicts, spring will arrive on March 21st as usual. February is the time to prune our roses back ruthlessly so they will get beautiful blooms this year. My forsythia bush has flower blooms ready to burst open. I should see daffodil leaves poking any day now.

**February 2, 2023**

Good morning, all 23. I'm off to see my dentist this afternoon but will be back by 4:30 p.m. before darkness descends. Just a quarterly cleaning and he had better not find any problems. How fortunate we are here to have good dental care. I was appalled the first time I visited England and saw what horrible teeth people had there, even our cheery tour director. Hopefully, since my trip 30 years ago, their dental care has improved.

**February 4, 2023**

Good morning, all 23. From 1 to 4 today I will be streaming the 90th birthday party given by three daughters of a *Bennett College* classmate. I didn't realize that she was a year younger than I. The Class of 1954 had members of different ages, the youngest being 15 and others older than I, with one married with a child.

I was surprised by another friend from N.C. whose grandmother had been a schoolteacher. At a very young age, Georgetta had attended school with her grandmother, and at age 14 she was ready for college. She entered *Johnson C. Smith University* at 15 and graduated at 19!

The *Washington Post* reported yesterday that signs of spring are appearing. You know that I am looking for them. How about you?

**February 7, 2023**

Good morning, all 23. I saw an interesting fact in the *Washington Post* this morning. Few people know that an African American woman, Marie Van Britton Brown, invented the home security system. I did not know this. There are many "hidden figures" we know nothing about.

**February 11, 2023**

Good morning, all 23. For Black History Month someone on this list shared information with me about African American Madam C. J. Walker. I first learned about her when I was living in N.J., and she had a home in Newark. I had the pleasure of meeting her great-granddaughter, A'Lelia Bundles at a book signing in Richmond, Virginia, where we both were autographing our books. She wrote a wonderful one about her ancestor, Dr. C. J. Walker, an amazing woman for her day. *Google* to learn about that successful Black entrepreneur who became quite wealthy.

**February 12, 2023**

Good morning, all 23. Today is my son's 60th birthday. My father teased me by saying that I should have named him "Abraham Lincoln Moss." I wouldn't be surprised that someone might have done that, but not me. In fact, I gave my eight-year-old daughter the privilege to name her new baby brother. He has never complained about her choice, so I guess she chose well.

**February 14, 2023**

Good morning, all 23. **Happy Valentine's Day**! Why do we send cards or celebrate in other ways? I like to learn the origin of customs. So, I Googled to learn about St. Valentine. Too much to discuss here, but if you who want to learn about him, the information is just a click away.

Yesterday my excitement was going with my grandson to pick out a new mattress for my bed. A spring in my very old mattress broke and was poking me, even though I did have a thick foam cover over it. I learned a lot about mattresses. One thing is that they are very expensive. Just like Goldie Locks, I tried several until I found the right one and then I was about to conk out on it. It will be delivered on Monday. Looking forward to a wonderful, long, uninterrupted winter's nap.

**February 15, 2023**

Good morning, all 23. Here I am at my computer where the news tells me that this is **Hippo Day**. So, what's the big deal about that? *"It is another day that God hath wroth."* In other words, it's another day to be amazed by our Creator's creativity. The stately, long necked giraffe is my favorite animal. *"The earth showeth His handiwork,"* Psalm 19:1.

**February 16, 2023**

Good morning, all 23. I woke up earlier on this dreary morning. No birds chirping and no children chattering. The Son awakened me to the sound of heavy rain falling on the roof and of cars splashing through puddles. I peeked through my bedroom venetian blinds and beheld several mothers escorting their small children to the school bus idling at my corner. The mothers carried umbrellas and tried to prevent their children from getting wet. I am curious about what they had on their little feet. Some kind of boots, I should hope.

I remember when I had to walk a mile to school in the rain. No one ever drove me. I carried an umbrella, of course. My outer clothing was not waterproof like fabrics are today. We did not have specific raincoats, just woolen coats that in the cold weather stank when they got wet. They were hung in a cloakroom to dry.

As far as boots, we wore "arctics" Those were rubber boots that we pulled up over our shoes. Of course, the boots came off as soon as we got to school and went into the cloakroom that every classroom had back in the day. When we returned home, the arctics came off immediately because no boots were worn inside. If people did, they'd go blind, according to the old folks. Later, fashion dictated that ladies would wear rain boots and then change into dress shoes when they reached their destination, such as a job. They had a special shoe carrier. My daughter gave me one recently. I guess they are back in vogue for the red-soled high heels I never could afford.

**February 19, 2023**

Good morning, all 23. **Happy World Whale Day**! Reminds me of my one-and-only whale watch boat ride in Massachusetts. I was taking a summer course at *Buzzard's Bay* to study plants and animals in a cold-water environment, as contrasted with the course I took at St. Thomas in the Virgin Islands in a warm water environment. I'm sure you know which one I enjoyed the most.

On my whale watching excursion, I swallowed a Dramamine tablet which made me very sleepy. I can still see me on the boat as our class was supposed to be watching for whales. Suddenly, someone yelled, "*There's one on the right!*" I woke up from my dozing just in time to see a large whale right next to us. It was so close it seemed that it was going to overturn the boat full of screaming passengers. But it did not. It was quite friendly. We only saw one that day. There was no school of whales which was what we were hoping to see.

A friend on my list, formerly from Pennsylvania, lives on Whale Watch Way in California. She sights whales when they are migrating. Oh, how I'd love to see that sight!

**February 20, 2023**

Good morning, all 23. **Happy Presidents' Day**, which is rather new on the American calendar. It was created to be a national holiday celebrated on a Monday like Labor Day, giving workers a long weekend. When I was a kid, schools celebrated Lincoln's birthday on February 12$^{th}$ and Washington's on the 22$^{nd}$. When I began teaching in 1958, our school system gave us a winter break during the week that included GW's birthday. Ed and I would take our kids on Caribbean cruises.

Then one year, out of the blue, that break was changed by the Board of Education to a long weekend. That upset the timeshares that several of my friends had during that February week. Fortunately, ours is the 16$^{th}$ week of the year. Our spring break was always during that week, and we went to Disneyland several times where our timeshare is located.

Who was the president when you were born? Franklin Delano Roosevelt was mine and he was reelected four times. It was because of him that the maximum number of two terms for the presidency became law. He was in his fourth term when he died.

**February 21, 2023**

Good morning, all 23 on **Fat Tuesday,** "Shrove Tuesday," or "Pancake Tuesday." I remember the men at *St. Marks United Methodist Church* in Montclair serving pancakes to the congregation and friends on this Tuesday before Easter Sunday.

I awakened this morning to the noise of tree trimmers and their equipment. I had slept so well on my new mattress that I was not aware that we had some rain during the night.

**February 22, 2023**

Good morning, all 23. 'Tis the 1st day of Lent, **Ash Wednesday** on the Christian calendar. Forty days of Lent until we celebrate the most important day ever, Resurrection Day on April 9th!

**February 23, 2023**

Good morning, all 23. I am "up and at it" after a wonderful sleep on my new mattress. Yesterday when I was in Old Town Alexandria, what did my eyes behold? A variety of Japanese cherry trees in full bloom and beautiful yellow daffodils in my church's flower gardens amongst smiley-faced pansies. My daffodils are still in the leaf stage, but I see blossoms beginning. This is my favorite time of the year, as you all know by now, because there is something new to see or hear, like robins in the morning. I heard one today declaring his territory.

**February 28, 2023**

Good morning, all 23. Leap Year's Sadie Hawkins Day is not until next year, when unmarried girls might propose to their reluctant beaus. Speaking of "leaping," Daylight Savings Time is just two weeks away. I hate the change. I have one clock that I never change so it is on DST now. I'm trying to make my body get on DST gradually, as my chiropractor has suggested. So, it's 9:00 a.m. in my mind, although only 8:00 a.m.

Tonight at 7:00 p.m. there will be a Zoom presentation about my father's unique anthracite coal art. If you don't get to see it, I have been informed that it will be recorded and probably posted on *YouTube* like a former presentation from the *Anthracite Heritage Museum* given several years ago. I was surprised to find myself on *YouTube* concerning a presentation C-Span recorded about 12 years ago. Please check them out.

**March 2, 2023**

Good morning, all 23. We had some rain during the night, but none now. If you missed the Zoom presentation about my father's anthracite coal art, it's on *YouTube* under the *Luzerne County Historical Society*. Several mistakes were made, such as the presenter saying that my great-grandfather had come from Louisiana, that my stepmother, Alice, was a nurse before she entered the WACS, and that he called my Uncle Harold "Harry," which was his father's name. But those mistakes do not take anything away from the overall presentation, which was very thorough. If you have questions, just ask the expert - ME at 703-780-7882 or www.journeyfromthepast.com.

And that's why I had to write a book about his work. Even though the presenter had it in his hand, he still made mistakes. Oh, well! *"What's done cannot be undone,"* said Lady Macbeth.

**April 15, 2023**

Good morning, all 23 on the **Ides of April**. 'Tis the middle of the month already. *Tempus fugit.* Next week at this time I will be visiting Plymouth, N.C., the place where at age 18, my great-grandfather, Crowder Patience, enlisted in the Union Army in 1864. It's going to be a very busy week for me. I thank you for your prayers that I may keep well enough to complete the task of dedicating a memorial in Edenton, N.C. that honors my ancestor and his older brother, Thomas.

I am very excited and thanking God for choosing me to be my family's eldest griot, which makes me the matriarch of the Patience family. Who'd have thought it? Little pig-tailed Juanita? Perhaps my Great Aunt Lillian Patience Cuff, who told me about her parents and siblings that led me to write my first book, *Created to Be Free*. Perhaps my father who had been proud of my accomplishments when he died in 1972. Since 2000 I have written nine books and am now working on a tenth. Neither he nor I would not have imagined that. Only God did, and He directed me.

**April 20, 2023**

Good morning, all 36 on this beautiful day in Edenton, N.C., where I am surrounded by good friends and family, some having travelled across the country to be here with me. The "mountain-top" experience today will be the unveiling of a joint monument honoring the memories of the two Patience brothers who served in the Union Army during the *Civil War*, Crowder and Thomas Patience. Information about the two is in my 9th book, *Deeply Rooted in North Carolina*.

What a blessing this is going to be! Many of our Patience/Lawrence descendants will be meeting each other for the first time, while others are renewing their connections. I believe that those of you who attended will never forget our wonderful weekend together. I'm thanking those who travelled far and wide to share this day with me. On my website under photos, the third set shows the dedication. www.journeyfromthepast.com.

**April 23, 2023**

Good morning, all 23. My pansies are happy. Yesterday I saw a beautiful red male cardinal and my first robin. I had heard him singing in the early mornings but hadn't seen him yet.

**HYMN: "THIS IS MY FATHER'S WORLD"**
*"This is my Father's world.*
*All nature sings and round me rings*
*The music of the sphere....."*

**July 15, 2023**

Good morning, all 32 on another hot day in the neighborhood. I'm sure Mr. Rogers would have taken off his cardigan today. When I was in grade school, I learned about Henry Ford inventing the automobile and Thomas Edison harnessing electricity, but I was not taught about who invented air conditioning. I am guessing that it was too soon for Willis Carrier to be in our schoolbooks.

No homes had air conditioning when I was a kid, but drapes were drawn to keep the indoors as cool as possible. Porches had awnings to provide some shade. Electric fans were found in some homes, but they were not the norm. I don't remember any ever being in mine. In churches the only fans were handheld. Didn't do much good. My favorite pew in my N.J. church was under an open window. When I moved to Virginia in 1958, there still was no air conditioning at *St. Mark's United Methodist Church*. However, in the church I joined in Virginia, Alfred Street Baptist Church, there was air conditioning which got turned off and on sporadically during the service. Women fanned themselves with handheld fans donated by local funeral parlors bearing a photo of the proprietors and their families. Such was the custom in many churches. Someone on this list is the son of one such funeral director.

I just mentioned to someone how grateful we are to the inventor of air conditioning, but I did not know his name to call. Of course, it was just a click away on my phone, but I was being lazy. Last evening on CNN a newscaster said to Anderson Cooper, *"Thank God for whoever invented air-conditioning."* He did not call the inventor's name, though. He should be acknowledged and so I am doing that here. Thank you, Willis Haviland Carrier (1876-1950).

**June 23, 2023**

Good morning, all 32. A cleansing overnight rain has made my deck beautiful by destroying ugly spider webs and bird signatures. I opened my back screen door to "air" the house. Takes me back to when my great aunts would open windows throughout the house in the mornings, to "air" it. Also, doing so after entering the house after being away from it for some time.

I haven't heard anyone use that verb lately, but you, too, may "air" something. In the olden days winter clothing that had been stored over the summer in moth balls had to be aired. Some woolen clothing taken out of closets might be draped over chairs on the back porch to chase that strong unpleasant odor away. And beds were always "aired" before being made up again each morning. Today some people may "air" their automobiles first instead of turning on the air conditioner right away.

I just read something interesting in the *Washington Post* this morning. It concerns a 7-foot 4-inch basketball player who will be playing for the San Antonio Spurs. Victor Wembanyama was described as a "skyscraper." I wonder what size shoe he wears. I look forward to seeing him play. I love basketball, but don't have a favorite team right now. I'll have to check out the Spurs' colors.

**August 8, 2023**

Good morning, all 44. Thankfully, I'm "up and at it" one more time! Mother Hubbard's cupboard is bare again, so, I will be making a supermarket run today. Good thing I don't have a doggie to feed. From what I see on television ads, though, dogs are eating very healthy food nowadays. Dogs in the olden days were fed table scraps which could be anything humans had not consumed, including bones. No chicken or fish bones, though. Too brittle and sharp for their digestive tracts.

Speaking of supermarkets, I am thinking about how presently we are toting our own bags to the store to be loaded. "Back in the day," every woman carried her own bag to a store because what was purchased would get wrapped in paper and then tied with string.

**August 27, 2023**

Good morning, all 44. Today would be my father's 117th birthday, having been born in 1906 in the borough of West Pittston, Pennsylvania. It's **National Cinema Day**. Back in the day, there were three movie theaters in our town. That meant we could go to the movies three times in one week and sometimes we did, especially when one feature lasted only for a day or so. When "going to the movies," we got see a main feature, an informative news reel, a hilarious cartoon, and a topic which was called "a short." Today it is called a documentary. Well worth the 25 cents spent on the ticket. If you wanted to see the feature again, you just remained in your seat.

I remember when my young daughter and her best friend who were in their early teens, went together to see a *Beatles* movie. They had not returned home at the expected time, and I had to go get them from the theater where they were watching the Beatles for the third time. People could come and go any time they pleased after the theater opened for business. I watched many movies twice. Ushers would seat us at any time, and we would just rewatch the movie, especially if we had arrived after it had begun. No problem. Yes, it was annoying when an usher with a flashlight made us stand up for latecomers.

**August 30, 2023**

Good morning, all 50. Sadly, what earlier was being anticipated by skywatchers with excitement now is adding to danger in Florida. Hurricane Idalia is about to hit the Tampa Bay area of Florida where I spent several years during the winter months. My heart is heavy for the people who live there. The super blue moon will reach its peak at 9:36 p.m. EDT on Wednesday, Aug. 30. It will be visible from most parts of the world, weather permitting.

**September 1, 2023**

Good morning, all 50. 'Tis the 1st day of *septimbre* 2023. I am up bright and early today even though I went to bed later than usual because I watched five episodes of *Blue Zones* on Netflix. The Zones are five different places in the world where a large population lives to be 100 years and older, including Okinawa, Sardinia and Singapore.

The commentator traveled to those places to talk with centurions to learn their secrets. In one spot gardening was one of their daily activities. In another, walking up steep steps in their town on an island off Italy kept them in good shape. All foods are freshly prepared such as the minestrone soup, a favorite in Italy and one of mine, too. The Americans studied were 7th Day Adventists in California who eat little or no meat and rest on their Sabbath which is Saturday.

One thing that each area had in common was community. Sharing their lives with others rather than being alone all of the time. Making new friends. Some just for a moment; others for longer. I have no problem doing that.

**September 2, 2023**

Good morning, all 50. 'Tis a beautiful morning in Alexandria. The sun is shining brightly. I'm off this afternoon to an event that will honor a member of my church who is exactly my age. General Leo Brooks is an African American retired general whose two sons are also generals, the only family in the U.S. to claim such fame. Should anyone be interested in learning about him, you can easily Google him.

**September 3, 2023**

Good morning, all 50. I remember when on the Sunday before Labor Day, I would be getting excited about school starting in a few days. It was never prior to Labor Day, either when I was a student or a teacher. As a student I would be anticipating what new subjects I'd be taking. When a teacher, I would be anticipating greeting the teenagers who would soon be meeting me in room 406 at Bloomfield High School. I enjoyed teaching the same subject (biology) for 33 years.

Recently, I was looking at my father's 1924 high school yearbook and saw a photo of Miss Isobel Poxon. It was her 2nd year at West Pittston High School where she taught Latin. What surprised me was her longevity. She was my Latin teacher in the 9th and 10th grades and my senior class homeroom teacher in 1949-50. Talk about longevity and love for her job! I have no idea when she retired. I loved her class.

I remember other dedicated teachers. Do you have a favorite one who took an interest in you personally? I have been blessed with several, including a second-grade teacher, Miss Hewitt, who was very kind to me. I had her again in the fourth grade. Years later I was encouraged by Mrs. Miriam Harris, my public speaking teacher, who suggested that I enter Wilkes College in 1950 after I had failed a nursing school physical examination due to a health condition from contracting scarlet fever when I was 10 years old. At Wilkes I entered a medical technology program where I fell in love with biology. Surprising because it had not interested me at all when I was in the 9$^{th}$ grade where we had no labs. We had to memorize a lot of facts. Boring!

**September 5, 2023**

Good morning, all 50. The *Washington Post* reported that a stunning meteorite was seen on Sunday night at about 9:30 p.m. between Richmond, Virginia, and New York City. I could not see it here.

I had a new bookshelf built yesterday, and now I have four divisions of books in my house: Black history, Civil War, religion, and miscellaneous others which include novels and non-fiction. Now, I will know exactly where to go to find a particular book, albeit they are not in alphabetical order either by title or author. When I have the time in my old age, I just might do that, but not any time soon. Would you believe that I have only one biology textbook left from my 33 years of teaching the subject which I will always love? Biology has not changed, but the way it is being taught has. I could not go into a classroom nowadays.

**September 6, 2023**

Good morning, all 50. I'm a little late this morning because my computer has been contradicting me. Every now and again, she gets ornery. "She's" getting old, too. The week is flying by quickly, as usual. I am still sorting my books into categories. I have soooo many. I always wanted a house large enough to have a library where I could read in peace and quiet. My whole townhouse is turning into a library with books stashed in every room. I know that modern folks like their Kindles and audios, but I prefer the feel of a book in my hands.

When did my love for reading begin? When my Great Aunt Lillie would read the Sunday comics to me before I was even school age. She really did not enjoy them and so she taught me to read them for myself. I had some favorites like Joe Palooka, Popeye, and Nancy. I was ready to read about Dick, Jane and Spot before some others in my first-grade class were. Interestingly, I have not read comics in years even though the *Washington Post* has a whole page full of them. They just don't catch my fancy anymore.

**September 8, 2023**

Good morning, all 50. Someone on this list asked me to send a photo of my Great Aunt Lillian (1883-1986). She was the most inspirational person in my young life. Not having any children or grandchildren of her own, she took me under her wing, and I am so grateful. All of my great aunts were very good to me. At one time I called myself Juanita Bernice Patience Cuff Garrett Lee which included them all.

Some of you from Pennsylvania and New Jersey may remember Aunt Lillie. Always the proper lady, she wore lovely hats and was a stylish dresser. She loved to shop. A devout Christian and pastor's wife, she introduced me to the *Bible* at an early age. Along with looking at her photograph album on Sunday afternoons, she read *Bible* stories to me. Thank you, Aunt Lillie.

**September 10, 2023**

Good morning, all 50. I am cutting out and saving an interesting section of the *Washington Post* today. It concerns where the best pizza can be found in the U.S. It is titled *American Pie*. I remember Christmas in 1951 when I spent a long weekend in Washington, D.C. with a *Bennett College* sister before returning to college for the 2nd semester. I was excited because it was my first trip to our nation's Capital when it was safe to walk the streets at night. At that time of year, it was dark at 6:00 p.m. Around 8:00 p.m. my friend asked me if I'd like to go somewhere for a bite to eat.

> *"Sure."* I said.
> *"What would you like,"* she asked.
> *"Let's go for a pizza."*
> *"What's that,"* was her response.

Surprisingly, she had never heard of pizza, and we could not find any place where it was being served. We probably settled for a hot dog and soda. Who in America does not know what pizza is today? Interestingly, the *Washington Post's* article mentions the town of Old Forge near my hometown close to Scranton, Pennsylvania, the hometown of President Joseph Biden. Even today, the kind of pizza I ate in my youth is still being prepared there. One orders a "tray" and not a "slice." It's square like the Sicilian pizza which is still my favorite of all I have eaten over the years. Pizza lovers might enjoy the article if you can Google it.

**September 12, 2023**

Good morning, all 50. I remember Jessie Owens today on his 110th birthdate. He was an African American track and field athlete who won four gold medals at the 1936 Olympic Games. In Germany Adolph Hitler was flabbergasted and very much chagrined that a Black man could win those awards.

I'm feeling "fine and dandy" today. Yesterday I had two very long telephone conversations with both a friend and a family member. They were just checking on me and I am thankful for their concern. Would you believe they do not have computers in this day and age? Consequently, they are not receiving morning messages, as you more fortunate folk are.

It's just like when my Great Aunt Florence refused to get electricity in her house *circa* 1945. That was until her soldier son, Nyles, returned home after World War II. He insisted on having electricity. I can still see in my mind's eye the bare electrical wires with naked light bulbs strung in the rooms on their first floor. There were none in the bedrooms. Neither was there any heat up there. Bedrooms in those days were used for sleeping only. In the winter, they were very cold. No reading was ever done there.

Florence's sister, my Great Aunt Rosa, had electricity in her home, but would not have a telephone that would have been a party line and very annoying with that ring going off all day. Any person Aunt Rosie wanted to talk to was living within walking distance of her home, anyway. She and Uncle Pete lived in the next block from me and around the corner from her nephew and his family. I learned a lot about gardening from Uncle Pete. He had a large vegetable garden in his backyard. He also played Chinese checkers with me. I spent a lot of time with older folk.

I spent many hours at their home after school when I listened to the radio with Uncle Pete. Aunt Rosie, as she was called, made the best homemade biscuits. Probably, she learned from her mother because her sister, Florence, made the best homemade bread. Slathered with butter and jam, they tasted as good as cake.

**September 13, 2023**

Good morning, all 50. I was awakened by the trill of a robin. Is he telling his mate for life that he's getting ready to go farther South for the winter? Might he be telling us that winter is coming sooner than usual? I sure hope not the latter.

My son asked me if I thought many of you knew what I was talking about yesterday when I mentioned "party lines." He didn't think his young daughter on my list would. He said I probably had told him about them. He has an even better memory about some things than I do. I don't usually ask for a response to my musings, but I am curious about which of you know about the telephone party lines of the past. They ceased all over the U.S. in 1980. They were a part of your grandparents' lives.

I *Googled* "party lines" to read about the history and I learned a lot, such as when they began, their purpose, and when they ended. This is how they worked. A certain number of people near each other would be placed on the same telephone line and given a mutual telephone # but with a differing letter on the end. Ours was 24R. Just how I pulled that out of my cerebrum from 85 years ago, I do not know. Each black, hand-held, corded telephone had a code ring like the Morse Code. Every time a call was made to someone on the same line, everyone on it heard the ring, but they were not to pick up the phone unless it was their own ring since the line was open to everyone on it. There were some cursory rules issued, but people being people broke them, such as not listening to anyone else's calls or talking for too long. It easily became an instrument of gossip.

I don't know when my father got his business phone. It was what I used in my teens to contact my friends. I just know that it was not on a "party line." People did not spend a long time chatting on telephones "back in the day." I never had a phone of my own. Unheard of for a kid back then.

**September 14, 2023**

Good morning, all 50. The only thing I found interesting in the *Washington Post* was an article about growing fruit trees in small spaces. I'm not inclined to do that, but I do remember the fruit trees in my backyard when I was very young. One by one, they died and were not replaced. Ours were apple, pear, plum, and cherry. The fruit would be canned and stored in the cellar because the "Mom and Pop" grocery stores in my hometown could not supply fresh produce during the winter. I am wondering if anyone has a fruit tree in their yard presently. It might be a nuisance with the fruit falling off and rotting. 'Tis the same in Florida with orange trees and in California with lemons.

Providing a food supply for their families for over the winter was a vital job for the women of each household. In my case, it was my great aunts' responsibility. Families did a lot of sharing. Mrs. Langford next door had a sour cherry tree, and we had a sweet one. Sour cherries make the best pies. For eating out of hand, sweet cherries are the best, and so the two kinds were exchanged by the neighbors over the fence every year.

Up North where I was reared, many people had gardens where they raised food to store in root cellars for over the winter months. Unheated root cellars in homes had floors which were dug to cover certain vegetables with soil. They would not sprout until spring. I'm sure you all have seen sprouting potatoes and onions. We just throw them away nowadays. During World War II, most back yards were converted into "Victory Gardens." People planted many kinds of vegetables which were shared among neighbors.

Our backyards were large and elongated. At one time each home had its own outdoor toilet that had to be set a certain distance away from the house. We called ours "Miss Jones." I remember her well. It seemed far from the house to this little girl. Tall holly hocks were grown on the outside wall seemingly to hide its purpose.

This time of the year reminds me of all the canning of food women had to do in 100+-degree weather with no air conditioning. They canned tomatoes, apple sauce and peaches which were considered essential foods. They pickled cucumbers and concocted relishes, as well as homemade jelly and jam. Women would brag to each other about how many jars of whatever they had "put up." It was like a badge of honor. What a task canning was, with flies buzzing around everywhere! Sticky fly paper catchers hung from ceilings. Fly swatters were kept busy. I happen to have a rubber one for the occasional fly that comes inside and annoyingly flies across my television and computer whose light attracts them.

Many homes had grape arbors erected in their backyards. Both Great Aunt Florence and Great Aunt Rosie had them. We often ate lunch beneath them on benches and at tables because they were shady. My great aunts made both grape jelly and jam. They were not wine-making folks, but some of my Italian neighbors were, with all the necessary apparatuses in their cellars.

I was sooo glad that frozen food had been invented when I married in 1952 because I swore I would never do canning in the fall, and I haven't. I do a lot of freezing instead. However, I do enjoy the endeavors of others. Thanks to my darling younger cousin (my flower girl in 1952) on this list who treats me with jars of homemade peach preserves each year. Yummy!

**September 15, 2023**

Good morning, all 50. Today, I find just the same dire news you see on your television. In the beginning of television, the news was only on at 6:00 p. m. Later a news program was added at 11:00 p.m. Now they are on for 24 hours.

Some of you remember life before remotes. The others of you cannot imagine getting up from your seat to change the channels by hand. At one time the television stations (only three) shut down at midnight after the *Star-Spangled Banner* was played. I have no idea what time they began in the morning. Perhaps 6:00 a.m.

Would you believe that at one time in a public speaking class I had to learn all five verses of the *National Anthem*? Written by Francis Scott Key, the last verse is very touching.

> *"O thus be it ever when freemen shall stand*
> *Between their lov'd home and the war's desolation!*
> *Blest with vict'ry and peace may the heav'n rescued land*
> *Praise the power that hath made and preserv'd us a nation!*
> *Then conquer we must, when our cause it is just,*
> *And this be our motto – 'In God is our trust,'*
> *And the star-spangled banner in triumph shall wave."*

In 1890 Agatha Christie was born. She is best known for *Death on the Nile*, a favorite of mine.

Today is **Rosh Hashanah,** which begins at sunset. I am sending a *Jacquie Lawson* card to a younger Jewish colleague with whom I worked for many years. We have remained friends and have kept in touch for all these many years. I remember how kind she was to visit my Great Aunt Lillie at my home on her 100th birthday in 1983.

I thank all of you "golden" friends for being in my life. My very first "golden" friend from when I was six and she was four is on this musing list. The new *23 and Me* and *Ancestry.com* relatives found in 2018 may have begun as "silver" friends, but now I count them as "gold" because they are more precious to me than costly metals. It is as if I've known them all of my life instead of just for a few years. Thanks, dear Cousins.

**September 17, 2023**

Good morning, all 53. Today is **International Mantra Ray Day.** I love watching sting rays swimming gracefully in large aquariums. The *Washington Post* has an interesting article today on "*embracing jetlag.*" I get it bad and need at least three days to get used to a new time zone. The author's ideas on the subject are interesting, but I don't know if they apply to me. I am cutting the article out to save with other articles I plan to read again one of these days.

Yesterday, I was speaking with someone on this list who was telling me about an old car she drove when she was a young woman. It was a 1939 model. I asked her if it had a rumble seat. Do any of you know about rumble seats in the back of automobiles? If not, *Google* to see pictures of them. My father's first car had one, but I was too young to ride in it. Trunks replaced them many years ago. Interestingly, they were dubbed in England as "mother-in-law seats." Very amusing. Now we are relegated to the back seat.

**September 18, 2023**

Good morning, all 54. This is **National Voter Registration Day.** I hope that each of you is a registered voter. I cannot believe the number of books in my house that I have to keep or give to a library. I still have books that belonged to my Great Aunt Lillie and her husband, the Rev. Charles Edward Cuff. He was born and reared in Mercersburg, Pennsylvania. Some of his books have his signature written in them. Because they are dusty and falling apart, I must discard many of them 88 years after his death in 1935. I always said I'd love to have a home with a library. My whole house has become one with books in every room. I used to have subscriptions for several magazines, but I have none presently. Too many advertisements nowadays and not enough content for the price.

**September 21, 2023**

Good morning, all 61. The frost will soon be on the pumpkin and everything else, as well. Leaves have begun changing colors here and falling to the ground. I'm glad our development has a lawn service that gets rid of the fallen leaves. We have lots of oaks and maples. This season was my Ed's favorite time of the year. It was the time for his favorite apple cider, which now can be found here year-round. He also liked apple butter, which I have not seen in recent years. It is a Pennsylvania Dutch creation. Delicious when mixed with cottage cheese and spread on toast. If I remember to rise early next week, I may meander over to see if there is any apple butter for sale at our local farmer's market. The secret is like that of the "early bird." One must get there early because by 10:00 a.m. the best "worms" may all be gone.

We frequented the local farmers' market on Wednesdays when Ed would drive me there and we'd load our van with all kinds of goodies, including an unsliced loaf of raisin bread with a thin topping of white icing. It is as good as any cake. To slice it, I used my serrated knife. There is a farmers' market about six miles from where I live, touted as the oldest farmers' market in the country. It was to this farmer's market that George Washington sent his produce from Mount Vernon to be sold. It is located on King Street in Old Town, Alexandria and is open every Saturday morning. Why is it called "Old Town?" Because originally the area belonged to the Distinct of Columbia which is formed like a rhombus—a diamond shape. The lower tip was in Virginia.

That large farmers' market sells beautiful flowers and other wares besides produce. It is an adventure being there with the large crowd of folks, many with dogs straining on leashes. I find the different breeds to be quite interesting.

Washington, D.C. freed its slaves in 1862. Virginia did not. However, the census records of my great-grandmother, Elsie Veden Patience, differ. Several report that she was born in 1858 in Virgina and others that she was born in Washington, D.C., showing the confusion at that time. Her story goes back to a smallpox outbreak. Like her, many children were orphaned. She had been born free in 1857 and was never a slave.

Through a Presbyterian program, she was given to a family in Dillsburg, Pennsylvania, as a "bound" child until she was sixteen years old. At that age, she married Crowder Patience, who was twelve years older than she. I lived in her home until her passing in 1940. What I remember about her is that she was a small woman who walked with the cane her husband had carved for her. It was passed to Great Aunt Lillie, who passed it to me. Hopefully, I will never have to use it.

**Crowder-Patience Clan**

**September 22, 2023**

Good morning, all 62. I awakened to the sounds of cheery children on their way to their bus stop. This is **World Rhino Day**. Sadly, many wild animals are in danger of extinction, rhinos among them. Their babies are cute, but aren't the babies of many species cute except for rats, bats and snakes?

It's time for a homemade apple pie. There are many different varieties of apples in grocery stores nowadays. My Great Aunt Lillie's favorite apple for pies was the Northern Spy found only in the fall. It makes a firm filling rather than a mushy one. My pies always consist of Granny Smith with another variety. When Aunt Lillie was baking pies 100 years ago, there was no such thing as a refrigerator. Even so, her secret to a successful pie crust was the very cold water she used.

Before refrigeration, where did she get ice? From the iceman, of course, who delivered chunks to homes. People placed a clock-like sign on the front door for the iceman to know what size chunk he was to place in the icebox. Ours sat on the back porch. It was my job twice a day to empty the pan underneath it, lest the water overflowed from the melting ice and rot the floor. Sometimes, when I had to run home for lunch, I forgot. Was I punished? I don't remember ever being punished for anything. Most of the time I was a good little girl. Got a lot of talking to, though. With her trusty ice pick, Aunt Lillie would chip pieces of ice for her "Flaky Pastry" recipe that would make two crusts. I use ice water and then place my dough in the refrigerator for several hours.

With my new fan dangled apple slicer, I can peel and core apples very quickly. I slightly cook the apples on top of the stove with ¼ cup of water. I use a non-stick pot and stir until the apples soften, but not to the point of becoming mushy. My final step is to squeeze lemon juice on the filling, something my Great Aunt Lillie may not have had access to "back in the day."

**September 23, 2023**

Good morning, all 65. **Happy Autumnal Equinox**! I am learning something new today. I thought the Autumnal Equinox always occurred on September 21st. I was surprised to see by my *Washington Post* calendar that this year it is occurring on the 23rd. The hours of light will become shorter each day until the Winter Solstice, which has the shortest hours of light. And there are people who love living in Alaska during the winter when the sun does not show at all! I'm looking forward to spring. Winter is not my favorite season. I am not a bear and do not enjoy hibernating. I wish I could spend my winters in St. Petersburg, Florida, at the beach, but my pocketbook does not allow me to become a snowbird like so many lucky Canadian and U.S. citizens, four of whom are on my list. I am obeying the Commandment, *"Thou shalt not covet."* Maybe I am a little bit, though. Please forgive my trespass, Lord.

I'm not longing for Phoenix, Arizona, though, where the temperatures this summer rose to 119 degrees. I have cousins who live there all year round, two who are on this list.

I awakened to rain and wind this morning, so I didn't hop up immediately, "hurkle-durkling" like in Scotland. That is just lying there for a while under the covers. I lay in my bed for a while listening to a neighbor's wind chimes. No kids' pealing voices, no noisy automobiles revving up in the parking lot and no loud airplanes flying above. It was still so dark and dreary at 9:00 a.m. that when I finally looked out my bedroom window, I saw that the streetlights were still on. Now at 10:40 a.m., I am ready to begin my day after sending my morning greeting to all of you across the country.

**September 24, 2023**

Good morning, all 68. This is **National Cooking Day**. It's an excuse to make something scrumptious, should you be so inclined. I had a nice day yesterday with the visit of a cousin who is on this list. We went to brunch, and I ordered red velvet waffles with chicken wings. I had never seen red velvet cake before visiting a church some years ago while wintering in St. Petersburg, Florida. Following the service, ladies of the church sold delicious baked goods. I was surprised to see slices of red cake with white icing. But, after tasting it, I was hooked, albeit I have never made one myself. The red velvet waffles are not as sweet as the cake, which I think is a good thing. The icing was served on the side. I brought two pieces home in a "doggy bag" to enjoy later.

Ever wonder the origin of the "doggie bag?" It began in the 1940s during World War II when people began taking home scraps for their dogs from restaurants. And so began the custom of taking leftovers for later human consumption, too. My husband Ed said that I liked going to restaurants, just to have a "doggie bag" to take home. 'Tis so true.

**September 26, 2023**

Good morning, all 72. 'Tis **Happy World Tourism Day,** especially for those of you on this list who are flying somewhere today. I'm up early this morning to put outside a pickup for the Wounded Vets. At 7:00 a.m. the Eastern sky was beautifully streaked with pink clouds as the sun peeked over the horizon. A portent of a beautiful day, hopefully. Concerning my message about cutting down on my salt intake, my daughter suggests that interested people might want to check out the *Penzys* salt-free combinations which she uses.

In an earlier message I discussed apples. Today's *Washington Post* has this article: *Sweet vs. tart? Tender vs. crisp? There's a breakdown of apples for baking.* Pictured is a Jewish bundt apple cake. It reminds me of one my Great Aunt Lillie baked and served with a warm lemon sauce. Yummy! I prefer a tart and crunchy to a super sweet and soft apple pie. For that combo, the *Washington Post* suggests the best apples are Goldrush, Paula Red, Northern Spy, Granny Smith, and Winesap. I am familiar with only the last three varieties. The last was one of my Great Aunt Lillie's favorites.

Another article is *You (usually) don't need to rinse pasta.* Why do I? Because that's what I saw the cooks in my family do. They were introduced to spaghetti by Italian neighbors many years ago in Pennsylvania, but I do not know about the rinsing part. I would not think that possible with home-made macaroni. Probably it became popular when companies began boxing it. The first documented pasta factory in America was established in Brooklyn in 1848, and by the *Civil War,* "macaroni," was fairly common on American tables. The *Washington Post* article suggests that the noodles and the sauce shouldn't meet for the first time on your plate and that the pasta should always finish cooking in the sauce instead. Do any of you do this? I have not but will the next time I prepare spaghetti.

**September 28, 2023**

Good morning, all 73. It's sweater time and there's a Harvest Moon tonight. What I remember most on this nippy morning are the *West Pittston High School* football games that I attended on Saturday mornings prior to my graduation in 1950. My girlfriends and I would pin green and white streamers on our lapels when we went to the stadium. We carried blankets and oftentimes wore heavy boots because we got very cold while sitting on the bleachers in the stadiums. The last game of the season was always on Thanksgiving morning when our competitor was the town of Forty-Fort, several miles away. We'd take a bus straight down Wyoming Ave. to it.

My friends and I would sit right next to the band to cheer along with the cheery cheerleaders who were freezing their legs off while being cute. I would be wearing blue jeans. My best friend, Marguerite, played the clarinet and wore a skirt. I had wanted to play saxophone in the band, but my father maintained that girls don't play horns. Why did he tell me this? I haven't a clue. Perhaps he could not afford to buy a sax for me, or perhaps it was because there had been no girls in the *West Pittston High School* band in 1924 when he played the coronet in it. My husband was a trumpeter in his high school band in 1946 ten miles away in Wilkes-Barre. The band leader there would not allow girls in his band at G.A.R. High School, either. I wonder if it had to do with uniforms. Girls were not wearing "trousers" back then. Just when the rules changed, I do not know.

After each home football game was over, we would follow the band as it marched through the West Pittston streets from the stadium to the high steps of our high school where we would always sing the *Alma Mater. "We are proud of football players, ......"* I wonder if that custom ended when our stadium got lights and the games were played in the evenings. That took place long after my graduation in 1950.

When reading this, my daughter will remember her experiences as a cheery cheerleader at Montclair High School. My son will be remembering playing a Sousaphone in the marching band eight years later and a tuba at the national Christmas tuba-fest at the Rockefeller Center in New York City. He borrowed it from his band leader who had encouraged him to attend. Other people carried their own tubas and sousaphones from across the country in order to participate. I remember that it was a bitter December morning. Ed and I were both freezing to death, but that's what parents do for their kids -- grin and bear it. Needless to say, to be supportive of our kids, we attended a lot of very cold high school football games. We always toted blankets.

**September 30, 2023**

Good morning, all 73. I failed to mention that yesterday was **Coffee Lovers Day.** I am one. Not strong coffee, just enough to perk me up . As a child, I was not allowed to drink coffee or tea. It would stunt my growth, so "they" said. My drink at meals was always a tall glass of cold milk. During my school workday, I would become very tired by the 7th period when I had one more class to teach. The school nurse suggested that I drink a cup of black coffee with my lunch. It did the trick.

'Tis hazy here this morning. Won't complain, though. I am feeling sorry for New Yorkers who were flooded due to *Hurricane Ophelia*. They are warned to stay at home, lest they drown. Some of you remember the flood in Wilkes-Barre in 1972 due to Hurricane Agnes when the Susquehanna River overflowed. My father had died just two weeks prior to it. The flood water was as high as the third floors in downtown buildings. When the water receded, Wilkes-Barre looked like London during World War II -- totally devastated. New York, fortunately, will not be like that, just a mess to clean up.

Where my stepmother lived was up a hill, and so she was not affected by the flooding. In fact, she had 15 family members and two dogs living with her for several weeks. Thankfully, she had a big house. I toted fresh water to them from New Jersey. I don't remember what kind of containers I poured it in. There was no bottled water back then like we have now.

**October 1, 2023**

Good morning, all 77. Today is **World Vegetarian Day** and provides 65 interesting recipes. I am not a vegetarian, but I have become less of a meat eater. I know the importance of protein in our diets. Some of you may not know that a protein contains eight amino acids. Meat, fish, eggs, and cheese contain all eight. Beans and other legumes contain four amino acids, while corn and grains such as wheat contain a different four. Therefore, combining a legume and a grain will equal the amount of protein found in beef, pork, fish, eggs, cheese, and poultry. Hence, the popularity of beans and rice, beans and corn, and pasta and beans in certain cultures. I love chili. Back in the day, I made chili con carne, which means with meat. I used ground beef., but no longer. I exclude the meat and now eat my chili with rice or pasta and save meat for another meal. It's more economical, anyway, with food prices skyrocketing as they are.

Sending a Happy 99th birthday greeting to President Jimmy Carter, the oldest-lived President. He is still smiling, even after entering Hospice care in February. With his wife of 77 years, he attended the annual Peanut Festival in Plains, Georgia, on Sept. 23, 2023. His trust is in the Lord.

**October 2, 2023**

Good morning all 79. This is **National Voter Education Week,** and today is the **National Techies Day,** which was begun in 1999. I am thinking about my stepmother, Alice today. In 1937 at Bennett College, voting was probably not on her mind when she took part in a boycott of a segregated movie theater in Greensboro, North Carolina. It was the first known boycott in the United States. It was organized by Bennett College women and was successful. But at that time, it was not to force integrated seating. No, that would not happen until the late 1960s. It was due to the positive roles of Black actors being cut from movies when they were shown in the South. Students from the North were "in the know" about that fact. In Greensboro, the practice ceased at the Carolina Theater after the successful boycott. It took place many years before gutsy Bennett College women would participate in boycotting the Woolworth's lunch counter in 1961 and again made history.

The *Washington Post* published this article today. *Sitting all day increases the risks of dementia—even if you exercise. Google* if you are interested. I certainly am. Some good news in the *Post* today is that the *Ringling Brothers Circus* is back, although sans animals. There is a new twist on circuses. A cousin on this list sent me a response to my message yesterday that I wish to share with you today because it is so sweet. *"I also agree you should publish your musings. They are uplifting and fun to read. I do look forward to this bright spot which links me to familiar memories and new info. Like a box of chocolates, never know what you're going to get, but it will be sweet."* Thank you, dear Cousin.

### October 4, 2023

Good morning, all 79. The only thing that interests me from the *Washington Post* today is a recipe for banana bread, which I love. It is made with raisins, chocolate chips, and walnuts. Three suggestions were made to ensure good results: very ripe bananas, spices, and not baking it too long. I will cut out the recipe to add to the many I plan to make one of these days. It will have to be for company, lest I eat it all by myself. Ever have pesky *Drosophila* (fruit fly) problems when you bring bananas into your house? Once they come in, it's hard to get rid of them because they multiply so rapidly. Perhaps some of you experimented with them in a college biology class. They are used for genetics experiments because one can study several generations in just one week. They multiply that rapidly.

The first thing I do with bananas after bringing them home is to wash them in a little soapy water. That seems to do the trick to kill any eggs lingering on the skins. However, if I see a *Drosophila* flying by my computer, which annoys me, I set out a small dish of vinegar and water. They dive right into it and drown. Thankfully, I have not seen any this summer.

### October 7, 2023

Good morning, all 79. The **Albuquerque International Balloon Fiesta** is taking place today. That is something I have always wanted to do -- go up in a hot air balloon. From seeing the photograph yesterday in the *Washington Post* of African American Viola Fletcher, age 109, there still may be hope for me to also do likewise. She is the last survivor of the *Tulsa Race Massacre of 1921, and* she looks like she is 80-ish because she has no wrinkles and is wearing red lipstick. Sound familiar? Anyone want to go up in a hot air balloon with me? I've got 18 years to catch up with Viola, who is still going strong, according to the article.

Happy news in the *Washington Post*! Ten years after her first world title, African American Simone Biles won her sixth in Antwerp, Belgium, becoming the most decorated gymnast ever.

### October 8, 2023

Good morning, all 79 on **World Octopus Day.** Anyone like calamari? I do. Several articles in the *Washington Post* grabbed my interest. Perhaps you may be able to ***Google*** them, should you be interested in the topics, too.

1. *Being vegetarian is easier for some--and that may be due to genetics.*
2. *In Alaska, internet-famous bears draw packs of fans.*

This is **Fat Bear Week** in Alaska. Bears must put on weight to survive their winter's hibernation. There is an annual contest in Alaska to determine which bear is the fattest. The article has great photos of really obese bears.

### October 9, 2023

Good morning, all 79 on ***Columbus and Indigenous People Day.*** I wonder who decided that they should be celebrated on the same day. Not the latter group, I am sure.

### October 19, 2023

Good morning, all 80. I am home and "back in the saddle" again. Since you last heard from me, I have been in Pennsylvania to receive an award from the *Luzerne County Hall of Fame* in my father's memory. Anyone interested in learning about him can do. *Google* Charles Edgar Patience. He is on several *YouTube* sites, too. Also, I have written a book about his unique anthracite coal art. To purchase it, please see my website. www.journeyfromthepast.com

Back home in Pennsylvania, I had lunch with three dear classmates from the *West Pittston High School* Class of 1950. We nonagenarians had a wonderful time reminiscing about the good 'ole days. I so cherish those first "golden" friends.

**October 20, 2023**

Good morning, all 81. I am wondering if any of you saw beautiful Venus in the east this morning. It was peeking through my blinds.

This is **National Pizza Month**. You youngun's do not know a world sans pizza. It has been a part of your life forever. Mine, too, having been born and reared in Pennsylvania among many Italian friends. To this day, my favorite is the square, which was the kind served in my hometown. I have not found it here in Virginia.

On my train trip North last week, I saw only yellow leaves replacing green ones. Coming back, I saw the reds and oranges joining in. This morning when I went outside to retrieve my newspaper, I saw several bright red trees which are red maples. In a few weeks all the branches of the deciduous trees will be bare again. Never, though, the evergreens like holly, fir, yew, spruce, and magnolia. I have a beautiful holly in my front yard.

I asked an Ethiopian young woman who had come to the United States to be a student at *Bennett College* what had impressed her the most here. I expected her to say, "*The snow,*" which had impressed my Puerto Rican classmate the most in 1950. Rather, she said, "*The leaves turning colors.*" She added that there was no way she could explain the phenomenon to the folks back home. That was a time when no one had a convenient way of sharing photos like we have today.

So, here is one more lesson for today. I mentioned in one of my musings that the reason the leaves are turning color is that green chlorophyll stops being manufactured, so, the green disappears.

There are three other pigments that may also be in the leaves, always the same each year. The leaves, according to their species, may be red due to anthocyanin, yellow due to xanthophyll, or orange due to carotene. Red maples always turn red and Norway maples always bright yellow. Do any of you remember the leaf collections you may have made in school?

I do know that some of you live in areas where deciduous trees do not exist. Some people take cruises North in the fall as far as Nova Scotia just to see the magnificent vistas along the way through New Jersey, New York, Connecticut, Rhode Island, New Hampshire, Vermont, and Maine. I have never been to the last three states.

**October 21, 2023**

Good morning, all 85. Lovely fall chrysanthemums are now decorating businesses and homes. My favorite shade is burgundy. It is time to plant bulbs and pansies for brightening dull winter gardens. Some people enjoy ornamental cabbages. I do not because they lose their glamour before spring arrives. They become scraggly. I first saw winter pansies when I was visiting England during a Christmas break from school. I was astounded when I spotted them growing all over London. Also, there were cyclamens and primroses planted in window boxes on buildings. Because homes are built out to sidewalks and have no yards, many people use window boxes full of flowers to brighten their world. It gets dark so early there in the winter, as early as 3:00 p.m.

I like a red cyclamen at Christmastime along with a poinsettia. Both will last for several months. Amaryllis are beautiful, too. Who is thinking about Christmas already? Home Depot and Lowes are, for instance, where Halloween, Thanksgiving and Christmas overlap.

By the way, my computer is working fine right now because a dear cousin on my list shared his computer savvy with me for a long time yesterday. Hopefully, "She" will continue to behave so I do not have to replace "Her" any time soon.

**October 22, 2023**

Good morning, all 86. *"This is the day that the Lord hath made. We will rejoice and be glad in it."* Today is **Wombat Day**. I wonder how many of you know anything about that small burrowing animal. It is an Australian marsupial with pouches for its babies, just like kangaroos and koalas. Not as cute as either, though.

When I traveled to Australia over 30 years ago with a group of teachers, we visited a Koala farm. I thought about having a photo of me holding a cute koala, which did not happen. We were not allowed to hold those cuddly-looking marsupials because they have long, dangerous nails. We could only visit them in their favorite habitat, very tall eucalyptus trees. I took a lot of pictures of them clinging to branches. They were to be used as part of my Australian slide show for my students.

**October 23, 2023**

Good morning, all 86. I am glad "She" is working again today, but "She" was mighty slow to open. Reminds me of my next-door neighbor's *Model T Ford* back in '38. Carmen Ciampi got up early every morning to go to work on his farm several miles away. At that time, his was the only car on our block. He had to use a pole-like contraption to crank up his car. It fit onto something on the front of the car. There are names for those parts, but I do not remember them, if I ever knew them.

I still hear in my mind the annoying sound of the grinding and grinding until the Ford sputtered and grumbled for a while before Mr. Ciampi could drive away. "She" does not make any noise but is just as stubborn. If you don't know who "She" is, she's my computer that may soon be replaced. I was not really annoyed by the noisy Ford in the mornings because Mr. Ciampi would take several of us neighborhood kids and his daughter, Helen, for a ride to his sister's farm, which still is in the same spot and is now run by her grandchildren.

Once, when I was in West Pittston attending a high school reunion, my old friend took me to visit her elderly aunt who remembered me as a child. No seat belts with five or more excited kids piled in my neighbor's black rectangular Ford. Our guardian angels were kept very busy, as Mr. Ciampi drove us carefully down the dusty, unpaved, bumpy roads to his sister's farm.

**October 24, 2023**

Good morning, all 86. No frost here yet to kill my flames, which are tall plants with red flowers that seed themselves every year in my small flower garden. I also have small fuchsia jonquils that bloom only in the fall. It's time for my winter pansies and new spring bulbs to be planted. I am ordering some uniquely colored daffodils that will be beautiful in April. No tulip bulbs, though, for the squirrels I see scurrying around my yard love them, but not the daffodils.

An article was in the *Washington Post* yesterday reporting that two beautiful flamingos have been sighted nearby. It is believed that they were blown off course during the last hurricane. Whether they can weather the cold this far **N**orth is to be seen.

**October 25, 2023**

Good morning, all 86**.** It's two months today 'til Christmas! The oldest known person lives in Spain and is 116-year-old Maria Branyas, who was a beautiful bride in 1932, the year I was born. She has no cardiovascular problems and can recall details of her youth back to when she was four years old. Scientists are studying her DNA to see if they can find some genetic clues to longevity.

I cannot remember anything from when I was four years old. Five, though, because I can remember longing to go to school with my older neighbors when they took off in the mornings, but I was too young. We had to be six years old. I was ready for school, but our small town had no kindergarten. At last, right after Labor Day in 1938, the big day came. I remember it well. I was so excited to enter the school building, escorted my Great Aunt Jessie who was my guardian. She was the one who signed my report cards because I was living with her in my great-grandmother, Elsie's home. Report cards had to be taken home quarterly for parental signatures. After Grandma passed away in 1940, we moved into my father's house, where he conducted his business. After that time, my father signed my report card with his beautiful signature. I have all of my report cards from the first to the 12th grades.

Another woman, age 104, is mentioned, too, on my computer. She says that her longevity is due to removing toxic people from her life, avoiding excess, and eating natural yogurt every day. The oldest person I have ever known personally is a *Bennett College* alumna, Helen Newberry McDowell, Class of 1924, who passed away at age 108. I presently know several over 100 years old. Someone on my list is 104 years old.

**October 26, 2023**

Good morning, all 86. The changing leaves are beautiful -- red, orange and yellow. My holly, covered in red berries, is bright green because it is an evergreen. Certain birds like robins will strip the tree bare when their food supply becomes scarce. Blue jays will, too. However, I do not see the latter in my neighborhood like I did in Pennsylvania and New Jersey. Today is **National Pumpkin Day.**

*"Oh, out in my garden some pumpkins I found.*
*They were big yellow pumpkins that lay on the ground."*

That's all I remember from the little ditty I learned as a child. My childhood Halloween pumpkin had its eyes, nose and a grinning mouth with teeth carved by hand. The top was cut off first and the seeds scooped out. A candle would be the light. It sat on the front porch steps before it collapsed after a couple of days. It's so easy to have a Jack-o-lantern nowadays. No mess or fuss, just plug a plastic one into an electrical outlet.

Halloween was a very simple event back in the day. We kids wore our costumes to school. We went out in the evening, usually chaperoned by adults until we were teenagers. We'd ring doorbells and sing songs or recite the poems we had learned in school, in exchange for some candy. Later churches began to have parties for us where we would dunk for apples and play games like Musical Chairs. The best costume might be awarded a prize.

Back then, pumpkins were always orange. I was very surprised when I was in California one fall and visited a pumpkin farm where I beheld white pumpkins. I had never seen them before in the East, but they have arrived here now. My Great Aunt Lillie always used canned pumpkin for her Thanksgiving pies. Her mother used Hubbard squash. My first cousin's grandmother used real pumpkin, which is very fibrous. I did not care for her pie, but I never told my cousin that. I just ate a piece of pie when it was offered to me, but I did not look forward to it like my cousin Jane did.

**October 27, 2023**

Good morning, all 86. After musing on October pumpkins, a North Carolinian on this list responded with information about peanuts that I am sharing with you. Many of us have never seen peanuts in the soil where they grow. I have not. I commented to her that I had heard that it was a very dusty enterprise to harvest peanuts. Here is her reply: "*You are correct about the dust! Lots of dust/dirt, when the peanut plants are turned in the fields and even more dust when the tractors 'pick' the peanuts!*"

I told her about my first trip to Edenton, North Carolina in 2001. Ed was "driving Miz Daisy" along a country road when we two northerners for the first time observed cotton growing in fields. Looked like snow from a distance. We also saw several women bent over as they picked something from fields. "Curious George" Juanita asked them what they were doing. They informed me that they were gleaning sweet potatoes to take to food banks. Very commendable.

The only time I had ever heard of "gleaning" was in the story of Ruth in the *Bible*. She had gleaned Boaz's field. Their love story was set up by Ruth's mother-in-law, Naomi. "Gleaning" is the removing of the leftovers from fields after they have been harvested by their owners. I asked a friend on this list about present day gleaning. She answered, *"Yes. People still glean sweet potato fields and share with food banks/food pantries."*

I asked her if the farmers rotate their crops because peanuts are legumes planted for the purpose of producing nitrogen for the soil after other crops like cotton and tobacco have depleted it. Her reply was, "*And yes, the farmers tend to rotate the crops - there is a field of cotton near my house."* Many of you are familiar with Dr. George Washington Carver's discovery of hundreds of uses for peanuts after Southern farmers began planting them following the *Civil War*. What were they going to do with all of those "goobers," they had asked.

For those of you who want to learn more about the genius who had been born enslaved, George Washington Carver, just *Google* away. Hope you enjoyed learning a bit of horticulture this morning. Of course, I enjoyed sharing it.

**October 28, 2023**

Good morning, all 86. I was awakened by the sound of roaring airplanes overhead. In this hour, I have been up and sitting at my computer while "She" took her time starting. I have counted 26 airplanes going to or from *Reagan Airport*, just a "stone's throw" from where I live, or perhaps going to or from *McGuire Air Force Base,* just 5 or so miles to the North. # 26 is passing over right now. Might they be the same airplanes practicing? Reminds me of how during World War II we'd run out of our houses to see fighter airplanes flying in geese formation over our heads. Where were the planes travelling that were flying over my house today? It was most unusual.

This is **National Chocolate Day**. When I receive a box of assorted chocolates, the first piece I eat is always the dark chocolate caramel. My least favorite is the almond one. I have never enjoyed *Almond Joy* bars. So that coconut one gets saved 'til last.

Seems that the peanut musing brought back personal memories for some of you. I received more responses about peanuts than any other topic I have discussed thus far. I learned a lot myself, never having seen peanuts growing or being harvested. But am a fan of eating them unsalted. I do not care for boiled peanuts, though. I am wondering if most people have any idea how peanuts grow. Perhaps they think they develop on arbors like grapes. Most people don't think about it at all when making a peanut butter and jelly sandwich for lunch. It's my mainstay when I travel because it will not spoil sans refrigeration.

Here are interesting responses from three women who really know all about how peanuts grow. Thanks, Friends, for your responses.

*1. "This picture really brought about some happy and not so happy memories about peanuts. Having grown up on a farm in the rural south, I shook a lot of peanuts and put them on stacks to dry. This was a tedious and labor-induced job that occurred each fall.*

*The happy memory about peanuts, as they had dried, was baking them in the oven, sitting around with my siblings eating those hot roasted peanuts. Occasionally, my parents would make peanut brittle out of all those peanuts, and we kids loved it. Simple treat, but so meaningful to farm kids."*

*2. "Though Georgia is known for its peaches, peanuts are a second favorite crop and grown on many farms. Two most popular ways to eat them are boiled and roasted. Jimmy Carter's father made a fortune on peanuts. My uncle's farm is near Plains and the Carter farm. He and President Carter were very well acquainted with each other.*

*Funny, for some reason I never saw peanuts harvested. If I recall correctly, they are ground vine crops that must be vigorously shaken to first get the dirt off of them. The boiled peanuts are cooked in salted water. I have never eaten any that way other than in Georgia."*

*3. "I had to reply to this message. Since I grew up on a farm and peanuts were one of our crops, I am well familiar with them. All the way from planting, chopping (weeding), thrashing and stacking to harvesting. My dad sold the peanuts, and the dried vines were fed to the cow and mule. My dad always loved a good pan of roasted peanuts."*

**October 29, 2023**

Good morning, all 87. Someone on our list recommended a site that tells me what is special about each day of the year. Today is **Internet Day, National Cat Day,** and **National Oatmeal Day**. I celebrate two of the three. I am eating my oatmeal with apple sauce and nuts, as I compose on my computer. I like cats. but my daughter is allergic to them.

Last night when I was closing my deck door for the night, I beheld in the East the beautiful Harvest Moon with the "old man" smiling down at me. A fantastic sight that has been there in the sky ever since *"In the beginning,"* whenever that was.

**October 30, 2023**

Good morning, all 89. Today is **National Candy Corn Day.** Yesterday I was pleasantly surprised at church. We had a guest preacher whom I knew from 35 years ago when we both lived in Montclair, N. J. When I spoke to him after the service, he looked at me as if he were trying to remember me. We both were delighted by the fact that Rev. Marvin McMickle and I knew each other from Montclair, even though I did not attend the Baptist church he pastored. We shared a mutual friend, though. She was Dr. Byerte Johnson, who some of you on this list from New Jersey also knew. She had served as his organist at St. Paul's. As they say, *"Small world!"*

**October 31, 2023**

Good morning, all 89. I was awakened by the sound of Canadian geese honking overheard, as they were flying to their breakfast. They are beautiful birds, but very messy. You don't want to walk where they've been. I bought some pansies yesterday and soaked their roots so that they can be planted today after lunch. It should be a perfect day for doing so.

Once, I was in London during my Christmas break from school. I could not believe my eyes when I beheld gardens filled with beautiful pansies, which are among my favorite flowers. No winter pansies grew where I had ever lived. Later**,** when I saw them at a nursery here in Virginia, I just had to have a few in my small garden. They will still bloom even when covered by snow, because they thrive on the moisture.

I am happy to be able to wish each of you a **Happy Halloween** because "She" was acting up yesterday. Something to do with the Wi-Fi not working properly. Thanks to one of my cousins on this list, the problem was solved before I went to bed. So here I am one mo' time. Should you not hear from me, think first that it is "She" and not Juanita who is having a problem.

Today is my household helper's day, so I have some decluttering to do before she comes. The most important thing she does for me is to change my bed sheets because I cannot lift the mattress any longer. Did you know that Jackie Kennedy insisted that her silk sheets be changed daily? When I was a kid, bed sheets were changed on Mondays, which was always wash day in my "neck of the woods." Before there was such a thing as a fitted sheet, there were identical top and bottom sheets on each bed. On wash day, the top sheet became the bottom sheet. Then the bottom sheet was thrown into the wash tub. And I mean "tub."

There had to be two. They were round and made out of corrugated tin. They were also used for Saturday night baths. On laundry day, one was for the washing and the other for the rinsing. No such thing as an electric washing machine when we had no electricity. Just two tubs and a washboard. Our first electric washing machine was a wringer one. That was such an advancement. However, my Great Aunt Jessie got her arm caught in the wringer once. I saw it happen, and I heard her scream. Fortunately, nothing was broken, just bruised.

All sheets were hung out-of-doors on a clothesline, and using fewer sheets would be the imperative, especially for large families. Sheets and towels and undies came only in white and had to be bleached and then rinsed in bluing for keeping them white and not turning gray. Bluing, laundry blue, dolly blue or washing blue was a household product used to improve the appearance of white fabrics. Women critiqued each other by what their laundry looked like hanging on the clothes lines. After being taken down and folded, sheets, towels, underwear, hankies, and even socks were ironed. Oh, our poor female ancestors! My father's mother died at age 35 after developing pneumonia while hanging clothes on the line. She had a lot of laundry to do with her husband and six boys.

**November 1, 2023**

Good morning, all 89. Seventy-one years ago, 25-year-old Edward Irving Moss and 20-year-old Juanita Bernice Patience were wed at the *Bethel African American Episcopal Church* in Wilkes-Barre, Pennsylvania. Our reception was at my parents' home in the backyard with refreshments. Today is **World Vegetarian Day,** which provides 65 interesting recipes. I am not a vegetarian like a goddaughter is, but I have become less of a meat eater.

**November 2, 2023**

Good morning, all 89. The temperature was 37 degrees, and I closed my two outdoor faucets, just in case freezing temperatures hit overnight. I certainly do not want any burst pipes. My new daffodil bulbs arrived in the mail yesterday, but they will have to wait for warmer days before they can be planted. They will be so beautiful in the spring. They are all new species to me and not the ordinary trumpet ones which I already have in my yard.

Today, "on-the-go" breakfast sandwiches are the favored early meal as cereal falls in popularity.

**November 3, 2023**

Good morning, all 91. I read an interesting article on my computer today. *What is the way of making daylight savings time permanent.* It discusses the history of Daylight Savings Time. I hate it. It's like jetlag for me. Both put me out of sorts for the better part of a week. I've tried different suggestions for how to avoid both, including food choices, but nothing works for me. Something about gaining or losing an hour does me in. It always happens.

I will turn my clock back an hour when I go to bed. The computer and television will do so automatically, but I will change the clock in my car. Forty-eight states and Washington, D.C. will be making the change. For anyone interested, the *Washington Post* has an article entitled *Why daylight savings time is worse for your body than standard time.* From a health standpoint, most sleep and circadian experts say we should stay at standard time. It's **National Bison Day**. The only time I have seen any up close was on a trip to Colorado. They are such majestic animals.

**November 5, 2023**

Good day, all 91. Today is **Donut Day** for you *Krispy Creme, Dunkin Donuts* and other brand lovers. When I was a kid, the only kind of donuts were round ones with holes. Some were heavily covered with powdered sugar that got on everything. I still prefer the cruller type dunked in steamy hot coffee, but I no longer can find them at *Dunkin' Donuts.*

**November 6, 2023**

Good morning, all 91. I got some daffodil bulbs into the soil yesterday. It took a lot of doing to turn the hard soil to be able to dig deep enough holes. Thanks to my young neighbor who is on this list, we were able to plant 18 daffodil bulbs. I have a few more to get in before the frosty weather comes back. No planting of tulips, though, because my hungry squirrel neighbors love them so.

Today, I am 91 1/2 years old. It's countdown now to 92, Lord willing. Today is **National Nachos Day**. I was first introduced to nachos in movie theaters. Our movie treat was a hotdog, bag of popcorn and a soda, all of which cost 25 cents, in addition to the 25 cents to get in. I saved my pennies to be able to go to the movies on Monday afternoons with my best friend Marguerite. My great aunts used to pay me for running errands for them. Students got out of school early because our teachers had meetings then. Marguerite and I were *Laurel and Hardy* fans, as well as *Abbott and Costello*. They were hysterical comedians. I wonder if I would find them funny now.

By the way, I did not know that carbonated drinks were called by different names until I went to North Carolina to college in 1951. When I asked for a "soda" at a fountain in a drug store, the waitress didn't know what I was talking about. After explaining, she said, *"Oh! You want a 'pop.'"* Some areas say, "soda pop." My favorite is root beer. May each of us be blessed today and may each of us be a blessing to someone else. Remember, *"When you're smiling, keep on smiling, and the whole world smiles with you."*

**November 7, 2023**

Good morning, all 92. Someone on this list sent me a website with special days in November. Thanks. Today is **World Pianist Day.** Some of you may not know that I can play the piano. I started taking lessons at age ten and continued until sixteen. Many children of my generation took piano lessons, both boys and girls. I never liked to practice. Sound familiar? I served as the pianist in my church when I was a teenager and then as the co-director of a youth choir at my church in N.J. for 17 years -- the Choralaires.

A number of you remember wearing your robes every 3rd Sunday and marching in the processional to *We've Come This Far By Faith*. The recessional was always, *Rejoice, Ye Pure in Heart*. Some others on this list may be familiar with those hymns. If not, you may be able to find them on *YouTube*. Since I moved to Virginia 32 years ago, my piano has sat patiently in my family room waiting for me to come back to it when I am ready. I had it tuned recently, so it is ready for me to play, but I've been doing lots of other things, lately, like musing.

Today is also **Cook Something Bold and Pungent Day**. I am going to prepare for my dinner Jamaican chicken curry using the recipe given to me by someone on this list. His mother used to make it. He provided me with a jar of real Jamaican curry. Thanks, dear Friend.

**November 9, 2023**

Good morning, all 92. 'Tis **World Freedom Day.** This day is an important one to each of us on this list of wonderful persons from the East to the West, North to South, male and female, young and old. It is also **National Scrapple Day**. I am wondering who does not know what scrapple is and who likes it as much as I do. It is a Pennsylvania Dutch (German) creation of pork, corn meal and seasonings formed into a loaf. It is sliced and fried until the outside is crispy. My husband, kids and I love it. One of my Soror sisters and church members loves scrapple, too. At one time my son could not purchase scrapple in California, so I froze some and mailed it to him. I'm not sure if he can get it there nowadays and if so, if it is the brand he likes—*Rapa*. He always has some when he travels East. Mostly, it is eaten for breakfast, oftentimes served with scrambled eggs and apple sauce.

A concoction called "mush" is cooked corn meal, sliced and then fried and served with maple syrup. This was probably a dish invented during the Depression when I was a little girl and people were poor. I am thankful that I never went to bed hungry. Anything that did not poison us was edible, even dandelion leaves, now sold by the bunch at *Whole Foods*. My great aunts boiled them. They were our "greens," along with mustard and turnip.

I remember in the late 30s seeing an Italian widow travelling up our street, all dressed in black and stepping onto people's yards to pick dandelions. A burlap bag was flung over her shoulder and a knife held in her hand. Her husband had been killed in the mines and left her with several children to feed, one being my age. Since she could not speak English, she did not pay any attention to those who yelled at her for digging in their yards. My Great-grandmother, Elsie, was one of them.

The burlap bag that Mrs. Tedesco was carrying might have been the same one she used to collect coal from the towering culm bank, which was debris from the coalmine. Poor women climbed to find pieces of coal to burn in their stoves. My great-grandmother and her daughters were not among them. My great-grandfather had a good job with the Carpenter brothers, and he worked for them over 40 years.

**November 10, 2023**

Good morning, all 92. Today is **National Forget-Me-Not Day** named for a beautiful little blue flower used for borders. I planted some when I first moved into my townhouse thirty-two years ago. I also planted *Lily of the Valley* along with them, but over the years they got crowded out by ferns and pachysandra. I will remember to sow some seeds in the spring. I love the beauty of both. *Lily of the Valley* is the month of May's flower. Perhaps that's why I love them so, having been born in May.

The *Washington Post* reports that the magnificent pandas on loan to the U.S. have been returned to China. The only pandas in the U. S. are in the Atlanta Zoo.

**November 11, 2023**

Good morning, all 92. Today is **Veterans Day**. For all the veterans on this list, we say, "*Thank you for your service.*" For all the veterans you and I are remembering today, we are grateful. I especially remember my Uncle Harold Patience, my stepmother, Alice Patterson Patience, and my 2$^{nd}$ cousin, Nyles Glover, all who served during World War II. Alice was a WAC (Women's Army Corps), Uncle Harold was wounded at the Anzio Beachhead in Italy, and Nyles contracted malaria in the South Pacific. Fortunately, they all survived the War. Nyles' son is on this musing list.

Of course, several on my list will remember the two Patience brothers, Crowder and Thomas, who served in the Union Army during the *Civil War*. One of my paternal cousins remembers one of her maternal ancestors who served in the *Revolutionary War*, and whose two sons served in the *Civil War* in the Washington, D.C. area. Who might others be remembering today?

It's also **National Sundae Day**. Don't forget to ask for real whipped cream and the maraschino cherry on top of your sundae. Haven't had one in years. Is there any such a thing nowadays as the soda fountain like I remember where we sat on tall stools and enjoyed sundaes served by a "soda-jerk?" *Woolworth's 5 & 10* in Bloomfield, New Jersey used to serve banana splits. Floating balloons had prices inside that would tell us how much to pay for the treat. We also enjoyed our root beer floats there, served with long-handled spoons. One of you reminded me of those fond N. J. memories.

**Sgt. Harold Lee Patience, Sr. WW II**

**November 12, 2023**

Good morning, all 92. Today is **International Pneumonia Day.** I am mentioning it because I had pneumonia twice while I was still teaching. It sneaked up on me both times, two years apart. I was "fine and dandy" one day and the next I was flat on my back. I was away from my job far too long while ill. I had to leave my students with substitute teachers who knew nothing at all about biology. The last time I was out for 28 days. I felt so guilty. But rather than have a third bout, I retired at age 60. I haven't had pneumonia since, perhaps because pneumonia vaccines have become available. Pneumonia is still a killer, even to young people. I am up-to-date with my necessary vaccines now, having had the 4th and last COVID yesterday. The pharmacist said that my arm might be very sore today. I don't feel anything yet. I'm tough.

My father died from pneumonia when he was only 65. It was because his lungs were so badly damaged from breathing coal dust all his life when he was carving his anthracite coal art. The tiny coal particles damaged the cells (alveoli) of his lungs, and when he caught pneumonia, it killed him. Thankfully, it did not kill me.

Today is also **International Chicken Soup for the Soul Day**. That goes along with what to eat when one has pneumonia or any other sickness, for that matter. Very easy to digest. I keep cans of *Campbell's* chicken noodle soup in my cupboard just for sick days which, thankfully, are few. It is quite salty, so I do not eat it any other time except when I am not feeling well. Lastly, today is **National Pizza Without Anchovies Day**. Anchovies are too salty for me. I am sure my body is on Standard Time now because I awakened at 8:00 a.m., a perfect time for me to rise. When I was working, I had to stand at my door to greet my homeroom students at 8:00 a.m. So, I rose at 6:00 a.m. to get my kids up. It was pitch black at 6:00 a.m. during the winter, just like it is in Alaska.

A *Bennett College* sister lives in Alaska because her husband was stationed in the Army there. Even after retirement, they are still living in Anchorage. Their children live in "the lower 48," though, so I suppose the parents escape the winter darkness when they wish to.

One more memory is seeing myself on my back porch when I was school age, with a blackboard that was placed on an easel. Neighborhood children came to "play school" with me, and I was always the teacher because the blackboard was mine. 'Tis interesting that I was the only one who would choose teaching as a career. A lot of girls in the early 50s became nurses. Several of my class did. I had planned to become one, too, but God had other plans for Juanita.

**November 13, 2023**

Good morning, all 93. Today is **World Kindness Day.** If all people were kind to one another, what a wonderful world we'd be living in. Kindness is becoming as "scarce as hens' teeth." Thanks to each of you for your kindness to me.

I have a poem to share with you about kindness. I used to read my favorite poems to my students when we were between chapters. They could begin the next chapter or listen to me read poems. You know what they chose! Nowadays, I would not be allowed to do that. A biology teacher must teach for the test that the students will take at the end of the year. No time for frivolity!

### THREE GATES

*If you are tempted to reveal*
*A tale to you someone has told*
*About another, make it pass*
*These narrow gates: First, "Is it true?"*
*Then, "Is it needful?"*

*In your mind give the trueful answer.*
*And the next is last and narrowest, "Is it kind?"*
*And if to reach your lips at last*
*If it passes through these gateways three*
*Then you may tell the tale, nor fear*
*What the result of speech may be.*
From the Arabian
*Best Known Poems of the American People* p. 613

My computer has articles today discussing the fact that the longest living people in the Blue Zones eat a lot of complex carbohydrates like beans and rice. Garbanzo beans (chickpeas) are said to be an excellent source of protein. I like them sprinkled on a salad. Remember that a grain plus a legume equals a whole protein. You don't need any meat when they are eaten together. I think I will make some chili today with the red kidney beans that are sitting on a pantry shelf. I will serve it over brown rice. White rice has little nutritious value. To me, it will taste best when about three days old.

**November 14, 2023**

Good morning, all 93. Today is **National Pickle Day, National Seat Belt Day** and **International Girls Day,** all three of which are of interest to me personally. I love Kosher dill pickles, as well as sweet ones. I also like relish, dill or sweet, in my tuna, chicken and potato salads. I even enjoy it on hot dogs with *French's* yellow mustard. I have not eaten one in a long time because of the nitrates and the salt they contain. Should I purchase some from *Safeway*, they would be *Nathan's* beef ones. I like them with sauerkraut.

As far as seat belts are concerned, they were new to my father's generation that balked at using them. My generation accepted them, although there were still those who rebelled. Present generations, by law, always buckle up first while telling their passengers to do so before the car moves. I always buckle up when I am riding in either the front or back seat of anyone's vehicle.

For **International Girls Day**, I am introducing you to a Delta Soror who is also a *Bennett College* sister in the Class of '42. Those of you who know her are wishing her a very happy 103rd birthday, too. She is not on our list because she does not use a computer, but she likes to talk on the telephone. The recent *AARP* bulletin that some of you got in the mail discusses "super-agers." She certainly is one of them who is blessed with good health and a very sound mind.

Girls on this list, do something special for yourself today! I'm going to get a bright red manicure with sparkles. My mother's generation did not have access to such a pleasure. Women painted their own nails. For years I had horrible nails because my hands were always in formaldehyde from dissecting. I did not wear gloves. Now they always look beautiful. Neither broken nor chipped.

**November 15, 2023**

Good morning, all 93 on the **Ides of November**. It's **National Raisin Bran Day** and **National Clean Up Your Neighborhood Day.** The first celebrates my favorite dry cereal. I brought my kids up on it. Because the number of raisins has decreased in a box, I will add an additional handful when I eat a bowlful with some almond milk. No added sugar. Speaking of sugar, that is what diabetes was called by people at one time. I know that "sugar" is still used by some older folk. Someone on this list reminded me that yesterday was **International Diabetes Day**. I had not mentioned it because, thankfully, I do not have diabetes. I wonder how many of you know that until insulin was discovered in 1921, diabetes was always fatal. "Curious Georges" might want to *Google* Dr. Frederick Banting to learn how he discovered insulin by accident. It may surprise you. Almost a miracle. Then again, maybe it *was* one.

I read something upsetting to me. You see, each October, my father would order four tons of anthracite coal from the town's coal man, John Dickerson. He was also the iceman in our small town. Coal was delivered to our house in a large truck that had a long chute to go through cellar windows. Coal was stored during the winter in a large coal bin built into home cellars. We had both a furnace and noisy radiators heating individual rooms. By October, homeowners with wood burning stoves would have chopped stacks of wood. On farms, silos would be filled with corn for animals. People knew how to prepare for the winter. Nowadays, people who use oil fill their tanks in their cellar. We had oil delivered by oil trucks in N.J., but I have electricity to heat my home now.

So here is what has upset me in the *Washington Post. Unsatisfied snow lovers may get their shot in 2024.* I am not looking forward to a snow-covered winter. My father had no such prediction as discussed in the article. It was just what cautious people did -- anticipate a very cold winter.

I envy the snowbirds from Canada who fly to my favorite St. Petersburg, Florida, and the folks from the North who take the Auto Train nonstop from Lorton, Virginia, to Sanford, Florida. Lorton is not far from where I live. The train leaves at 4:30 p.m. and arrives the next morning at about 9:00 a.m. It's the best way to go to Florida if one is staying for several months and needs a vehicle. Ed and I took it with our van for several years when we would spend winter months with someone on this list but who no longer resides there. That was heaven on earth. Old folks were out and about in the sun all day long. We loved it, especially our early morning walks along the St. Petersburg Beach.

**November 16, 2023**

Good morning, all 93. I think I'm back on standard time now because I went to bed last evening at 9:00 p.m. and awakened bright and early today at 7:00 a.m. The sun was just rising. I am going to make the most of the daylight today. Today is the **International Day for Tolerance**. How we need that around the globe! "*Thy kingdom come. Thy will be done,*" is my prayer.

It is also **Fast-Food Day**. So here is an excuse to go out and purchase a favorite treat for yourself. But don't make it a habit, though. My favorite is a Reuben. I can get one from a nearby restaurant called "Mama's Kitchen."

My computer lists the "dos and don'ts" of the garbage disposal. I am guilty of some don'ts. The *Washington Post* has this interesting article entitled, *"Why you should buy clothes to last (almost) forever."* I am guilty of having clothing in my closets from my working days more than thirty years ago. They have held up much better than some things I have bought in recent years. I need to purge!

## November 17, 2023

Good morning, all 93. It is **National Apple Cider Day**. I love a nice glass of cold apple cider. When living in Pennsylvania and New Jersey, we could purchase cider only at this time of the year, but now I see it being sold at other times. There was a farmer's stand where we would drive some distance to purchase a gallon of fresh cider. I like it heated, too, served in a mug with a cinnamon stick.

Back in the day, we could find cranberry sauce only at Thanksgiving and Christmas times. Now I buy my whole berry *Ocean Spray* sauce all year round. Love it. I also like cranberry juice, but that's high in sugar since cranberries are very bitter. Who knows about cranberry bogs? I first saw those bodies of water in Massachusetts when I was visiting Plymouth and the Mayflower replica. Wisconsin is the #1 grower of cranberries with Massachusetts as #2 and New Jersey as #3.

South Jersey has cranberry bogs in the Pine Barrens where there are also several unique species of frogs and unusual plants. *Ocean Spray* headquarters was in South Jersey for years before moving to Pennsylvania. Speaking of holidays, in my youth there were no turkeys except for Thanksgiving and Christmas.

## November 18, 2023

Good morning, all 93. Today is **International Men's Day** and **Gettysburg Address Day**. I remember having to memorize that short speech in high school. How about you? *"Four score and seven years ago....."*

I've been to Gettysburg, Pennsylvania, several times on "Remembrance Day" in November. I've had the opportunity to be among other authors selling books about the *Civil War*. Black and White Re-enactors galore attend and march with their comrades. Some are accompanied by bands. Many wives will join their husbands, and sometimes lively balls are held. My publicist and I were invited to one of them once where we delighted watching couples in period clothing merrily dancing jigs from the *Civil War* period. It can be quite cold in Gettysburg in November, and so they were wearing heavy attire. The men's uniforms can be very hot in the summertime.

There were male re-enactors. One was Frederick Douglass, who wears his thick hair just like Douglass did. Once there were two General Grants at the same time. A great camaraderie exists between the re-enactors and no competition. Even two Abraham Lincolns in top hats were in a parade.

Speaking of reenactments, one of my mountain-top experiences took place in Alabama. It was at the dedication of a tombstone for a Black *Civil War* veteran who had died 99 years before. There were a lot of reenactors present on a very hot day.

I was asked to speak briefly at the dedication. Interested people can *Google* the ceremony that took place on July 11, 2011, in the Sykes Cemetery in Decatur, Alabama. Like my Great-grandfather Crowder, Amos McKinney had served in an integrated regiment, the 1$^{st}$ Alabama Calvary. Historians told me that there were no Black soldiers serving in White regiments, but I knew better and wrote two small tomes about them in which I named hundreds.

## November 19, 2023

Good morning, all 109. My college-aged neighbor informed me that today is the 352$^{nd}$ day of 2023 and that only 13 days remain before a leap year when February 2024 will have 29 days. People born on February 29$^{th}$ will be able to celebrate their birthdays once again.

Today is **National Bake Cookies Day**. My young neighbor and I celebrated a day early because we made some cookies yesterday. I introduced her to some of my Great Aunt Lillie's cooking skills, such as cracking an egg into a small dish before adding it to a batter. Do you? I always do.

**November 20, 2023**

Good morning, all 96. This is **Universal Children's Day.** Also, it is the beginning of travel for Thanksgiving. The *Washington Post* reports that already air travel has increased since last year. My early memories of Thanksgiving include high school football games in the morning and the sumptuous turkey meal in the afternoon. My later memories in N.J. include the same, only I was the one preparing the dinner for perhaps ten neighbors and others who were friends of my children.

As far as high school football games, a rivalry existed between the town in which I worked (Bloomfield) and the town where my children attended school (Montclair). When the two were young, I could take them to the Thanksgiving game with me and we would sit with my colleagues on my students' side of the stadium. But when my children got older, I had to sit on Montclair side. Once when I was walking towards that side, one of my students saw me and asked where I was going. When I tried to explain, she called me a "traitor." She said that I should be cheering for my students. She had a smile on her face, though. That rivalry ceased when television football games took the attention away from small town rivalries. They had been such fun—homecomings for alumni to meet and greet each other after returning home from college.

**November 21, 2023**

Good afternoon, all 96. It's **National Entrepreneur Day**. Some of you are entrepreneurs, including my dear publicist. Enjoy your special day. I have several friends who do not use computers. Therefore, I must send them Christmas cards via snail-mail. I mailed one to my 103-year-old Delta Soror/*Bennett College* sister yesterday saying that I am hoping mine is the first card she receives this year. At her age, every day is super precious.

**November 22, 2023**

Good morning, all 96. Today is **Go For A Ride Day**. This applies to those who are driving back home for the Thanksgiving feast or driving to pick up something forgotten for dinner tomorrow, such as the requisite can of cranberry sauce (whole for me), or the jar of green olives stuffed with pimento, or the marshmallows for the sweet potato souffle.

Today is also **National Jukebox Day.** I wonder if everyone on my list knows what a jukebox is. Of course, if you do not, it's just a click away. When I was young, I loved to go to Greek diners where there was always a small jukebox in each booth. I loved to purchase a pastry there called a horn that has an almond filling and chocolate dipped ends. Yummy! Still do, although real Greek diners are as "scarce as hens' teeth" nowadays, especially here in Virginia. There are several "pseudo" diners in this area. I call them that because they may have a Greek cuisine, but the buildings are not the railroad diner shape. The history of diners in the USA is an interesting one for any inquiring mind. Just a click away.

**November 24, 2023**

Good morning, all 96. *"We gather together to ask the Lord's blessing."* Soon, Thanksgiving Day will be here. I hope I am one of the first to wish you a happy day. 'Tis "Turkey Day" across the states. Ethnicities galore will serve their favorite dishes. Many will serve a plump turkey, except for the vegetarians. If you've ever seen wild turkeys running around, you'll see that they are anything but plump. They look rather scrawny, just like what the Pilgrims would have caught.

An interesting holiday meal was served to me on a bus tour for Americans that I took in Scotland one summer. On the 4th of July we stopped at an inn for dinner. The owner greeted us graciously and announced that he was preparing a special American holiday meal just for us on that 4th of July. We thanked him for his kindness and readied our palates for hot dogs, hamburgers, buns, and perhaps some baked beans. Instead, he served us a delicious turkey dinner with mashed potatoes and other sides. No one had the heart to tell him that he had the wrong holiday. I don't remember if he served pumpkin pie for dessert. I doubt it.

Here's a tip to save yourself the need to peel white potatoes for mashing. Some people peel, cube and then boil. Others boil the potatoes in their skin and then peel. But I saw an even easier way today. Use a pair of scissors to make a ring around each potato and then throw it in a pot of water to cook. When done, each potato is placed in a bowl of ice water. In minutes the skins are peeled by themselves. Russets are the best potatoes for mashing. Some people add cream with the butter to make them creamier. Anyone still using your Grandma's hand potato masher? I have one. Who knows what one even looks like? Anyone make potato pancakes with the leftover mashed ones? Good for breakfast served with scrambled eggs, bacon or a piece of ham and apple sauce.

## December 5, 2023

Good morning, all 100. I'm "back in the saddle" again, hopefully, with my new *Dell* laptop. It has been quite an undertaking with so much to learn new on *Windows 11*.

I had been wondering who would be #100 on our list. I received an e-mail from her last week and invited her. She has been a real joy to know since she was a teenager. And her name is JOY. I don't think she will mind my sharing her name with you, especially during this joyous season. Several of you know her from when you were singing together at St. Mark's U.M. Church in Montclair, N.J. *"We've Come this far by faith, leaning on the Lord...."*

## December 6, 2023

Good morning, all 100. My new computer tells me that I missed **Pie Day** on the 1st, **Basketball Day** on the 2nd, **Let's Hug Day** on the 3rd, **Cookie Day** on the 4th, and **Blue Jeans Day** on the 5th. Today, the 6th, is **Mitten Tree Day.** Each of these days can apply to me, but I will write only about the teen basketball player, Juanita, and her blue jeans. My female classmates and I had to purchase ours at the Army and Navy store that was geared for men and boys. Denim jeans did not fit girls snugly until Gloria Vanderbilt introduced her brand for women and Brooke Shields advertised them. That was years after my generation bought jeans that had to be held up by a belt, and whose legs were rolled up at the bottom. It was forbidden for us to wear them to school and to *Bennett College* in 1951.

According to our university President, Dr. David D. Jones, *"Ladies do not wear trousers."* He had a daughter a generation older than I. I wonder if Frances ever did. She and my stepmother, Alice, were "besties" at *Bennett College* in the late 30s. I was in the next generation when American teens in the 1950s started to call denim pants "blue jeans," and they became the rage. They still are.

I have a lot of work to do so I can find lost documents. *Que sera sera.* For instance, I retrieved a letter that I had received in December 2010 from *Kings College* in Wilkes-Barre, Pennsylvania. I presumed it was a solicitation for yearly contributions. My only connection to *King's College* was that my father had carved a magnificent anthracite coal altar that resided in a small room in the college's chapel. It now sits majestically in the college's new chapel that used to be a Presbyterian Church in Wilkes-Barre, Pennsylvania. When I finally opened the letter, I saw that it was an invitation for me to be awarded a Doctorate of Humanities at Commencement in June 2011. Talk about surprises! Indeed, *"Yes, of course I would accept."* Thank you, *Kings College*.

**Juanita Patience Moss Receiving Honorary Doctorate from *Kings College***

**December 7, 2023**

Good morning, all 100. Today's date is one that I'll never forget -- Dec. 7, 1941. It is **Pearl Harbor Remembrance Day.** It is also the birthdate of one of my granddaughters. I was nine years old and in the 4th grade when the Japanese bombed Pearl Harbor, Hawaii early one Sunday morning. The next day the United States entered World War II which had been going on in Europe since Germany invaded Poland in 1939. Every able-bodied male from age 18 to 34 was drafted. Many boys as young as 16 with parental permission quit school to join. Sadly, soon in the front windows of many homes small flags were hung with gold stars for the fallen. The war would last for four long years until the dropping of the atomic bomb on Hiroshima in 1945. I was 13 and attending a Girl Scout camp when the war was officially declared over. I remember that we were allowed to stay up late that night. In my mind's eye, I can remember all of us young campers gathered around a bonfire, too young to know all that had happened during the past four years, but happy that our boys would be coming home soon.

**December 8, 2023**

Good morning, all 100. The last two days here have been dreary. I need bright sun and fresh air. My deck door is standing open, and I am going to put my winter coat on and drink my cup of hot coffee on the deck while I manufacture some Vitamin D.

Today is **National Brownie Day**. I love brownies made with walnuts. I know that some people are allergic to nuts, and many people do not include them when serving brownies for dessert. My Original Toll House cookies and oatmeal raisin ones always include walnuts. But if you were coming by for a visit, I would make some special ones sans walnuts just for you. You'd just have to tell me ahead of time that you are allergic to nuts. Fortunately, no one in my family is. It's Christmas cookie baking time again. What are some of your favorites? Last year I discovered a recipe for delicious shortbread cookies. They take a little time because they must be rolled out. I cut them into a star shape and top them with a pale-yellow lemon icing. Pretty and delicious. They also freeze well.

It was 70 years ago when my father and father-in-law were living that I would make for them a large assortment of Christmas cookies. It was like being an artist. After they passed away, my interest waned because if I bake cookies, I will eat them. *"Yield not to temptation."* My iced lemon stars are very tempting. Two years ago, I cut a sprig from a Christmas cactus in my chiropractor's office. His plant blooms beautifully each year in his office. Last Christmas mine did not bloom, but this year it is, and is delighting my soul.

**December 9, 2023**

Good morning, all 101. Sending Christmas cards can be very expensive now. On special occasions you will be receiving a lovely *Jacquie Larson* card from me via e-mail. Don't be afraid to open it. Should you wish to send a reply to the card, please include your full name since the company does not provide that information. Also, some of you have the same first name. In fact, four of you do.

Yesterday, when I was on my deck while drinking a cup of coffee and observing my very quiet neighborhood, one of my four-footed neighbors came hopping towards me along the top of the fence surrounding my backyard. It was the melanistic (black) squirrel living in the *Village of Gum Springs.* I kept very still as it approached where I was standing on my deck. It stopped suddenly, its tail swishing up and down as it sensed my presence, perhaps smelling "human." He and I stayed in our spots until he finally retreated. I noticed that my small garden was full of holes. I don't know if they were from that squirrel or the other gray squirrels vying for the same territory. I have never seen so many large squirrel nests as I did this year. I hope they aren't forecasting a cold, snowy winter.

**December 10, 2023**

Good morning, all 101. Today is **World Choral Day.** Reminds me of *We Are the World,* directed by Quincy Jones and sung by multiple vocalists including Lional Richie, Smokey Robinson, Stevie Wonder, Michael Jackson, Bruce Springsteen, Diana Ross, Ray Charles, and many other popular musicians. Even though I do not sing well, I have been in several choirs during my 91 ½ years, first to fill a space in a small children's choir, and then with a church choir consisting of both teenagers and adults. No one was accomplished enough to be a soloist. We all sang to praise the Lord. I also sang in the high school glee club where, in my sophomore year, Miss Catherine Fear taught us all the words to *"Twas the Night Before Christmas."* Still know them. It includes the names of all Santa's reindeer except for one. For you who may not be aware, the red-nosed Rudolph came along many years later. He was not among the original**s** when the song was written.

I even remember an added verse beginning with "*'Twas the night after Christmas and all through the house, not a creature was stirring, not even a mouse.....*" Being able to read music because of my years of piano lessons allowed me to sing in the choir at Wilkes College during my freshman year and at *Bennett College* during my sophomore year. I didn't have to audition for either, just show up. So, I did, and I have the photo to prove it.

I wish I were an accomplished alto like my Great Aunt Lillie. She and her tenor husband sang duets in churches. A tenor and alto combo present such a lovely harmony. Not that I ever heard them sing together because he died when I was only three. But I once knew a couple in Montclair with that beautiful sound. Several of you on this list may know the Spiveys who were members of *St. Paul's Baptist Church.* All this to say that I love choral music. It is now time for me to pull out my Handel's *Messiah* CD to listen to the beautiful voices on it. It is in two parts. I once thought that the *Hallelujah Chorus* was the finale, but it is not.

One last memory for today. On the 2nd Sunday of December 1951, when I was merely 18 years old, I met my future husband at a Christmas party. Two years later we married and lived "happily ever after" for 62 years. As you can imagine, I am missing him right now as are others on this list who also knew and loved him.

**December 11, 2023**

Good morning, all 102. This is **National Bagel Day**. One of my favorite breakfasts is lox (smoked salmon) and bagels with cream cheese, a slice of tomato, a piece of lettuce, and a few capers. Yum! I always have it at least once when I go to Virginia Beach each August, and definitely whenever I visit New York City. I could make my own combo, should I desire, since *Whole Foods* sells the lox. But it would not be on a New York bagel, which is special. They are not at all like *Lenders* pseudo-bagels.

**December 12, 2023**

Good morning, all 102. This is **National Poinsettia Day**. Most people mispronounce the flower's name. It is poin-set-tia. I once saw masses of red ones growing on the Island of St. Lucia in the Caribbean during one February when my family was on a cruise ship that stopped there. I was amazed to see how tall the shrubs can grow. Nowadays, one can find other shades, such as pink and white. Horticulturists have hybridized them. Why do I call poinsettia a shrub? Because its stems are woody and grow in width like trees, forsythia and lilacs. You are all aware of annual rings. Native to Mexico and Central America, the poinsettia was first described by Europeans in 1834. It was named after the first U.S. Minister to Mexico, Joel Roberts Poinsett, who introduced the plant to the U.S. in the 1820s.

**December 13, 2023**

Good morning, all 103. Today 'tis **National Violin Day, Ice Cream Day** and **National Cocoa Day**. All three can apply to me. My favorite ice cream is butter pecan and I enjoy a hot cup of cocoa. Not too particular about marshmallows in it, though. As for the violin, I never played one, but my son did for a short time when he was a pre-teen. His instructor in N.J. had been one of the fiddlers in *Fiddler on the Roof* on Broadway. I just saw it on *Turner Classics* a few days ago. It's one of my favorites. *Tradition*!

One of my favorite poems is in *The Best Loved Poems of the American People,* called "The Touch of the Master's Hand." It compares the worth of a violin with the worth of a person. My son and I performed together several times at church services when I read the poem, and he played *Morning is Breaking* on his violin. He was an interesting child with many interests, all of which his father and I encouraged. When he discovered the computer while in the 6th grade, he found his life's work. At that time, I had never heard of a computer. I had an electric typewriter, which was an advantage over a manual one, which was an advantage over a fountain pen, which was a step above dipping a quill pen into India ink for writing and labelling biology diagrams. I've experienced them all. What's next in technology? What might make computers obsolete?

I found an article in the *Washington Post* that I will share, entitled *I'm not Jewish, but I love my mezuzah.* As you may know, this is **Hanukkah**. What is a "mezuzah," you may ask? I was introduced to one when I bought a Dutch colonial house in N.J. which several on this list have visited. I had lived in it for a number of years before I gave a party for some colleagues on the day before school opened in September. One of them was a young Jewish woman with whom I am still close friends. When I opened my front door, she noticed the painted-over mezuzah nailed to the left doorpost. I had no idea of its significance, but the house had been built by a Jewish businessman in the 1940s. I bought the house from a Black person in 1974.

A mezuzah is important to Jewish people. It has a blessing stored inside. People touch it like a kiss when they go out and return home. After I learned what it was, our mezuzah stayed in place for the entire 33 years we lived at 32 Oxford Street. I wonder if it is still there hidden under paint and with its meaning unknown to the owners who purchased the house for over one million dollars last year. Ed and I paid $40,000 for it in 1974 and sold it for $225,000 in 1992.

Before COVID, I attended a religious play at the *Sound and Sight Theater* in Lancaster, Pennsylvania. There I saw pseudo-mezuzahs for sale and purchased one. That is, it has been Christianized. Its message reads: *"God's blessing rest upon this house and all who dwell within. May all who enter this house also be blessed."* It hangs on the door of my computer cabinet as a reminder of the constant presence of God. *"He walks with me, and He talks with me and He tells me I am His own"* which are words from the hymn *In the Garden.*

## December 14, 2023

Good morning, all 103. Today is **Roast Chestnuts Day**. I mentioned before about my Great Aunt Lillian's love for roasted chestnuts. *"Chestnuts roasting on the open fire,"* sung by Nat King Cole, is from a song you may be familiar with even though you have never tasted chestnuts. It may be an acquired taste, I think. Four species of chestnuts and several hybrids are grown in the United States today. On the streets of New York, vendors sell them in brown paper bags.

Back in the day, *Radio City Music Hall* would show a movie along with the Christmas show featuring the famous Rockettes. The movies ended possibly 45 years ago, because my daughter was a teenager when they no longer were shown. The reason, so I heard, was because Hollywood was not making movies suitable for family audiences.

## December 15, 2023

Good morning, all 105 on **Bill of Rights Day**. In case you do not remember from your civics classes, that pertains to the first 10 amendments to the *Constitution*. Today also has a more frivolous side, being both **National Cupcake Day** and **International Tea Day.** The latter two can be compatible for those who **enjoy both**. Cupcakes are what mothers would make for birthday parties for their grammar school aged kids. I have been told by someone on our list that because of dietary restrictions, that practice has ceased. Cupcakes are showing up nowadays at different venues, even weddings. No longer is cutting a fancy cake with a long sharp knife happening. My favorite cupcake is a yellow one with a thick chocolate icing. I also like a red velvet one with a vanilla icing.

As for **International Tea Day**, I'm not a regular tea drinker, but every now and again I drink a cup of green tea sans sugar. My Great Aunt Lillie always drank a piping hot cup of Orange Pecot tea following her dinner. She liked a lot of sugar, along with lemon juice when it was available. I never joined her because I had not been allowed to drink tea or coffee when I was a child. Instead, I drank lots of milk. Perhaps that's why, even though I have fallen several times during my life, I have not broken any bones.

A milkman used to deliver bottles of milk to homes very early in the mornings. He had a truck. The horse and wagon delivery had ceased by the time I came along, even though a farmer's wife still drove hers to town to sell her wares on Saturday mornings. The milk in those days was pasteurized, but not homogenized, and so the cream rose to the top of the bottle. A paper top closed it tight. In some homes, the bottle of milk would immediately be shaken so the cream would be mixed with the skim milk. In my home, however, no one was allowed to do that until my father poured off some of the pure cream into his coffee. Then the remainder of the bottle could be shaken and poured over oatmeal or drunk from a glass.

Back to my Great Aunt Lillie's tea. Lemons were not always available. A tangerine would be a special Christmas stocking treat. I remember the first time I had one. I was delighted that it peeled so easily. Some oranges are difficult to peel. Consequently, they were usually quartered and still are. I just purchased some easy to peel clementines yesterday. Love them.

**December 17, 2023**

Good morning, all 108. With rain being predicted, this would not be the type of day the Wright Brothers, Orville and Wilbur, would have chosen for their experiment in 1903. They made the first controlled, sustained flight of a powered, heavier-than-air aircraft with the *Wright Flyer* four miles south of Kitty Hawk, North Carolina. If any of you have visited the museum there, you know why that windy spot with extremely high sand dunes was chosen by the Wright brothers. I visited Kitty Hawk once and was amazed by the intensity of the wind. It was difficult even to walk.

Imagine a life without airplanes, as my Great Aunt Lillie's was after she was born in 1883. Such a life probably was also my father's, born a generation later in 1906. No noisy "aero planes" woke him like the ones I heard yesterday morning flying over my home.

My first flight was in 1960 with my five-year-old daughter to visit my brother and family in Winston-Salem, N.C. and my husband's sister at *Bennett College* in Greensboro. At that time in the South, buses and trains were segregated, as well as their stations. Airlines, however, were never segregated, including the newly opened Greensboro-Winston Salem Airport in 1960. So, my little daughter and I flew to N.C. from N.J. My two longest flights have been to Australia and Egypt. My most exciting flight, though, was on a 6-seated Cessna that flew through the Grand Canyon. Such flights were stopped years ago after too many accidents had occurred. At the time I took lots of photos to make a slide presentation for my students.

One of these days, I need to check my slide projector to see if it still works. I'd like to look at my slides again, especially of my trips to Egypt and Australia where I petted a kangaroo. It stank! It was not until World War II that military airplanes would fly over our houses. We'd run outside excitedly just to see them. Now we do not bat an eye. *"What hath God wrought"* in the last 120 years? I am borrowing that phrase from Samuel Morse, inventor of the telegraph who was the first to transmit a message using the Morse Code on May 24, 1844. He sent a biblical transmission from Washington to Baltimore. *"What Hath God Wrought?* (Numbers 23:23)." Interpreted as *"What has God created?"*

**December 19, 2023**

Good morning, all 109. Today is the 352$^{nd}$ day of 2023 and there are only 13 days remaining before a leap year when February 2024 will have 29 days. People who were born on February 29$^{th}$ will be able to celebrate their birthday once again. Why is there a Leap Year? Because years are really 364 1/4 days, so, every four years an extra 24 hours are added to the next year. It's **Bachelor's Day,** where women propose marriage to men.

'Tis also **National Bake Cookies Day**. My young neighbor and I celebrated the day early because we baked cookies yesterday. I introduced her to some of my Great Aunt Lillie's cooking skills, such as cracking an egg into a small dish before adding it to a batter. Why? Because she was from an era when eggs were purchased fresh from a farmer if one did not have her own flock, which she never had. Unfortunately, eggs sometimes were rotten. So, after a batter already had been prepared, the cook would not want it to be wasted due to a rotten egg.

Aunt Lillie would crack each egg individually before adding it. She did that even when preparing scrambled eggs. In all my cooking experiences, I have never come across a rotten egg, and none of you have either, I would presume, since we purchase them from a grocery. Still, my habit is to crack my eggs one at a time in a side dish, just in case. How about you?

I have not been to a mall this year to see the decorations and hear the bells jingling, but I might be able to when I go to my daughter's home in Connecticut this weekend.

**December 20, 2023**

Good morning, all 109. This is **Poet Laureate Day, International Solidarity Day** and **Sacagawea Day.** Sacagawea was a young Lemhi Shoshone woman who helped the Lewis and Clark Expedition in achieving their chartered mission objectives by exploring the Louisiana Territory, travelling from North Dakota to the Pacific Ocean. She traveled with the two for thousands of miles. In my teens, I became fascinated by her story, which you who are interested can *Google* without having to go to the library like I did when writing a book report about her for a high school English class. I wrote it in long hand because I did not have a typewriter until I got a manual one during my freshman year at *Wilkes College*. Dr. Davies, my English professor, complained about not being able to read my handwriting.

It's **Go Caroling Day,** which brings back a memory from my teens when my church secured a horse to pull a straw-filled wagon for our youth group to carol for elderly, sick and shut ins. Afterwards, we went back to the church for hot chocolate and donuts. My last remembrance of group caroling is with several of you who sang with the Choralaires. We would carol at nursing homes where the residents were happy to see us. One resident told me that she had not seen a child in two years. I felt so sad for her and others in the same lonely situation.

**December 21, 2023**

Good morning, all 110. 'Tis the *Winter Solstice* and the first day of winter in the Northern Hemisphere. Only three months 'til spring, my favorite time of the year. Until that time, I am in hibernation, not quite like a bear, though. I do step out of my townhouse, every now and again. For instance, I had a wonderful time at my church's "Seasoned Saints" Gala yesterday. Those are senior citizens 65 years and older. We were all attired in beautiful white, even some of the handsome older gentlemen. It was delightful watching agile old folks dancing the "Electric Slide."

'Tis the first day of summer in Australia and New Zealand and all places in the Southern Hemisphere. I'd love to see the Christmas decorations "down under," to see the similarities and the differences. I was in Mexico one December and Christmas there did not look like here.

I loved geography when I was a child, so, that's why solstices, equinoxes, hemispheres, longitude, and latitude are fascinating to me. I don't think that subject is taught nowadays. Too bad. When I was a kid, many homes had a world globe sitting in the living room. The names of countries on modern globes may be different from what they were on mine in the 1940s, but the sizes and shapes of continents have not changed. I'd like to have one with a light in it. The earth will tilt on its axis today and slowly return to an equinox on March 21$^{st}$, just as it has done since *"In the beginning God created the heavens and the earth"* (Genesis 1:1).

**December 23, 2023**

Good morning, all 111. I did not send a message yesterday because I was travelling with my grandson to Connecticut where I am now. Traffic was very heavy and slow. It took longer than the usual six hours. At about 5:00 p.m. we crossed the *Tappan Zee Bridge* connecting N.J. with N.Y. It was so dark that it felt more like 9:00 p.m. That's another reason why I do not like winter. It reminds me of the time I was in London once at Christmastime. My stepmother, Alice, and I were shopping at *Harrod's* at about 3:00 p.m. when darkness began to descend. Over the loudspeaker came this message that is reminiscent of the Charles Dickens' play *Oliver*. It was, *"The pickpockets are out. Watch your pocketbooks."*

**December 24, 2023**

Good afternoon, all 116. I went out yesterday to a Mall. Just wanted to see Santa and enjoy watching some adorable, excited kiddies. Some were all dressed up for their photos with Santa. Many of you may plan to attend a church service this evening, especially Christmas Eve Mass. Be blessed. I am interested in the traditions and customs of different ethnicities. If you are, too, you might like the *Netflix* movie I recently saw called *Feast of The Seven Fishes,* about a custom carried on by some Italians on Christmas Eve. The setting is near Pittsburgh where many men from Europe had migrated to work in bituminous coal mines. As many of you know, I grew up on the other side of the state where many Italian men worked in anthracite coal mines. Bituminous coal is softer than anthracite. Even though I had Italian friends, I was not familiar with the *Feast of Seven The Fishes* until I moved to New Jersey where one of my colleagues told me about it. I hope I will receive some responses to this from my Italian friends on the list. I'd like to hear about your memories of Christmas Eve.

### *A Response: Merry Christmas Eve, Dr. J.*

*Responding to your musing today. We did not eat seven fishes for Christmas Eve and probably many of the Italians you knew as a child did not, so that's why it was new to you. It's a regional tradition of southern Italy and Sicily. My family was from Tuscany, pretty far from there in miles and culture, and many of our neighbors were from neighboring regions - Morgantinis, Bertis, Barnis, Bovanis, Chiavaccis…it's like the difference between southern and northern U.S cuisine.*

*Both sides of my family were from the areas around Florence. No seafood since they were from the landlocked hills . Our big meal was/is on Christmas Day as opposed to Christmas Eve. And we had homemade ravioli, capon, ham, lots of sides, always salads, and ricotta cheesecake with strawberry topping for dessert. Also, chestnuts, and a platter of oranges and nuts in the shell with a silver nutcracker - a very old tradition. Homemade wine / but we had small juices glasses of it, not big stemware like today. And everyone had some. The kids had 7-Up with a tiny bit of wine in it to make it pink. That was a thrill for us. Wine was a part of the meal but not a drink to get drunk or tipsy on. And then different varieties of homemade cookies. Always my mother's biscotti.*

*The ravioli was made ahead of time and frozen. It was a family and friends' operation since it was labor-intensive, and we made a large quantity. Whatever your traditions are, we hope you enjoy them and enjoy being with family this holiday.*

Thanks, Dear West Pittston Friend but now living elsewhere.

**December 25, 2023**

Merry Christmas, all 117. May each of us be blessed today with wonderful memories of Christmases past with loved ones who have gone to be with the Lord. Remember that the real "reason for the season" is found in the scripture John 3:16-17: *"For God so loved the world that he gave His only Son, that whoever believes in Him shall not perish but have eternal life. For God did not send his Son into the world to condemn the world, but to save the world through Him."* Thanks be to God.

**December 28, 2023**

Good morning, all 118. I am back home again and sending a musing today, but none tomorrow. Today is **Call a Friend Day** and **National Chocolate Candy Day.** Thanks to one of you on this list, I am celebrating with the box of chocolate candy that arrived from a high school classmate while I was away. Thanks to her. I will just say to each, *"Be blessed today."* If you have a friend whom you have not heard from for a while, this is the day to make a call. You will be a blessing to that person.

**December 30, 2023**

Good morning, all 122. On this day in 1803, the U.S doubled in size when it formally took control of Louisiana. It was bought from France for $15 million dollars. Also, today is **National Bacon Day**. Yeah, for a BLT lathered with *Hellman's* mayo! That is, unless you are a vegan or a non-pork eater. I am neither but do go easy on meat. One of my favorite meals is fresh pork ribs and sauerkraut served with white potatoes and applesauce. It is a German meal.

**December 31, 2023**

Good afternoon, all 124. 'Tis **Make Up Your Mind Day**. It may pertain to making New Year's resolutions. Being kinder and more considerate to others is my resolution for 2024. The first **Watch Night Service** was celebrated in Black communities in America on this date in 1872 when slaves and free Blacks gathered in churches and private homes all across the nation, awaiting the news that the **Emancipation Proclamation** had become law. It was on January 1, 1873. Thanks be to God!

**January 1, 2024**

Good morning, all 124. Seems like it was just 2000, which was amazing to write on a check for the first time 24 years ago. I did not stay up to watch the ball descend on Times Square last evening as I had so many times through the years. Before retiring, I remembered some of the New Year Eve parties I attended in my young married years in Wilkes-Barre, PA and then later in Montclair, NJ., where it was a "must" to attend a party at someone's home. We'd be dressed "to the nines."

Oftentimes, someone who had moved away but was visiting their parents for the holidays came to these parties. After 1958, Ed and I were among that number. The older "set," which included my parents' friends, often hosted movable New Year's Eve parties. That is, cocktails at one home, heavier food at someone else's home, and desserts at a third home. I remember when Ed and I were finally considered old enough to be invited to a "grown-up" party at an aunt and uncle's home. I have black and white photos from before there was color photography. They held up much better than the later colored Polaroids which were all the rage for a while. Immediate photos. It was a miracle! But they are mostly faded now.

I have a lovely black and white photo taken in 1957 of 12 couples who were members of *Club 402*. We were the younger "set" in Wilkes-Barre. I am the last one still standing in 2024, thanks be to God. Many of you may celebrate family traditions on New Year's Eve, so enjoy! Once a colleague in N.J. took Ed and me to his West Indian mother's house for "hog head cheese." That is souse made from pickled pig parts in a gelatin base. I liked it. Ed did not. Other Black homes may serve chitterlings and pig feet. I will eat the latter but not the former.

**January 2, 2024**

Good morning, all 124. Yesterday I watched the Rose Bowl Parade. I remembered when Ed and I took our two children to it in 1969 during our school's Christmas break, which was always the longest when Christmas was on a Thursday. And so, we planned a bus trip south along the Pacific Ocean from San Francisco that ended in Los Angeles. We were all bedecked in London fog raincoats. My kids thought we looked silly, but we were well protected from the elements. First, we planned to tour in San Francisco for a few days. Our hotel room was on the $27^{th}$ floor. We arrived during the night and in the morning when we woke up, I opened the closed drapes to look out. All I could see was fog. It took three days before finally we could see a bridge in the distance. "*On a clear day I can see forever…..*" Then I understood the meaning of that song.

It was the first time I had tasted sour dough bread, for which I developed a love. We visited Muir's Woods to see the giant redwoods there. Amazing to behold. Then we went to Fisherman's Wharf where I ate clam chowder from a bowl made out of bread. Delicious. I saw enormous cones from sugar pines. Craftsmen craft various articles from them such as ducks.

Later we traveled to Pasadena for the Rose Bowl Parade. We had to arrive very early in the morning, so we parked our rental car before dawn to get seats in the bleachers, first come, first served. It was a very, very cold January $1^{st}$. We shared blankets because we had been forewarned about how low the temperatures might dip. They did. Once out there in the winter is enough for me. "Been there; done that." What I can see at home of the Rose Bowl Parade on my television is simply marvelous. Beauty and ingenuity can be admired without my being cold.

My son reminds me that we tasted tacos for the first time on that trip to southern California and fell in love with them. It was at a goddaughter's home in Palm Springs. Both she and her sister are on my musing list. We arrived there lugging our London fog rain gear. How ridiculous we must have looked when we deplaned at the airport.

**January 3, 2024**

Good morning, all 125. This is **Glaucoma Awareness Month** and **Cervical Cancer Awareness Month.** On a jollier note, it's **Festival of Sleep Day** and **National Chocolate Covered Cherry Day.** My father always gave me a box of chocolate covered maraschino cherries for Christmas. Haven't had any in years. Too sweet. But I will always remember that special treat from him. You may wonder why I talk only about my father and never my mother. It is because when they got divorced, my mother returned to where she had been born in Tacoma, Washington. She took my younger brother with her, while I remained with my father's family, including his grandmother and aunts. He was single until he married my stepmother, Alice, when I was sixteen. I then lived with them until I married Edward Irving Moss.

**Festival of Sleep Day** is all about rest and relaxation. Getting enough sleep is important for our health and well-being. I get plenty. Just like chickens. Early to roost. Early to rise.

**January 4, 2024**

Good morning, all 125. It is **National Spaghetti Day, National Trivia Day** and **World Braille Day.** Louis Braille invented a tactile reading and writing system that transformed the lives of countless people with severe vision impairments or blindness. Blind himself, while still at school he was the first with the idea of a form of writing that one can read by touch. Spaghetti will be for my dinner today. Angel hair is my favorite pasta and marinara my favorite "sauce," which I learned to love in PA but called "gravy" in N.J. This day reminds me of my many Italian friends and neighbors in West Pittston, Pennsylvania, as well as many students in Bloomfield, N.J., several whom are on my musing list.

**January 5, 2024**

Good morning, all 125. Tomorrow is *Dia de Los Reyes* (Three Kings Day or Epiphany). **Epiphany,** one of the oldest Christian feasts, has been celebrated since the end of the Second Century, prior to the Christmas holiday being established. What a boon to our modern existence! No more pouring through encyclopedias like I had to do not so long ago. Anyone have a set of *World Book* in your home? I sold sets for a while in the late 50s. It was delightful and stimulating, as was the accompanying *Child Craft* for young children. Both were popular because they were beautifully illustrated, which the children and their parents enjoyed. I know that I did.

**January 6, 2024**

Good morning, all 127. Today is **Dia de Los Reyes (Three Kings) Day**. I got a little ahead of myself yesterday. Someone on this musing list sent me some interesting information about his pet blue jay. I had no idea that they could be so happily caged. Blue jays, cardinals and robins are birds I know in both PA and N.J. where they are plentiful. I like to watch birds at the seashore, but I am not an ornithologist and cannot identify many as they are skittering along the sand on their long legs as they search for food. I have never gone "birding" with binoculars, but I am not averse to doing so with other people who know what they are looking for. I love swans, eagles, herons, flamingoes, puffins, canaries, and penguins. Some birds are so beautifully colored. Owls are the only birds with eyes in front of their heads like humans. Are they really wise? All birds have feathers and lay eggs, but not all birds can fly. Consider the stately ostrich and the funny looking road runner from out west. They are categorized as "flightless" birds in ornithology.

One of my favorite *Bible* verses includes the soaring eagle.
*"But they that wait upon the Lord will renew their strength.*
*They shall mount up on wings as eagles.*
*They shall run and not be weary.*
*And they shall walk and not faint."* (Isaiah 40:31).

We saw soaring eagles on our Alaska trip in 2002, celebrating our 50th wedding anniversary.

**January 7, 2024**

Good morning, all 128. Today is **Orthodox Christmas** for certain Eastern Orthodox churches, including those in Russian and others that follow the ancient Julian calendar, which runs 13 days later than the Gregorian calendar that is presently used by Catholic and Protestant churches. Some other Orthodox, including those in the Greek tradition and some Ukrainian churches, now celebrate Christmas on the same date as Western churches.

I received some interesting responses about birds. I have photos of the caged blue jay I mentioned, swans in N.J. and a beautiful male peacock in Santiago, Chile, where one of you was vacationing. Thank you. Another told me about the birds she watches from her deck: owls, falcons and eagles, and masses of starlings flying in their unique manner. We saw thousands of them in Maryland when we drove from Virginia to N.J., usually in the fall when they are gleaning food from the fields after the corn and other crops have been harvested. I was so amazed when I saw them for the first time. I am now pulling from my cerebrum all the birds whose names I am familiar with. I am surprised at how many I know without looking in a bird book or *Google*, which I can easily do. But I want to exercise my brain.

Someone from West Pittston, PA, has told me about her chickens. The hens, all personally named, provide her with morning eggs. They would not be allowed where I live, especially not noisy roosters. I missed mentioning the sparrow, but one of my favorite hymns is "*His Eye is On the Sparrow.*" It reminds me that if God's eye is on the little sparrow, so it is on me. African American singer, Ethel Waters, many years ago sang that hymn during Billie Graham Crusades. She would end it by changing the last word "me." Rather, she sang, "*And I know He's watching we.*" And so He is. I know that He has watched over me.

**January 8, 2024**

Good afternoon, all 128. January 8th has no particular significance, so I am going to include a paragraph from the explanation I send when inviting people to my list.

You are young and old friends and family members, mostly cousins. Male and female; Black, White, and Latino; Catholic, Protestant, Jehovah's Witness, and Jewish; hailing from the Northeast, middle America, South, and West and from Jamaica and Tobago; goddaughters; Bennett College sisters; Wilkes College alumnae; Delta Sigma Theta, Inc. Sorors; present and past church members; work colleagues; former students; high school classmates; neighbors; a daughter; daughter's friends; a son; son's friends; grandchildren; a sister; nieces; nephews including one great; in-laws; a bridesmaid; a flower-girl; and much younger St. Mark's U.M. Church Choralaires from Montclair, N.J. Some of you fall into more than one category and each of you is beloved.

I have received several more interesting responses to the birds' messages. Forgotten birds keep popping into my head, such as the toucan. This is good exercise for all of our cerebrums. It reminds me of a childhood game we children played long before television came into our homes. It was hop-scotch on sidewalks which we would divide into squares with chalk. I can't remember the rules, but I do remember it was good exercise for our developing brains. Did anyone else play this game? We younger kids learned from the older ones when we all played together "back in the day."

**January 9, 2024**

Good morning, all 128. Today is **Play God Day**. My computer did not discover any new information on the meaning or purpose of this day. What we know is that **God is good** all the time. Therefore, I believe that this is a day to do something good and extra special. Reminds me of a hymn that says, "*Make me a blessing, Oh, Savior, I pray. Make me a blessing to someone today.*" Every day should be a **Play God Day**. I like that concept.

As for the hopscotch which I mentioned yesterday, perhaps the game my friends played was not hopscotch at all, but that is what my West Pittston friends called it. I was remembering how we played it. We bounced a ball in each square after announcing what our topic would be when it was our turn. If we lost control of the ball, we lost our turn. We were just little kids and that could easily happen. We would say something like "fruit" and then name as many as we could. I don't remember how a winner was determined. Makes me think of other pre-television games—jump rope, jacks and marbles. One of my male cousins collected a bag of beauties. I wonder what happened to those marbles of yesteryear. If I had any I would place them at the bottom of a vaseful of flowers.

**January 10, 2024**

Good morning, all 128. It **is National Save the Eagles Day, Houseplants Appreciation Day, Bittersweet Chocolate Day,** and **Cut Your Energy Costs Day.** One or more of these choices might suit your fancy. The houseplants are right down my alley. I've always had some in my home. In N.J. so many plants were placed in front of my living room windows that Ed called it "the jungle." It had a wonderful southern exposure. Some of you may remember my beautiful plants in N.J. Many friends adopted them when I moved to Virginia where I had to begin anew. I have a much smaller home and just a few plants now. My favorite is the Christmas cactus that was in bloom right on time in 2023. Why should you have some houseplants in your home? Not just because they may be pretty, but because their leaves manufacture oxygen for you to breathe. How many of you remember learning about photosynthesis in your biology class? I am confident that my former students on this list will remember.

I had several responses about how we little kids played hopscotch. Seems that rules may have differed from region to region, just like "soda" and "pop."

Yesterday's *Washington Post* had an article, *Your first test of 2024: Are you fit for your age?* Today's article of interest to me is *5 tips for shaking the salt habit.* That's because I have a "tetch" of high blood pressure for which I take amlodipine and losartan. I never sprinkle salt on my food at the dinner table. In fact, you would be hard pressed to find a saltshaker in my home. Same for a sugar bowl. I do have both, should you request them.

**January 11, 2024**

Good morning, all 128. "She" does not tell me much that caught my interest today. The *Washington Post* has an article in its Local Living section titled *8 ways to get a cleaner house in 2024: The path to a tidier, more organized space doesn't have to be overwhelming.* I will read it the day after I return home from "lunching" with someone I have not seen since BC which used to be "Before Christ," only. Now it is "Before COVID" which, thankfully, I have not had.

As you know, I've been fascinated this year by the activity of the grey squirrels in my neighborhood. A neighbor told me yesterday that he saw about ten running up and down trees at one time. I have five or so who visit me on a regular basis. Since fall, I have been predicting a hard winter because of their increased activity when hiding their stash of acorns and building large nests in tall trees. It seems some sections across the country are having very bad weather right now. Hopefully, it will not be so here.

**January 12, 2024**

Good morning, all 128. One of you sent the following message which my computer did not inform me about. Just read a *Huffington Post* article that stated: *Today is known as 'quitters' day,' which is apparently when people who make New Year's resolutions have already cast them aside or abandoned them.* Very interesting. I never make resolutions because I know I will break them.

This also is **National Pharmacist Day,** honoring pharmacists and recognizing their important roles in medical care. I will make a special trip to CVS to wish my pharmacist **Happy Pharmacist's Day**. I'll be surprised if he knows what I am talking about. Today is also **National Tea Day**. Enjoy your cup. My favorite is green tea sans the sugar.

**January 13, 2024**

Good morning, all 128. I spoke at length on the telephone last evening with a former colleague who is the same age as I. She is not on my musing list because she does not have a computer. Never wanted one. Can you imagine that? I have several older friends who do not, and I might not have if I had not helped my blind stepmother publish her memoirs in 1998. She had become blind due to glaucoma. There was a history of it in her family. She fought it for years but lost the battle seven years before she passed away.

I was transcribing her words from a tape recorder when my son visited me from California. He was appalled that I was using an electric typewriter. He said, *"You need a computer."* And the rest is history. Even though I balked at first, he sent me my first computer from California and taught me how to use it from afar. How gratifying it is when parents can learn from their children.

Yesterday, I had the local *Critter Control* inspect the spot on my roof where a determined squirrel has been trying to get into my house via a gutter since summer. I live in a four-story townhouse, and it is difficult for anyone to get onto my roof to check. I had a raccoon in my attic several years ago. A male was successfully trapped and taken away. Today the technician took pictures of my roof with a drone so I could see where the squirrel may have entered my attic and made a comfy nest. Not that a nest can be seen by the drone, but the point of entrance into my roof can be.

Because I am on a waiting list, the entrance will not be sealed until next week He assures me that a lot of damage has not been done yet, but that squirrel is quite aggressive and may cause havoc if not taken care of NOW. My daughter has photos of it as it tried to stare me down menacingly back in August. The nerve of it! That squirrel's got to go!

I have mentioned seeing many squirrels this year and the many holes they have dug in my garden, even to uprooting my beautiful winter pansies. The technician's explanation is that oak trees produced a "bumper crop" of acorns this year, providing an ample diet for many to live. He said that this happens every five years. Well, I've lived here for 32 years and not noticed so many squirrels before. I will take him at his word. I just don't want them in my house—ever.

**January 14, 2024**

Good morning, all 128. Today has National significance in the U.S.A. It is **Ratification Day** that annually recognizes the act that officially ended the American Revolution. On a lighter note, January 14th is also **Dress Up Your Pet Day.** You might want a coat and booties for your doggies, should snow fall in your area. Then they could get dressed up when going for their walks. What are dog owners in Iowa doing today in 24 below zero-degree weather?

**January 15, 2024**

Good morning, all 128. This is **Martin Luther King Jr. Day**. The holiday is like other holidays set under the Uniform Monday Holiday Act. Several years ago, I chaperoned a group of teenagers, including my oldest grandson, on a bus trip to Atlanta, Georgia, where we toured areas pertaining to Dr. King's life, including the home in which he grew up, his church—the Ebenezer Baptist Church, a small museum, and his tomb. He was still a very young man at age 39 when he was assassinated in Memphis, Tennessee. His memory lives on, but so does his dream. We still are asking, *"How long?"* For what? That all men and women are created equal!

On a lighter note, today is **National Hat Day**. My computer shows a photograph of rows of men's hats that remind me of the ones my father's generation wore. Men were usually attired either in casual clothes, which included work clothes like dungarees, or in dress clothes like suits. Their dress hat often was a *Fedora*. Baseball caps became the rage years later when men began dressing informally for most occasions. My Ed always wore a *Fedora* as a dapper young man in the 40s. Even little boys wore dress hats to church. Took them off, of course, when they entered the edifice, as well as just about everywhere else inside. Men tipped their hats to ladies, and Catholic men respectfully took their hats off whenever passing a Catholic church, even while riding on a bus. That is where I observed the custom, when I rode a bus from West Pittston to Wilkes Barre during my freshman year at Wilkes in 1950. There were several Catholic churches along the way.

A lot of thought went into a man's picking out a dress hat. It had to fit just right to look good. Specialty hat shops catered to stylish men. The *Fedora* went out of style in the 50s but comes back in style occasionally when men want to dress formally, especially during the winter. I like them on spiffy gentlemen. Young men do not take their baseball caps off nowadays but wear them everywhere. They do not wear them in my church, but I don't know about others.

### January 16, 2024

Good morning, all 129. My highlight of yesterday was to see a brown female cardinal sitting alone with her bright red mate at 4:30 p.m., both roosting in the same tree. Unbelievably, in the very same tree sat a lone robin. I thought to myself, *"Go out front and take a look at your holly tree."* Sure enough, it had been stripped clean of its red berries. The last time I noticed robins in the winter was during a snow-magedon about 12 years ago. Surprisingly, at that time I beheld a flock of very large robins in my holly tree. They had stripped it clean, so, I wanted to check it out yesterday afternoon. Was it the robins or the cardinals who had a great meal? Or all three?

### January 17, 2024

Good morning, all 129. At 6:00 this morning I peeked out my 3rd floor bedroom window to see if it was snowing again. What my wondering eyes beheld in the East looked like a bright diamond sitting on the top my neighbor's roof. I knew immediately that it was Venus, the so-called "morning star." After admiring it, I lay down to go back to sleep but could not. A half hour later I was compelled to peek at Venus again. It had risen to what seemed to my inquiring eyes about an inch. I still could not go back to sleep. So, at 7:00 a.m. I peeked again to see Venus even higher as the sky brightened at sunrise. Soon it disappeared. *"How great Thou art!"*

Several of you know that I love to look for Venus in the southwest sky in the early evenings. It cannot be seen at the same time everywhere, although I have seen it in many locations. It has its own rotational path, as does our Planet Earth, never to collide with another since *"In the beginning God created the heaven and the earth." (*Genesis 1:1). How Great is our God!

When my Ed and I used to winter in Florida with someone on this list, we always looked for Venus. In the early evenings, the planet would be directly to our left as we entered her front door. Throughout the years, I've pointed the planet out to many others and encouraged them to become Venus's admirers, too. Consequently, some of you on this list are. *"The heavens declare the glory of God."* (Psalm 19:1).

### January 18, 2024

Good morning, all 130. Going back to Monday, I did not exactly "do nothing." I read some. I have hundreds of books in my home library which is really my whole house. Books are everywhere. Some I have read more than once, such as several of James Mitchner's. He is one of my favorite authors. Discovered among my books was one describing ten favorite backyard birds. From it I have picked up some new information about each species, especially the blue jay, which the author describes as being very intelligent and mischievous. The book is *America's Favorite Backyard Birds* by Kit and George Harrison.

When I was teaching biology, I had a small library in my classroom for students to use to write extra credit reports. I was determined that everyone would pass my course, and most did. The bird book is one that I kept when I transitioned thirty-two years ago from biology to genealogy.

As for real New York bagels, one of my New York-born 2$^{nd}$ cousins on this list has provided this website for purchasing real deal bagels: hhbagels.com. Included is the description of the company's special way of making real Jewish bagels. I will make an order of lox and bagels as a 92nd birthday treat to myself on May 6th. They are sort of expensive, so it has to be for a very special occasion.

**January 19, 2024**

Good morning, all 130. I'm emptying my freezer and pantry before grocery shopping again. I'm eating to live right now, not living to eat. Chili with beans and rice or pasta is a great winter protein meal. Remember that a legume and a grain make a whole protein that consists of the eight essential amino acids. No "carne" is ever needed. Add some cornbread and apple sauce to create a very healthy meal.

In 1883 the first electric lighting system employing overhead wires, built by Thomas Edison, began service in Roselle, N. It was built by Edison as part of an experiment to prove that an entire community could be lit by electricity from a shared generating station. Forty lucky homes, 150 streetlights, and a railroad depot were wired. How exciting that had to have been!

My house did not have electricity until 1938 when I entered first grade. I can see the tall electrical poles being put up along our block. Electrical wires were strung to and from houses. We kids watched brave linemen go up and down the poles. Initially, only the first floors had naked light bulbs hanging along the walls. The kitchen got wired first where there was warmth from the anthracite coal-burning iron stove. Everyone in the household congregated in the kitchen to stay warm during winters. Kitchens were big in those days because it was where all the family gathered to keep warm. Many families were large. There were ten in my great-grandparents' house.

An antique that's sitting in my home is my Great-grandmother's rocking chair in which she sat while keeping warm near the kitchen stove, with a blanket covering her knees and a shawl around her neck. I was eight when she died. No heat or electricity was in the bedrooms until later. I moved in 1940 to a house with electric lights. There still was no central heating, so, for bedrooms to be kept warm, people had to sleep under layers of quilts that a mother may have created herself. Women formed quilting circles just for that purpose. I still have a quilt belonging to my Great Aunt Lillie. It must be over 125 years old!

**January 20, 2024**

Good morning, all 130. Yesterday was **National Tin Can Day**. The tin can was invented in the early 1800s and is perhaps one of the greatest inventions in history because it revolutionized the storage of perishable foods. Housewives who canned food to last over winters were elated because tin cans changed the way food was stored. On January 19, 1825, Thomas Kensett and Ezra Daggett received the U.S. Tin Can Patent, and in 1858 the can opener was invented by Ezra Warner.

Today is also **National Cheese Lover Day.** I am sure each of you has a favorite cheese, that is, if you do not have a lactose intolerance. My father loved a lump of blue cheese with his apple pie. I like feta on a Greek salad, parmesan sprinkled on pasta, and extra sharp cheddar in scrambled eggs or on a toasted cheese sandwich. I enjoy provolone or Swiss with ham, beef or turkey on rye bread. I love horseradish cheese with pastrami on sour dough bread.

Today is also **Penguin Awareness Day.** Many people think penguins and polar bears live in the same place. No, the bears are at the North Pole and the penguins are at the South Pole. The way parent penguins take care of their young is fascinating. The female lays an egg and leaves it with her mate to sit on his foot as he drags it along for nine weeks while the young develops in the egg. Where is the female? She's gone off to feast on fish. In due time, she will return and then care for her young. All God's handiwork.

**January 21, 2024**

Good morning, all 130. 'Tis **Squirrel Appreciation Day!** I haven't seen any squirrels in several days. I certainly do not appreciate them! They are keeping warm somewhere, hopefully not in my attic. I'm still waiting for *Critter Control* to come, but bad weather has kept them away. Squirrels look as though they don't have a care in the world, frolicking up and down trees, but they must be on the lookout for predatory birds like eagles, hawks, falcons, and owls who will try to swoop down and grab them for a tasty meal.

It is also **National Hugging Day**, but since COVID is still around, we best hug via our computers or telephones. So, today I am sending a virtual hug to each of you. I appreciate your responses. I am learning a lot from you, which makes me very happy.

### A Response From a Cousin a Generation Younger:

*I just love all your beautifully written emails. As I have said before, I'll say it again, "You are an amazing Orator!" I look forward to your emails. They harken back to a bygone era, as if I were expecting an envelope sealed with wax and tied with a ribbon.*

*In my younger years, I used to read the newspapers before leaving home for the day, whether it was beauty school, modeling, or a job that I was heading to. My favorite was The New York Times because it was based in Manhattan. I loved reading about fashion. Trying to complete daily crossword puzzles was a real challenge.*

*The local paper that my Mom subscribed to was, Long Islands' own,* Newsday. *I loved the Funny Section. My favorite cartoon was Ziggy. I could relate to him. I paid close attention to the classifieds, always looking for that next great job. My brothers were paperboys for* Newsday. *I remember them getting the circulars a day before the bundle of newspapers were delivered hot off the presses at the crack of dawn to our front door. They would stuff them with circulars, on a couple of occasions enlisting my services. I figured, if I could bag groceries in record timing, I could help them start their paper route on time.*

*It was a time before all this technology that I miss. A time when kids knew their place. A time when most families broke bread at the dinner table at the same time. An occasional TV dinner, the new processed food, not like today's microwave age.*

*We were tuned into our tv sets, to watch The Mickey Mouse Club, The Little Rascals, Wonder Rama, The Wide World of Sports, Boxing, and National Geographic. The US Space Shuttle Systems launched Rocket Ships and watched for days until the Astronauts returned safely home. Eyes glued to the tv watching NASA put the first man on the moon. TV shows like The Ed Sullivan Show; The Nat King Cole Show; The Della Reece Show; Bat Man; watching Eartha Kitt play Cat woman; The Andy Williams Show; The Red Skelton Show; The Honeymooners; The Twilight Show; One Step Beyond; Land of The Giants; and Star Trek. I loved Soul Train and Wolfman Jack, and all the game shows, too many to name. Just an amazing time for television and music. If only I had a Time Machine….*

Thanks, dear Cousin, for reminding me of all those old television shows. I enjoyed them, too.

**January 22, 2024**

Good morning, all 138. One of you reminded me of an article that was in yesterday's *Washington Post*. It is the "musing" of a senior citizen. Why would you want to read it? Because you are hoping to be one someday. The *Post* states, *Age makes the miracles easier to see.* The author also wrote, *I spend a lot of time looking out the window. Age has given me this time and intention. I didn't have so much of either when I was younger.*

Neither did I, scurrying from one task to another every 24 hours. I had a lot of energy in those days. Being a wife, mother, teacher, Sunday School teacher, and children's choir director was my life during much of my younger years. I also belonged to a club called the *Highlighters*. We were all young mothers who annually gave an outdoor luau for friends. It was a lot of fun, with delicious Polynesian chicken wings and outrigger rice being served. We were all bedecked in muumuus and wore leis around our necks. A former *Highlighter* in California is on my list. At that time, I remember how difficult it was to purchase chicken wings by themselves. We had to go to a poultry store to specially order them.

After retiring 32 years ago, I had planned to learn Spanish fluently, learn to play the organ, and take up quilting and oil paint. I have done none of those things. Instead, I have published nine books. Right now, I am enjoying musing about life with all of you for a tenth, if the Good Lord wills. If you are reading this, He did. Thanks be to God.

**January 23, 2024**

Good morning, all 150. Today is **National Pie Day**. We all have our favorites. Mine includes apple, blueberry, cherry, sweet potato, and lemon meringue, which was also my father's favorite. He liked his tart. Also, this is **National Handwriting Day.** My computer suggests that we send a "snail-mail" message to someone today. Handwriting has become a lost art due to typewriters first, and now the computers. I am guilty of relying on the latter, because as a left-handed person, handwriting has always been tedious for me. Some left-handed people write with a decided slant to the left. I never could do that. My hand would become cramped. Needless to say, writing reports was an ordeal for me until I got a manual typewriter when in college.

Right-handed elementary teachers taught us penmanship on the blackboard that was in front of the classroom. Some of you older folks will remember a time when blackboards were on all the walls in classrooms. They were when I began teaching in 1958 but had disappeared when I retired in 1992. There was no longer the need for blackboards after printers were invented. *"What's a blackboard?"* young'uns may be asking. It was made of black slate and preceded the white boards with which you may be familiar. Blackboards were also called "chalkboards," which may be green nowadays. I have no idea what classrooms look like in 2024.

Back in the day, students were taught the *Palmer Penmanship* method. Consequently, everyone's handwriting was similar. The handwriting of older generations is generally beautiful and very legible. With only an eighth-grade education, my Great Aunt Lillie had beautiful penmanship because it was mandatary for all students. She loved to write long letters, which she did when I was at *Bennett College*. My father, too, a generation later, had beautiful penmanship. My teachers taught us to write by drawing circles and slants that went to the right on the blackboard. I don't know how left-handed teachers were able to do that. Maybe they had all been changed, as was the custom. A child's left hand was tied behind his or her back. No one was allowed to be left-handed.

How do I know this? Because that is what happened to one of my father's brothers a generation before mine. The custom had stopped in my school system by the time I was in first grade in 1938. There were several of us lefthanders in the Class of 1950. When I was older, if I ever had to write anything in ink, I always smeared. Some older people when using a quill or fountain pen would use a blotter to press over their writing to prevent smudging.

### A Response Concerning Handwriting

*I wanted to share just a few sentences about handwriting/penmanship and my aunt. My dear Aunt Ramona, who has long been gone on to glory, was one of the most important persons in my life. She was a teacher who had the most beautiful handwriting I have ever seen. People who knew both of us used to say that I wrote just like her, but we both knew it wasn't true. But I worked hard to improve my handwriting/penmanship because I so admired her.*

*Auntie started a school in Chicago and had to sign lots of letters and other documents, and to help her after school, I would sign letters for her after my "forgery" of her signature improved. LOL. I think of her often, especially when I meet people from Haiti because Aunt Ramona was the first and only person I knew who went to that poor country to help the people improve their lives by starting a bakery and a few chicken farms. Every time I sign my name, I remember how she would instruct me to hold the pen and not lift it from the paper until it was time to dot the "i" or cross the "t."* Thank you for the response.

## January 24, 2024

Good morning, all 152. It's **Compliment Day**. Please make someone happy by surprising them with an unexpected compliment. A cousin has sent me some information about crows during the winter in Minneapolis, Minnesota, where she lives. Since we had been discussing birds, I'd like to share her information with those of you who may be interested in an amazing phenomenon:

*"Up To 10,000 Crows Invade Minneapolis In Minnesota Every Winter And It's A Sight To Be Seen' By Betsy Rathburn | Updated on December 03, 2022 (Originally published November 28, 2022). Murder isn't too common here in Minnesota – unless it's winter and we're talking about a murder of crows. There's one that descends upon Minneapolis, Minnesota, every year, and it's one of the strangest sights you'll ever see. The flock is thousands of crows deep, and it only keeps growing. Evidence of the crows is all around. They can be spotted on power lines and fenceposts, circling the sky, or gathered in trees. Their caws fill the skies, and their droppings cover the sidewalks – and even some unlucky cars."* I wondered why the word "murder" was used in the article. Seems that a large group of crows is called a "murder," just as a large group of geese is called a "gaggle." During winters sometimes a "mega murder" of crows is seen."

Dear Cousin, thank you for sharing this interesting information.

## January 25, 2024.

Good morning, all 153. I was just thinking that if my morning musing is a blessing to just one person today, then my living is not in vain. I thought this article from the *Washington Post* yesterday might interest some of you. *Are you hoping to save more money in 2024? Try these three strategies.* To answer that question, *"Yes, I'd like to be able to save the suggested $1,378 for an unforeseen emergency or for taking a trip."* Already an unforeseen emergency for this year is having *Critter Control* deal with the squirrels trying to get into my house. Since the snowstorm four days ago, I have not seen one squirrel. Where are they? I just know they are not in my attic!

I like the article's suggestion of *Eat out of your house*. I do that already. I make very interesting concoctions that perhaps no one else would eat. But as I've said before, I am eating to live and not the other way around. I'm not a picky eater. Another article in yesterday's *Washington Post* was *Tips for baking better brownies, whether from scratch or from a mix.* Ten top mixes were suggested with *Trader Joe's* being deemed the best.

**January 26, 2024**

Good morning, all 154. Today is **Spouse's Day**. Many of you are fortunate enough to still have a spouse, so do something special for him/her today. It is also Australia Day where "down under" the Equator is summer. I visited there during my summer and its winter, which is nothing like ours here in Virginia. It was more like Florida or southern California. I visited Australia during the month of August. Farther south is New Zealand. Several people from my group were planning to go skiing, for which they had packed their gear. While visiting New Zealand, we had to wear our heavy winter clothing. Needless to say, I was carrying a large suitcase for all the necessary changes of clothing. We had stopped first at Tahiti where the weather was hot. Couldn't do that today with all the airplane restrictions on the amount of baggage we can tote.

*Critter Control* paid me a visit yesterday and all is well with the squirrels. I have seen only two scurrying around my yard since the heavy snowstorm. Trap doors have been placed on my roof so the squirrels cannot return to their nests in late afternoon, should they have made a home in my attic. They are diurnal and not nocturnal pests like racoons. When the sun goes down, they go home. Not in my attic, though.

An interesting article was in yesterday's *Washington Post. How a day of rest can help give you (and the world) a break.* It tells the history of the day of rest from the Jewish Shabbot that begins on Friday at sundown and ends on Saturday at sunset. It is integral to their religion. Christians created their day of rest on Sunday because of Jesus' resurrection, calling it the Sabbath.

Back in my hometown in Pennsylvania, most families were affiliated with a church, whether they were regular church attendees or not. Most funerals were religious. I have attended many to pay respects in my almost 92 years, ever since my great-grandmother passed away when I was eight and she was only 83.

"Blue Laws" were adopted back in the day that forced people to "keep the Sabbath," whether they were church goers or not. Those laws certainly were not as stringent as the Jewish laws are with their many "*Thou shall nots*" concerning what is considered to be "work." When I was a child, there was no serious shopping done on Sundays because there were no stores open except for the "Mom and Pop" stores selling the Sunday paper and perhaps bread. Supermarkets or department stores were not in existence yet, and there were no shopping centers or Malls to be closed on Sundays. I can remember when a new Acme opened in my hometown. To be able to push a shopping basket through the store and pick out what we wanted was such an improvement on grocery shopping.

On Sundays, women would never hang laundry on their outside lines. No major housework was ever done inside either. Men ceased their labor except if they had animals to care for. My Great Uncle Walter Glover had animals but managed to drive his wife, Florence, to church from their farm every Sunday morning. Wives were not driving when I was a little girl.

For church, everyone wore their best "Sunday-go-to-meeting" clothing. Great Aunt Florence was a seamstress, so she was always spiffily dressed from head to toe. She worked for several wealthy women in town and used their dress patterns to create her attire.

Many people took naps on Sunday afternoons. Such was my young life. I still like to take afternoon naps. For some church-going folks, there were Sunday evening services. During my mid-teens I attended them and was the pianist. I can read music so I could play from the hymnals. God did not give me the gift of being able to play by ear. The *Washington Post* article on rest may be of interest to those of you who just need to slow down. It discusses the advantages to your health and to our world, as far as climate change is concerned.

**January 27, 2024**

Good morning, all 154. Yesterday I ventured out of my townhouse to do some shopping. Mother Hubbard's cupboard was getting bare again. My van, "Blue Belle," hadn't been driven since the snowstorm. Back in the day with their horses needing to be tended to, their owners could not hibernate like I did this week. "Blue Belle" needs no special care.

It was a lovely summer day here yesterday in the middle of winter. The temperature rose to 80 degrees, would you believe? The *Post* says that it was the hottest January day ever recorded in Washington, D.C. history. People were outside in tee shirts, but I was not one of them. I had on a lightweight purple jacket, my favorite color. 'Tis pneumonia weather. To ward it off, I'm taking Vitamin C and Elderberry before retiring. I had pneumonia twice when I was still working, so, three strikes and I might be out!

You will never believe what I saw when I went outside yesterday. I beheld peeking out of the ground the daffodils I had planted in early November. The warm weather has caused them to shoot up two inches already. I am going to have great joy watching them grow. I am used to seeing daffodils peeking up in February, but not in January. They are very hardy, not to fear. The expected return of winter's low temperatures will not harm them. Right now, they are just preparing to show their glory in March, or perhaps even earlier with this unpredictable weather.

Today is **Chocolate Cake Day**. Yummy with a fudge icing.

**January 28, 2024**

Good morning, all 164. When I awakened early, it was pouring down rain which ceased by 8:13 a.m. I don't know if the old wives' tale about wet feet causing colds is true, but I'm not taking the chance. We all used to wear arctics. Someone on this list used the term "galoshes," and others say "over- shoes." Whatever, they were ugly rubber boots pulled up over our shoes. They were taken off as soon as we went inside. Later the style was to carry a bag just for shoes to be changed when we arrived where we were going. My daughter recently gave me one to carry, should I decide to go to church and have to walk on wet sidewalks.

You can see that our number has jumped a bit, thanks to the old and new friends who attended the birthday party yesterday. A good time was had by all, especially the "birthday girl." Yesterday was **Chocolate Cake Day** and guess what was serendipitously served at the party? Dark chocolate, only with white icing. Still yummy, though.

I can't believe February 1st is only a few days away. 'Tis the first day of **Black History Month** and the first day of the shortest month of the year. Do you remember this little ditty? I learned it in elementary school along with "i" before "e" except after "c" or when pronounced like "a" as in "neighbor" or "weigh."

*"Thirty days hath September, April, June, and November.*
*All the rest have thirty-one, excepting February alone,*
*And that has twenty-eight days clear,*
*And twenty-nine in each leap year."*

People born on February 29th will celebrate birthdays again. If it were my birthday, I'd be 23 years old this year, with my dark brown hair just beginning to show hereditary premature white and being a little plumper than I am now. My prayer is that each of us will be blessed according to our needs on this "day of rest." Take a nap. It will do you good. I will take my own advice.

**January 29, 2024**

Good morning, all 164. I awakened late after staying up last night to watch a riveting *Netflix* movie. This day is important for several reasons. 'Tis **National Carnation Day**, **Corn Chip Day** and **National Puzzle Day**. I do enjoy a jigsaw puzzle. One needs a special table, though, to work it on. Unfortunately, I do not have room for one in my house.

In 1844, Edgar Allen Poe's *The Raven* was published. Many on this list may have read the poem in an English class, as I did in 9$^{th}$ grade. I also loved his *Annabel Lee* when I was a teenage romantic. She was his wife who died young from tuberculosis (consumption). My Great Aunt Lillie's youngest brother, Niles, died from it, too, at 27. Young Uncle Niles had gone to Rochester, N.Y. to work. No coal mines for him! The cure for tuberculosis was found by Dr. Edward Trudeau, a physician in New York City who came down with it. His own physician told him that he had six months to live and to go somewhere to die. He travelled to the Adirondack Mountains by himself where he rested, sunned and fished. At the end of the six months, he was still alive and feeling pretty good. He returned to NYC to visit his doctor, who was amazed to see him. *"What have you been doing?"* he asked. That was the beginning of sanatoriums for tubercular patients and control over the disease.

In 1886, the patent number 37435 was applied for by Carl Benz for his "vehicle powered by a gas engine." It may be thought of as the birth of an automobile. In 1954, Oprah Gail Winfrey was born in Kosciusko, Mississippi. She is an African American talk show host, television producer, actress, author, and media proprietor. *The Oprah Winfrey Show* broadcasted from Chicago and ran in national syndication for 25 years-1986 to 2011.

**January 30, 2024**

Good morning, all 164. Someone sent a response to the *Post* article concerning getting enough rest. She introduced the Scottish term "hurkle-durkle," from 19$^{th}$ Century Scots, which is to linger under the covers of a warm bed long after it's time to get up. Long live "hurkle-durkling!"

**January 31, 2024**

Good morning, all 168. I didn't have the time to "hurkle-durkle" this morning because I have a meeting later today. I wanted to say, *"Good morning,"* to all of you, though, before I left my home.

I've visited Scotland in the summer and returned once in the fall to see the moors covered by the lovely lavender colored heather. North, in the Highlands where men don the kilts of their clans, the wind was fierce, even in the summer. I can only imagine what it is like in the winter. That is why the Scots are so famous for their woolen garments. I saw sheep whose wool is woven into garments and blankets, as well as many other clothing articles like hats, gloves and scarves. The sheep were herded to their spot by very intelligent dogs. Sheep are not very bright, but those dogs certainly were.

**February 1, 2024**

Good morning, all 168. I should have been born during February because its birthstone is Amethyst and purple is my favorite. Those of you who know me know that I have a lot of purple in my wardrobe.

February is **Black History Month** and also **National Freedom Day, Car Insurance Day, Change for Password Day, G.I. Joe Day, Heroes Day,** and **Optimistic Day**. Which day will I choose to acknowledge? Certainly, **National Freedom Day** that celebrates freedom from slavery in 1865 at the end of the *Civil War*. This day recognizes that America is a symbol of liberty, honoring the signing by Abraham Lincoln of a joint House and Senate resolution that later became the 13th Amendment to the U.S. *Constitution* that forever abolished slavery.

I also chose **Car Insurance Day** for "Blue Belle," **and G.I. Joe Day** as I remember the soldiers from World War II. Certainly, **Heroes Day** enumerates heroes in American history, including the G.I. Joes and other military, as well as Martin Luther King Jr. **Optimistic Day helps me look** forward to admiring my beautiful daffodils in the spring, peeking up each day.

I had a wonderful trip yesterday to the *Smithsonian Museum of African American History and Culture* in Washington D.C., with two younger cousins on my musing list. We had lunch with my favorite curator, also on the list, who created the display of my father's work. I was so proud of it. My cousin reminded me that yesterday was **Inspire Your Heart With Art Day**, which was exactly what we did at the Museum while admiring the work of the African American artist Jacob Lawrence. One of my favorite things to do when I visit my father's display is to go up to someone who is looking at it. I approach them with, "*Do you recognize anyone there?*" In a collectors' display case on Concourse 1 is a photo of me with several of my father's sculptures, including a gleaming Patience heart with four leaves carved on it, which was the Patience signature. There were other coal carvers in the Valley besides my father, but no one else gained the notoriety that he did, for instance making a necklace for the Queen of the Netherlands, or being in *Who's Who in America in 1972*, or having a display at an Expo in Canada.

When people turn to see who is speaking and see me, I point to my photo. One man was so excited to meet someone who had actually donated to the Museum that he took a selfie with me. I became a celebrity for a moment. The curator informed me that my display will be taken down soon. When it was put up in 2016, it was to be only for two years. I am satisfied that thousands of folks have been introduced to the unique anthracite coal art of my father, Charles Edgar Patience.

My grandfather, Harry, had begun whittling coal hearts when he was a young breaker boy working at a local mine at age 13. Breaker boys were youngsters who worked at the breaker, a large building where large lumps of coal were broken into smaller pieces. It was very dangerous work. Boys of 6 and 7 years worked there, and many died from accidents or tuberculosis. People were enthralled by Harry's gleaming black hearts, so, he began whittling them for purchase. Another favorite was a cross. After an injury at the mine when he was 17, Harry began his own business of carving anthracite articles. He passed the skills on to his six sons, including my father and his youngest brother, Harold, who continued in the business for their lifetimes.

Also, in the cabinet at the Museum is a pair of pliers used by both father and son. The third article is a copper plate that was used to create Harry's catalog in the 1920s. I found a number of those plates in my father's shop after his death. Then I was able to find someone with an obsolete printer who printed the catalog pages that are found in the book I wrote *Anthracite Coal Art of Charles Edgar Patience*. You can purchase it from my website. www.journeyfromthepast.com.

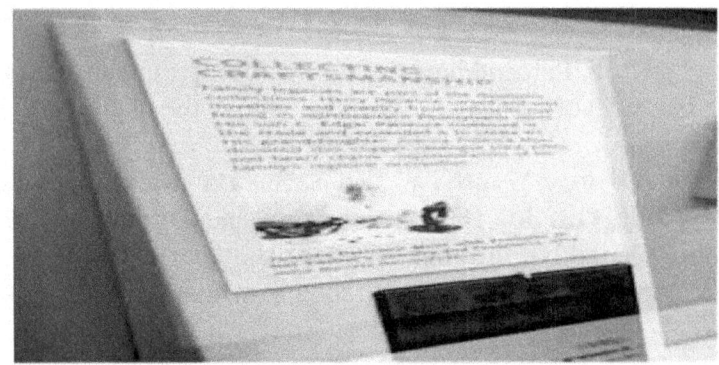

**February 2, 2024**

Good morning, all 169. When I opened my front door to bring in the newspaper, I spied in my yard a whole uneaten ear of corn! Question? Could a squirrel have dropped it there? Seems too large, but they are very clever little critters. It might have been a nocturnal raccoon that got it from a neighbor's trash can during the night. My question, though, is, *"Who eats corn on the cob in February?"* Not I! I don't eat it until June.

**February 3, 2024**

Good morning, all 169. I failed to mention yesterday that it was **Ground Hog's Day**. Being a born-and-reared Pennsylvanian, how could I forget that? What did Punxsutawney Phil, the famous groundhog weather-watcher, awaken to see yesterday? He did not see his shadow, meaning early spring.

Today is **Feed the Birds Day, National Carrot Cake Day,** and **National Wedding Ring Day.** Concerning feeding birds, Ed wanted to put up a bird feeder when we moved to our brand-new development in 1993. He always had one in our large N.J. backyard. The Homeowners Association here had a rule that there can be no birdfeeders because they attract squirrels. We knew this to be true because Ed was always chasing them from his bird feeders in N.J.

As for carrot cake, it is my favorite, homemade with raisins, walnuts and cream cheese icing. Yummy! My wedding ring anecdote goes back to 1942. For the war effort, we kids collected discarded tin cans. People would clean them, remove the labels, and carefully cut off both ends. Afterwards, the cans would get flattened by a stomping foot. We went around town collecting the cans and taking them to our elementary school, where a wired outdoor area had been built for the janitor to deposit our collections which we carried in brown paper bags. I don't remember if we just told him how many cans were in our bags, but he trusted us. I just know that I would have been too scared to cheat.

A contest was created by the School Board to encourage the students. Whoever collected the most tin cans in a certain time period would receive a $25.00 War Bond, costing $15.00. Ten years would have to pass before it could be cashed in for the full amount of $25.00. I wanted to win that contest, so my younger cousin and I dragged his little red wagon door-to-door through our neighborhood, and guess who won the contest? 5$^{th}$-grader Juanita Patience. In my mind's eye, I see it well when the announcement was made in assembly, and I had to go to the stage to receive the envelope containing the bond. I was soooo proud of myself! The next ten years passed quickly. I was 20 years old and about to be married in 1952. I cashed in the bond and used the money to purchase Ed's wedding ring. So, indeed, today is special to me.

**February 4, 2024**

Good morning, all 169. Today is Rosa Parks' birthday, born in 1913. "Mother of the Civil Rights Movement," she invigorated the struggle for racial equality in 1955 when she refused to give up her bus seat to a White man in Montgomery, Alabama. Her arrest launched the *Montgomery Bus Boycott* with 17,000 Black citizens participating. I also remember one Sunday afternoon in 1951 when I was a sophomore at *Bennett College* in Greensboro, N.C. Would you believe that I, Juanita Bernice Patience at age 19, refused to move to the back of a Greensboro city bus?

Some friends and I were going to be late for the dinner served promptly at 1:00 p.m. in the college dining hall. Earlier, we had attended the St. Matthew's Methodist Episcopal Church, which was within walking distance of our campus. When the service ended later than usual, we knew we were running late. No one wanted to miss the Sunday fried chicken dinner, and if we walked back, we would. We were starving college students, and our next meal of hotdogs and beans would not be until 6:00 p.m. There were no fast-food restaurants nearby. The president of our college had forbidden us to ride the city buses where Blacks were mandated to sit in the back, but there we were, confronted with "*To be, or not to be.*"

Unanimously, we made the choice to board the "forbidden" bus. Hailing from Pennsylvania, I had never been on a "Jim Crow" segregated bus and did not know that Blacks were to purchase their tickets from the driver up front, then get off the bus to reenter it through a door near the rear and then sit in the back. I watched my friends but decided not to do what they did. After buying my ticket, I plopped myself on the seat right behind the driver. What was I thinking? I was not thinking that I could be sent home by President Jones the next day for breaking his rule.

The driver ignored me. Someone has suggested that he didn't know who I was. He had to know that I was with my *Bennett* friends, all of us wearing our mandatory hats and carrying gloves by which *Bennett* women were easily identified. I like to think that perhaps he just didn't care. If that were so, then God bless that bus driver. My guardian angel must have been given charge over me that day since I was daring to do a "Rosa Parks" stunt four years before her brave rebellion. Seems I was not on the Civil Rights Movement timetable, since courageous *Bennett College* students were jailed nearly a decade later. One of them is on our list. My friends and I arrived at the dining hall before the 1:00 p.m. deadline, before the chimes sounded, before the doors closed, and before the "Grace" was chanted. That dinner sure must have tasted extra special good to us on that Sunday, for all we had to do to get it!

**February 5, 2024**

Good morning, all 170. February is **Canned Goods Month, Great American Pie Month, National Cherry Pie Month, National Library Month, National Hot Breakfast Month, National Bird Feeding Month.** 'Tis also **Women's Heart Week** and **African Heritage and Health Week.** It is also **Western Monarch Day.** I enjoy different kinds of pies, especially sour cherry. Cherries are good for women's health. I eat a lot of Bing cherries in the spring and early summer. They grow in California, Washington and Oregon.

As for my hot breakfast, most of you know that I am an oatmeal lover. I put all kinds of toppings on mine, including blueberries, raisins and nuts, even peanut butter. I prefer almond milk because I am allergic to the lactose in cow's milk. Not always, thankfully, because I love ice cream but must chew a Lactaid tablet first. Cherry pie ala mode. Yummy!

The migration of monarch butterflies each year is another marvelous phenomenon in nature. Homeowners are encouraged to plant milkweed to feed them on their journey. I do but never attracted any beautiful monarchs. Maybe I am not on their flight pattern. Monarch butterflies have the most highly evolved migration pattern of any known species of butterfly or moth. Unfortunately, their number is decreasing, and they may be put on the endangered species list.

Here is more of the continuing saga of the clever squirrels in my yard. As you know, *Critter Control* placed contraptions on my roof so squirrels cannot get back into my house once they leave for their daytime activities, being diurnal, should they have built nests in my attic. So where do the poor critters go? No, I'm not feeling sorry for them.

A neighbor came by to visit me yesterday afternoon. His eagle eyes spied a brand-new squirrel nest built in my holly tree where he had knocked down a gigantic one last summer. After he destroyed the new one, we watched as three squirrels indignantly scurried through the holly branches. They quickly ran across the street. Change of address. They no longer will be able to set up housekeeping in my holly!

**February 6, 2024**

Today is **National Frozen Yogurt Day, Safer Internet Day** and **National Chopsticks Day.** I have never mastered those, even though I am a lover of Chinese food. My son is quite adept with his left-handed self. I enjoy frozen yogurt but have not had any in a while. As for Internet safety, we all know that scammers are just a click away. Someone on this list has shared that for my Catholic friends, 2024 is being called "Love Beyond Words," and that this is **National Marriage Week.**

**February 7, 2024**

Good morning, all 170. When I was teaching, I'd give extra credit assignments to my biology students. One was what I called "Forcing in February." I hope my former students on this list will remember it. They were to cut branches from forsythia bushes growing in their yards. To the "average Joe," no signs of spring are evident yet. But to those "in the know," forsythia shrubs form tight flower buds as early as January, depending on the weather. All they need is some warm weather. At my desk I'd have a vase of beautiful yellow forsythia long before it was blooming outside everywhere.

Spring is my favorite time of the year. Have you ever noticed that forsythia and trumpet daffodils are the same shade of yellow and bloom at the same time in the spring? Bet you never noticed that dandelion flowers are the same shade, too, but we do not welcome them in our verdant grassy yards. Should you like to force some forsythia to bring sunshine into your home in February, after cutting the branches, place them in tepid, not cold water. They will bloom in a few days. Be sure to recut the branches on a slant like you would a bouquet of flowers. Watch your fingers! I wonder if pussy willows grow in Virginia like Pennsylvania and N.J. I have not seen any since I moved here in 1992. After being removed from the water in a vase, the catkins will dry and last for a long time.

On another topic, certain fruits eaten before bed help you to stay asleep. Not that I need this because I sleep "like a baby." It is for those who have difficulty staying asleep. I might eat these fruits for breakfast -- banana, tart cherry, pineapple, kiwi, orange, papaya, and apple.

One bit of advice from centenarians in yesterday's *Washington Post* article is to cherish our friendships as I do with all of you. Included were these two songs. *Thank You For Being My Friend,* from the television show *Golden Girls* and *You Are The Sunshine of My Life by Stevie Wonder*. I first saw the gifted blind "Little Stevie Wonder" when he was 12 years old playing his harmonica on the Steele Pier in Atlantic City.

**February 8, 2024**

Good morning, all 171. Yesterday, I was ZOOM-ed by a television station in Wilkes-Barre, Pennsylvania. Through the years, I have been asked during Black History Month to discuss my father's unique anthracite coal art, including this year. Check out *YouTube* to see my father, Charles Edgar Patience. Several of you have visited the *Anthracite Heritage Museum* in Scranton, Pennsylvania, where it was filmed.

Today **is Boy Scout Day, National Kite Flying Day, Molasses Bar Da**y, and **Opera Day.** Also, **Laugh and Get Rich Day**. It says to *Laugh yourself into better spirits and enrich your health and happiness.* It is also **Fat Thursday,** which is associated with Lent that begins next Wednesday. Lastly, today is **Propose Day**, just in case you might have that on your mind. It's Leap Year, so girls can propose. Also, did you know that the Smithsonian Institute Building (The Castle) first opened on February 8, 1855, on the Mall in Washington D.C.**?**

**February 9, 2024**

Good morning, all 180. This is **Chocolate Day, National Pizza Day** and **Bagel and Lox Day**, all my favorite foods. Someone on the list said yesterday was **National Girls and Women in Sports Day.** However, my computer did not inform me that her granddaughter is the Women's Basketball Head Coach at *Grambling State University*. Thank you for that information to share.

**February 10, 2024**

Good morning, all 187. **It's Umbrella Day**. On this cloudy day, folks may need an umbrella, should we get some rain later in the day. Invented over 4,000 years ago, umbrellas were used in early civilizations in China, Egypt, Greece, and Assyria, originally used as parasols to provide shade from the sun. Traditionally, an umbrella protects us from rain, while a parasol protects from sun, even though the terms continue to be used interchangeably. The first waterproof umbrella was invented by the Chinese as protection from the rain. They waxed and lacquered their paper parasols. Umbrellas would become a feminine accessory as parasols, beginning in the 16th century in Europe.

**Lunar New Year** begins this weekend. The *Smithsonian American Art Museum*'s annual **Lunar New Year Family Celebration** spotlights different Asian cultures as they ring in the New Year with activities. There will be lots of umbrellas in view. In celebration of **Chocolate Day,** two of you shared your favorite brands of chocolates. They include Ethel M and Sanders' dark chocolate sea salt caramels. They come in milk chocolate, as well. I will give them a try. They will test my willpower.

There's a rule of thumb that says spring moves North 13 miles a day. It's on its way! Some varieties of daffodils are in bloom in Williamsburg, Virginia, 142 miles south of Alexandria. I was informed of early daffodil varieties already blooming by the person who sold me the ones I planted in November. I asked her if this is early for them and she replied that seasoned members of her daffodil club say, *"Yes."* She has joined my musing list.

The *Washington Post* says not to think that winter is over yet, even though the temperature rose to 61 degrees yesterday. Even though I hear several species of birds trilling their songs, snowstorms can still hit this area. I remember a snowstorm on Easter Sunday in N.J. Remember that Easter is a moveable holiday but always on the first Sunday after the first day of spring (March 21$^{st}$) after the first full moon.

**February 11, 2024**

Good morning, all 187. It is **World Marriage Day**. It is also the **International Day of Women and Girls in Science,** and **National Fried Chicken Wings Day,** which goes well with Super Bowl Sunday. On our list is a college girl majoring in biology who teaches me about things I did not learn back in the day. The study of biology has changed from when I took it in 9$^{th}$ grade in 1947. Believe it or not, it hadn't interested me at all back then. God is full of surprises for His children. In history, Thomas Edison was born in 1897, and Nelson Mandela was freed in 1990 after twenty-seven years as a political prisoner in apartheid South Africa. Something else fantastic happened today. Someone at the ripe old age of 104 has joined our list. Welcome, Dear Friend.

**February 12, 2024**

Good morning, all 188. I wish on this day a very happy birthday to my son. No, I did not name him after Abraham Lincoln whose birthday is February 12$^{th}$, also. Someone else on this list is having a birthday, too. Happy birthday to you, Friend.

Today, some Virginia fourth graders recited the *Gettysburg Address* at Ford's Theatre in Washington, D.C., the historic landmark where the 16th President was shot. *"Four score and seven years ago......"* Among other celebrations today is **National Grapefruit Day, Clean Out your Computer Day, Georgia Day, Hug Day, National Football Hangover Day, Oatmeal Monday,** and **Shrove Monday** which is 48 days before Easter. The last two are not always on the 12th, but they are always on a Monday.

We probably all need to clean out our computers. I haven't eaten grapefruit since I began taking high blood pressure pills. I like pink grapefruit sprinkled with sugar and a maraschino cherry in the middle. I still have serrated silver grapefruit spoons that belonged to my Great Aunt Lillie.

I eat oatmeal most mornings. Using my microwave, it takes but five minutes to prepare. Sprinkled with walnuts, it equals perfect protein. I use no sugar, but fruit, such as apple sauce and blueberries. Remember the legume + grain formula=a protein? We should have some protein with each meal. A donut and a cup of coffee does not hack it.

Someone on our list tells me that 33 years ago snow fell here in Alexandria in April on Easter Sunday. Perhaps no frilly Easter bonnets were worn to church on that Sunday. My great grandfather was a farmer. His daughter, my Great Aunt Lillie, told me that he called snow in April "onion snow" because he planted his onions in April. They are bulbs just like the daffodils I am watching grow in my yard.

**February 13, 2024**

Good morning, all 188. Today is **Radio Day, Pancake Day, Black Love Day, National Cheddar Day, Kiss Day,** and **Galentine's Day,** which brings women together to celebrate each other on the day before Valentine's Day.

I have not had homemade pancakes for years. *I-Hops* are okay if I am craving a strawberry covered pancake. I used to have my Great Aunt Lillie's iron griddle, but I don't know what I did with it. It was long enough to sit on two burners simultaneously. It was for the coal and wood stove days, long before electric or gas stoves. She made a small cheese cloth bag to hold some salt. She would rub the bag on the griddle before pouring the batter. She used no grease. I have no idea what the rubbing of salt did. Today is also **Fat Tuesday, Self-Love Day,** and **Ferris Wheel Day.** It's too chilly for a Ferris Wheel ride at the National Harbor in Maryland, not far from my home, even though it is enclosed and heated. Two summers ago, my son took me up and I enjoyed the ride.

**February 14, 2024**

Good morning, all 190. **Happy Valentine's Day.** This is the first day of **Lent** and **Ash Wednesday** on the Christian calendar. Someone reminded me that I forgot to mention **Mardi Gras** yesterday. I am sure New Orleans was as exuberant as ever. Today is **National Women's Heart Day, Race Relations Day, Frederick Douglass Day, National Library Day,** and **International Book Giving Day**, all significant to me. Concerning pancakes, I received several responses that gave me permission to use my heavy iron skillet. The salt bag used by my Great Aunt Lillie was to clean the griddle between the cooking of each pancake.

An article in the *Washington Post* yesterday discussed the merits of dark chocolate, which is full of flavonoids. There is no solid cocoa in white chocolate. The lighter the chocolate, the lower the amount of cocoa and the higher the amount of sugar. The title of the article is *The benefits of chocolate are easy to love, but you must choose carefully.* Interested people may Google it.

I will be going to *CVS* to purchase a can of unsalted mixed nuts and the smallest heart-shaped box of chocolates in remembrance of my Ed, who gave me one every year for 62 years, plus the two when we were dating. I've seen the boxes shrink and the number of chocolates subtracted as the price accelerated. At one time, candy boxes were so beautiful that ladies would keep one on their dressers for small items, especially "hankies" which are practically nonexistent today. Every woman carried a pretty hankie somewhere on her body or in a pocketbook. They had to be washed and ironed, until *Kleenex* changed things. Now I carry tissues wherever I go.

**February 15, 2024**

Good morning, all 192. 'Tis the Ides of February. Every month has its Ides, always the 15th day. I learned that fact when I was studying Julius Caesar in my 10th grade Latin class. "*Et tu, Brute?*" This is the birth date of Suffragist Susan B. Anthony, who devoted more than fifty years to woman suffrage. The 19th **A**mendment granting women the right to vote was passed by Congress on June 4, 1919, and ratified on August 18, 1920.

For us nature and animal lovers, this is **World Hippo Day**. Hippopotami are the third-largest land animals. Even baby hippos are cute. I think all baby animals are cute, being miniatures of their parents. "*Beauty is in the eyes of the beholder.*" The rhino is the second-largest land animal, and I don't have to tell any of you that the blue whale is the largest of all animals.

Someone else has responded to my question about Aunt Lillie's bag of salt used when she made pancakes. *Preventing food from sticking- Rub a pancake griddle with a small bag of salt to prevent sticking and smoking. From:https://cooking.stackexchange.com/questions/16945/why-would-heating-salt-in-a-pan-prevent-food-from-sticking#:~* 'Tis enlightening to know the reason.

**February 16, 2024**

Good morning, all 194. Today has some interesting celebrations, including **National Caretakers Day, National Random Acts of Kindness Day, National Public Science Day, My Way Day, World Human Spirit Day, National Tennis Pro Day,** and **National Almond Day.** Many of us have been caretakers, as I was for both Great Aunt Lillie and my Ed before they passed away. **My Way Day** reminds me that one of Ed's favorite songs was Frank Sinatra's *My Way*. We played it during his Homegoing service in January. We had agreed that if we died in the winter we would be cremated and buried in Pennsylvania during warm weather. So, I chose his birthday, which was August 1st. His extended family and I gave him a wonderful send off on a beautiful summer day.

I wonder what random act of kindness I will do when I go to the Post Office. Perhaps just opening the door for someone with a cane. I am thankful not to have to rely on one just yet. In 1923 the burial chamber of King Tut was unsealed in the Valley of the Kings in Egypt by British Archeologist Howard Carter. His discovery was one of the most celebrated contributions to Egyptology. I went down into the empty King Tut's tomb when I visited Egypt in 1988. His body, however, is at the Museum in Cairo, along with his famous mask decorated with beautiful blue lapis lazuli. While in Egypt, I took a cruise up the Nile which flows from South to North. We had to pass through four hand locks where the boat was lowered each time. Later, it became electrified.

In 1937 Dupont Chemist Wallace Hume Carothers patented nylon, which was important during World War II to produce parachutes when silk was no longer available from Japan.The industry switched to nylon in 1942 after Adeline Gray's first jump using a nylon parachute. Nylon became a boon for women. Everything that changed was said to be "for the duration," until the war was over. For a while afterwards, some women wore undergarments made from reprocessed nylon of parachutes.

In 1903 the American Ventriloquist and radio comedian Edgar Bergen was born in Chicago. He is the father of actress Candice Bergen. Anyone remember Charlie McCarthy? I loved listening to "them" on the radio. When I was a little girl, I had a Charlie McCarthy puppet that sat on my knee, and I moved his arms and legs. Couldn't make him talk, though, hard as I tried.

Regarding the largest animals in the world, I need to clarify what I wrote yesterday. Animals are divided into water and land animals. The largest animal of them all is the blue whale. The largest land animal, of course, is the elephant, followed by the rhino and hippo.

**February 17, 2024**

Good morning, all 193. It is **National Pancake Week, Celebration of Love Week,** and **National Frankfurter and Kraut Week.** Indeed, I enjoy a hotdog at sports activities, although most of the time the kraut is absent. The best hot dogs I ever ate were from *Nardone's Restaurant* on Exeter Ave. in West Pittston. West Pittstonians on my list probably all have eaten hot dogs from there, too. Dominick's special chili sauce and onions did the trick.

Ed swore that the best hot dogs were from a small restaurant in Wilkes-Barre. *Abe's* is still in business and whenever I am in town, I will purchase two hot dogs from there. One is never enough. When travelling, I enjoy *Nathan*'s hotdogs with sauerkraut and yellow mustard. Some rest stops have a *Nathan's* in the food court. We stop at one on the trip to Connecticut, but I can purchase them at a nearby *Safeway* store. It was founded by a Jewish man, so no pork inside.

Today is **World Whale Day**. There are 91 species of whales known to scientists. Returning to *Jell-o*, I used to eat a lot of it for dessert with fruit cocktail made into a mold. Fancier desserts developed, such as ambrosia with marshmallows and nuts. A *Jell-o* mold was always present at a "potluck" meal or funeral repast.

**February 18, 2024**

Good morning, all 193. It is **National Eat Ice Cream for Breakfast Day** and **Crab-stuffed Flounder Day.** I have none of those foods in my fridge, but if I did, I would enjoy eating them both for breakfast. This meal is intended to break one's fast since last evening's dinner. Culture and custom have determined what is appropriate, which varies all over the world. Once when I was in London, a group of young Japanese nurses who spoke little English were at the same hotel. Breakfast was served cafeteria-style in a large room. There were stations with "our" kind of dishes: bacon, eggs and such. The English always served a broiled tomato and sliced blood pudding, which I do not care for.

There was also a station of Japanese food. "Curious George" me decided to try it. There was kelp (seaweed) soup and a tiny legume (seed) dish. Nothing suited me, so I went to the English station to fill my plate with what I was used to. Guess who was also there? The Japanese nurses. I hope they enjoyed the English food choices far more than I would theirs.

Another breakfast surprise happened in Atlantic City. Next to the Liberty Hotel where Ed and I stayed, there was a small restaurant, and on the menu were fish and pork chops. I never was served those foods for breakfast, where oatmeal or *Cream of Wheat* were the norm. We enjoyed the fish and pork chops and returned each morning to the same little "hole in the wall" for the tasty food. I've enjoyed them instead of bacon. If I had some of my favorite butter pecan ice cream in the freezer, I'd put a dollop on my oatmeal. Why not?

**February 19, 2024**

Good morning, all 196. Back in the day, someone always had to rise early to get a fire burning in the kitchen stove before everyone else got up. When I was a little kid in the latter 1930s, we did not have a furnace in the cellar, so the house was cold in the mornings. I wonder how women living alone managed back then. Widows and single women had to be taken in by their families. Such was my Great Aunt Lillie's fate after her husband died, and she was in her early 50s. She returned to her mother's home but soon went off to Buffalo to help a friend run a tea shop. Family members, such as my father and his brothers, were quite surprised by her gutsiness.

Once upon a time, school children celebrated President Abraham Lincoln's birthday on February 12th and President George Washington's on the 22nd. I don't remember if we ever had either day off from school. When **Presidents' Day** was first celebrated, the holiday was meant to celebrate George Washington. It has become a celebration of all U.S. chief executives. I would bake a sour cherry pie for my son, even though I knew the story about young George Washington and the cherry tree was a myth. Interestingly, I live now on what was once George Washington's property—Gum Springs. Legend has it that he watered his horses here where sweet gum trees grew. They are tall trees with brown balls hanging on them over the winter. They are the fruit of the tree, opening in the spring to blow pollen all over the place.

My school system gave us a week-long winter break in February. That's when my family would take our Caribbean cruises. The first two were on sister Greek ships—the Regina and the Romanza. Opa! Our first cruise left from the Dutch Island of Curacao, to which we had to fly from New York City. Imagine this sight. There we were deplaning while lugging our winter coats and boots since we had left N.J. during a snowstorm. The first thing to catch my attention was the tall cacti growing everywhere. It grows only in warm climates where coats and boots are never needed. The next year we left our heavy winter garb with Ed's sister in the Queens section of New York City. Fortunately, there was no snowstorm, and she lived a short distance from the airport. Most memorable about my first cruise was that I was sea-sick for three days. The ship's doctor told me to take Dramamine before I get on ships. I followed those orders on later trips, although I now take Bonine that does not knock me out. I take it when I fly, too.

In later years my winter break was shortened by the Board of Education to two days as a recognition of the two presidents born in February. No more winter cruises for the Mosses!

This is also **Daisy Galson Bates Day.** An African American, she organized the "Little Rock Nine" by selecting nine Black students to integrate *Central High School* in Little Rock, Arkansas, in 1957. She was posthumously awarded the *Medal of Freedom* in 1999. **Daisy Gatson Bates Day** coincides with Washington's birthday and is a public holiday in Arkansas, where schools, government offices and many businesses are closed on this day.

**February 20, 2024**

Good morning, all 199. I wondered who will win the brass ring at #200. Carousels used to have brass rings for the riders to grab for a prize. The *Washington Post* has two interesting articles today. *Remember our brains are built to forget* and *There's a reason the office thermostat is the subject of many heated debates.* Every year on February 20th the **World Day of Social Justice** promotes the importance of fair and just relations between the individual and society. It also addresses gender equality, exclusion, poverty, human rights, and social protection.

'Tis also **Muffin Day, Cherry Pie Day, National Love Your Pet Day,** and **Clean Out Your Bookcase Day**. My favorite muffins are blueberry, bran and lemon/poppy seed. *Publix* in St. Petersburg bakes the best bran muffins. Today I could enjoy a slice of homemade sour cherry pie, but I am not going to bake one because I'd "pig out" if I did. If my son lived nearby, I'd bake one for him, latticed top crust and all. He aways enjoyed my cherry pie when he lived home.

Perhaps some of you have pets. For you, every day is **Love Your Pet Day.** As for cleaning out my bookcase, I had to do that for my income taxes for my business Journey From the Past. I must report how many books I had in my inventory on December 31, 2023. I keep my inventory in an antique lawyer's bookcase that belonged to my father and perhaps his father. It sat in our living room when I was growing up. He kept a set of encyclopedias behind the windows that open and close to keep dust off precious books. I was a fortunate kid to have a set at my fingertips. Perhaps that's why I was so gung-ho about selling the *World Book* encyclopedias years later.

**February 21, 2024**

Good morning, all 199. The *Washington Post* has an article about Virginia Ali, the 90-year-old owner of the famed *Ben's Chili Bowl*, a landmark in Washington, D.C. Some of you may have eaten there. I have and love the famous hot dogs. There is an interesting connection between Virginia and me because I had met her late husband when he was a student at *Scranton University* when I was 16. My cousin had a party and invited three students who were from Trinidad to it. She also invited me. I remember well the handsome young fellows. Deceased now, Ben Ali's photo hangs on the wall of the restaurant, and one day I introduced myself to Virgina to tell her the "small world" story.

Today is **National Sticky Bun Day** and **Real Bread Week.** I haven't eaten a sticky bun in years, but I remember my father bringing them home for a treat. They were sticky due to being drenched in a delicious, rich brown sugar butter caramel sauce and covered with pecans. My favorite bread is sour dough from *Panera. Fisherman's Wharf* in San Francisco has the best, though. The first time I tasted sour dough bread was there many years ago and I fell in love with it. For years after my son settled in California, he always brought me a large, unsliced round loaf. He also mailed one to me. But after *Panera* opened nearby, I purchase a loaf any time I desire.

Perhaps some of you may not know why the bread is called "sour dough." Before commercial yeast was invented in the 1880s, bakers would leave dough out and let yeast from the air begin the fermentation process. Sour dough French bread, with its distinctive tangy taste, was invented in San Francisco in 1849. I enjoy toasting mine and slathering it with butter.

Famous people born on February 21st are singers Tony Martin and Nina Simone; politician Barbara Jordan; and astronaut twins Mark and Scott Kelly. In 1848 the world's first telephone book was issued in New Haven, Connecticut. In 1885 the newly completed *Washington Monument* was dedicated.

**February 24, 2024**

Good morning, all 198. Today is **National Tortilla Day**. I enjoy eating chips with salsa and guacamole. I don't remember when I first tasted it, but certainly not in Pennsylvania where I spent the first 26 years of my life and where there were no Spanish-speaking people living at that time.

In 1582, Pope Gregory XIII announced the Gregorian Calendar. In 1711, George Frederick Handel's opera *Rinaldi* premiered at the Haymarket Theater in London. Handel also composed the *Messiah* that includes the famous *Hallelujah Chorus*. Sadly, he was blinded by botched eye surgery at the hands of a flamboyant quack. The same thing happened to Johann Sebastian Bach at the hands of the same man. Handel died in 1769 at age 74. In 1823, Ludwig van Beethoven proclaimed Handel to be the "greatest composer that ever lived." Perhaps so, since we are still revering his music, especially at Christmastime.

In 1857 the first perforated U.S. postage stamps were delivered to the government. In 1863 the Arizona Territory was created. In 1868 the first U.S. parade with floats was at a Mardi Gras in Mobile, Alabama, years before the first Tournament of Roses began in Pasadena, California, in 1890. It was a parade of flowers, followed by an afternoon of chariot races, jousting, foot races, and tug-of-war. The Macy's Thanksgiving Day Parade originated in 1924. My family experienced the Rose Bowl parade in 1971. It had been my first trip to San Francisco where for three days we could not see the distance from our hotel room on the 27th floor. *"On a clear day, you can see forever."* 'Tis true. We could not see a bridge at first in the distance.

In 1921 the first transcontinental flight with 24 hours flying time arrived in Florida. U.S. Army 1st Lt. William D. Coney of the 91st Aero Squadron completed the flight of 22.5 hours' flying time from San Diego to Jacksonville. Not that I know anything about this event or the airplane, except to say that it had to be very important at the time. It was only fifteen years since the Wright Brothers had taken their exciting first short flight at Kitty Hawk, N.C. I'm off today to have lunch with my *Bennett College* sisters. If tortilla chips are on the menu, then I will order some to celebrate the day.

**February 25, 2024**

Good morning, all 200. Today is **National Chocolate Covered Nut Day, Peace Corps Day, Let's All Eat Right Day,** and **Quiet Day.** I can relate to all of these, not because I served in the Peace Corps, but I know someone who did. She was my next-door neighbor in Montclair, N.J. and grew up with my children.

This year **Quiet Day** occurs on the Sabbath that used to be a quiet day when I was a kid. Some very religious parents forbade any serious work or play. I was not even allowed to ride my bicycle on Sundays or roller skate on the sidewalk. Mores certainly have changed during my lifetime. I like the quiet. My television is on only when I am watching something like a *Netflix* movie to which I give my undivided time, or the *News* which I can stomach only once a day. I enjoy *The View* with Whoopie Goldberg. When doing housework, I listen to music on *YouTube,* especially peaceful hymns since doing housework is not my favorite thing. Otherwise, my house is totally quiet, and I can think. No television is on while I am writing this musing. I used to tell my students that our brains can do one thing at a time. They could not do their homework and listen to a radio. They may think they could, but one would suffer, usually their homework. So, it is with a television.

**February 27, 2024**

Good morning, all 212. Today is **International Polar Bear Day, National Protein Day, The Big Breakfast Day, National Strawberry Day, National Susan Day,** and **Retro Day.** When people share with me what they are having for a meal, I might ask, "*And where is your protein*"? You should have some with every meal. **Big Breakfast** and **Protein Days** can easily be combined.

Happy special day to the several Susans and Suzannes on this list from "sea to shining sea." I'd love to see the polar bears in their national environs at the North Pole along the coasts, inland streams, and lakes of Alaska, Canada, Greenland, Norway, and Siberia. But it's too cold up there for me to sight-see them. I hope they will not become extinct due to global warming, since ice floes are shrinking. I have only seen them up close when there was a special water zoo for polar bears in *Central Park* in New York City. That was many years ago, and, sadly, there are none there now. They were such fun to watch swimming in their pool of water.

Ask my granddaughter what her Granny's favorite homemade dessert is. Strawberry shortcake with real whipped cream. Yummy! I use the *Bisquick* biscuit recipe on the box for the shortcake. I do not like sponge cake or pound cake. They get too soggy from the strawberries.

Lastly, **Retro Day** describes my musings that take you to my "back in the day" experiences. No electricity? I don't think many of you can imagine that. Just look around your house and subtract what is powered by electricity. To begin a day, first light a fire. "*But how*?" you are asking. If my Ed were living, being the oldest son, that was his chore before the rest of the family got up. There had to be a coal fire in the iron kitchen stove for his mother to make breakfast for the younger children before they got dressed and set out for school.

Someone on our list told me that she is beginning to record her memoirs. Very commendable. Others should do likewise because, when you are gone, so will your stories be. Become your family's Griot. You have no excuse with a computer. When I began recording anecdotes prior to the year 2000, I was writing in longhand with a pencil in a spiral bound notebook for easy erasing. Now, I compose on my computer and am particularly happy with its "cut and paste" feature. Thanks, Son, for insisting that I learn how to use one.

**February 28, 2024**

Good morning, all 212. For *A.K.A.* Sorors on my list, today is **National Pink Day** for the lovers of the pink and green. It is interesting to me that it is **National Chocolate Souffle Day.** I love anything chocolate. It is also **National Floral Design Day** and I love beautiful arrangements of flowers. It is also **Inconvenience Yourself Day, National Random Acts of Kindness Day in February, World Kindness Day in November,** and **National Do Something Nice Day in October.** This last one offers a delightful excuse to just be a person who makes things just a little nicer for someone else. It might be surprising someone with a bouquet of flowers or a box of candy, as some of you have done for me.

Monday's *Washington Post* published an article about Howard University's competitive rowing crew that became the first all-Black competitive rowing team in America in 1964. The article is *From pioneers to champions.* I enjoy sharing what I have learned with you, and I love learning from you. I had never met a rower before I met one on my list. I've seen crews practicing on the Potomac River and on the water in Philadelphia and Boston.

**February 29, 2024**

Good morning, all 213. Our schools did not close for anything weather-related. All teachers were required to live within walking distance of the schools. Most were women who were not driving automobiles back then. Some boarded with families. No apartments were available to single women, which many of them were. So, sunny or snowy, wet or dry, we all were always in school.

Happy birthday to all "leapers." I don't believe I've ever known any. Are any of you? If so, enjoy your special day when you can celebrate your birthday once again. Dinah Shore was born on February 29, 1916. She was an American singer, actress, television personality, and the chart-topping female vocalist of the 1940s. I was a fan.

Yesterday, the *Washington Post* published in the Food Section an article that for me was another "small world" surprise. There was a photograph of the cover of a cookbook called "Spoonbread and Strawberry Wine," with two young women who are sisters. Why did they immediately catch my eye? Because I own that same cookbook that was published in 1978. It sits in my father's lawyer's bookcase. That cookbook was often given as a shower gift for a new bride who could not cook. I gave a copy to a friend who married the summer after her high school graduation and couldn't cook. She would have five children, so, I guess she learned. I remember when I purchased "Spoonbread and Strawberry Wine" at a book signing in Montclair, N.J. where I lived and where the two sisters had grown up. The sisters were younger than I and older than my daughter. Even so, how and why they created their unique cookbook is interesting to me because they travelled to the South from N.J. to become their family's Griots, as I've been to mine. The Darden sisters' cookbook is partly a scrap book that documents their family history via recipes and photographs. You can *Google* the article.

**March 1, 2024**

Good morning, all 213. Today is **National Peanut Butter Lover's Day**, **Share a Smile Day, National Pig Day,** and **National Salesperson Day.** Someone on our list reminds me that this is **Roots Tech Day,** which interests me as a Griot and amateur genealogist.

The Local Living section of the *Washington Post* yesterday published, *Don't think of them as pests. Squirrels can be good neighbors.* A very interesting article for those of us who are being "pested" by them. My message is short today because I am inviting you to open the interview that I gave about my father's unique anthracite coal art for Black History Month 2024. He was featured in the *EBONY* magazine in March 1970 and also listed in *Who's Who in America* in 1972.

Thanks to a dear former West Pittstonian friend on my musing list who sent this site to me from her present home in Florida. I hope you can open it.
https://www.wnep.com/article/news/local/black-history/learning-perseverance-from-patience-black-history-month-anthracite-heritage-museum-coal-art-sculpture-c-edgar-patience/523-b4373df7-a941-4689-bfee-f2fc2b292c41

Unfortunately, my father passed away before seeing his name published in *Who's Who in America* in 1972. I have the volume sitting on one of my numerous bookshelves. Not the lawyers' one, though, where I keep my inventory. Just in case some of you are not aware, I have written a book about his beautiful work called *Anthracite Coal Art by Charles Edgar Patience."* Any interested people may want to check it out on my website. www.journeyfromthepast.com.

**Charles Edgar Patience Sculpting George Washington Bust ca. 1945**

**March 3, 2024**

Good morning, all 239. Wow! The number shot up after the *Delta Sigma Theta, Inc.* luncheon yesterday, thanks to my Sorors. This is **National Reading Month, Irish American Heritage Month,** and **Women's History Month,** as well as **Celebrate Your Name Week.** This day, among others, is **World Wildlife Day, National Anthem Day, Namesake Day, World Hearing Day, National Canadian Bacon Day,** and **33 Flavors Day.**

**The 33 Flavors Day** has caught my fancy. My favorite ice cream is butter pecan. I'm not particular about many new flavors. I haven't had peach in recent years, which I enjoy with chunks of peach in it. Am I dreaming of the day when a cone with one dip cost 5 cents and two dips 7 cents at the soda fountain in Dressler's Drug Store? Possibly.

In 1845, Florida was admitted as our 27th state. It had been a slave-holding territory, so, Iowa was admitted as a non-slave state. In 1931, the U.S. adopted the *Star-Spangled Banner* for its national anthem. The words were written by Francis Scott Key during the British bombardment of Fort McHenry at Baltimore during the War of 1812 with Great Britain. In 1969, *Apollo 9* was successfully launched. Apollo 9 (March 3–13, 1969) was the third human spaceflight in NASA's Apollo program.

As for famous people's birthdays, we have Alexander Graham Bell (1847), Scottish-born Canadian, American inventor, scientist and engineer credited with patenting the first practical telephone. Jacqueline Joyner-Kersee (1962) retired African American track and field athlete who ranked among the all-time greats in the heptathlon, as well as the long jump.

**March 4, 2024**

Good morning, all 239. This will be my last musing until March 23rd, when I return to Virginia from my "Selah" (rest) in Florida. On March 6th I will be 91 and 5/6 years old. Amazing! Please keep me in your prayers while I observe my "Selah."

In 1770, while being harassed by a mob, Crispus Attucks, who was of mixed African and Indigenous ancestry, was killed by the British military. He was the first person killed in the Boston Massacre, and therefore the first American killed in the American Revolution. In 1797 John Adams became America's second President. In 1861, Abraham Lincoln became the 16th President of the United States. In 1924, *Happy Birthday to You* was published by Claydon Sunny.

March 23, 2024

Good morning, all 241. My daughter and I lucked out because we saw nary a drop of rain in the two weeks we were in Naples, Florida. Each day was picture perfect—sunny and warm. I met several "snowbirds" who soon will travel back to their homes in the North.

My favorite activity was enjoying the palms, and the plants, including New Guinea Impatiens, Petunias, Hibiscus, and Bougainvillea. I only recognized the Tamarind tree. You northern lovers of flowers are enjoying Daffodils, Forsythia, Japanese Cherry trees and Bradford Pears. Each blooms according to its DNA. This is my favorite time of the year, as you already know.

**March 24, 2024**

Good morning, all 242. Christians all over the world remember Jesus Christ riding on a donkey into Jerusalem to prepare for the Passover on Thursday. People stripped palm leaves to wave at Him and exclaim "*Hosanna!*" This is the beginning of "Holy Week," from Palm Sunday to Resurrection Sunday (Easter). Many churches distribute palms, and mine distributes crosses created from palm fronds. When I was a kid, people folded fronds into crosses for their lapels.

On this list are six former Choralaires from *St. Mark's United Methodist Church* in Montclair, NJ. Today, you surely will be remembering Palm Sunday afternoon concerts when you were teenagers 45 years ago. I remember which of you always sang *The Palms* so beautifully. The first half of the program was performed in choir robes. For the second half, girls changed into formal wear and boys wore tuxes. The program concluded with Mendel's *Hallelujah Chorus*. The audience stood and some sang along. No one ever made a mistake during the "tricky" ending, even by the younger Celestials who were itching to turn 13 and become Choralaires. After the concert, we went somewhere special for a formal dinner. Great time for Dr. Johnson, me, and all!

Because King George II stood when Handel performed the *Hallelujah Chorus*, everyone stood, and it became the custom. St. Mark's was always packed when you talented Choralaires presented concerts for Christmas and Easter. I was honored for seventeen years to be your co-director, along with my dear friend, the late Dr. Byerte W. Johnson. All five of our children were in the choir. Your choir's favorite hymns were *We've Come This Far By Faith* and *Hold Back the Darkness.*

**March 25, 2024**

Good morning, all 250. My niece in Colorado reminded me that I missed mentioning the Bird of Paradise growing in Naples, Florida. From traditional Neapolitan pizza to fresh seafood delights, Naples is a food lover's paradise. My daughter and I ate several meals at a Mexican restaurant where the seafood soup was chocked full of shrimp, calamari, mussels, and clams. I took a doggy bag home.

Naples is best known for Italian restaurants that serve delicious pizza and a large variety of fresh seafood dishes. Many fine establishments dot the main streets, and so it is difficult to choose one. As many of you know, I love Italian food, having been introduced to spaghetti (macaroni), ravioli and pizza as a child in northeastern Pennsylvania. My daughter and I are already planning to go back in March 2025.

Today is the **Day of Remembrance of the Victims of Slavery** and **the Transatlantic Slave Trade,** as well as the anniversary of the 4-day, 54-mile march led by Dr. Martin Luther King, Jr. in 1965 from Selma to Montgomery, Alabama. This is also **National Medal of Honor Day**. Awarded by Congress, the Medal of Honor is awarded only to military members.

Bruce Anderson, born June 19, 1845, was an African American Union Army soldier in the *Civil War*. In 1914, he received the Medal of Honor for his actions during the Second Battle of Fort Fisher. Twenty-five other Blacks who served in the *Civil War* were awarded the Medal of Honor, some posthumously.

For you Marylanders, this is **Maryland Day** that commemorates March 25, 1634, the day 120 English settlers disembarked onto Maryland soil from two small sailing ships—the "Ark" and the "Dove." It is also **Lobster Newburg Day**. I love anything made with lobster. Last is **International Waffle Day.** I love waffles covered with fresh strawberries, blueberries and banana slices with a smidgen of maple syrup. Yum!

In 1954 the first color television set went on sale. The first television Ed and I bought in 1955 was black and white. We were happy on Saturday nights to watch *Jackie Gleason* and on Sundays *Ed Sullivan*. *Tennessee Ernie Ford* came on weekdays at noon. I don't remember the year when we splurged for a colored TV. What a thrill it was! Out went the old black and white.

My all-time favorite movie, *Random Harvest*, is in black and white. *Turner Classics* are wonderful. I am so happy that someone had the foresight to store films. Tonight, when you stare in awe at the full moon, rejoice and sing, *"Oh, Lord my God, how great Thou art."* Reflect on the fact that the moon has been revolving around the earth ever since *"in the beginning"* when the Creator placed it there before He created humankind.

**March 26, 2024**

Good morning, all 251. Today is **National Spinach Day**. I grew up being told that eating spinach made me strong. 'Tis true that spinach contains iron and other essential nutrients, but I don't believe my parents' generation knew that. They just ate what was available and didn't kill anybody. I did not like spinach as a child because it was bitter to my tongue. Farmers have improved its taste through hybridization. Now I enjoy spinach scrambled with eggs and also sprinkled in salads, along with other tasty greens. This day reminds me of *Popeye the Sailor Man*, a comic strip that I read daily when I was young. I learned how to read via comics before entering first grade in 1938. I no longer read comics but still love to read books, especially historical novels.

Right up my alley is **National Science Appreciation Day**. Each day I appreciate science, especially the biology I taught for 33 years at *Bloomfield High School* in Bloomfield, N.J. That's a lot of dissected earthworms, crayfish, perch, and frogs. I never dissected cats in my classes, but my daughter did at *Montclair High School*. I was surprised when she chose an advanced class in biology. I was the only parent who allowed a dissected cat in their house. I remember when several of her friends came by to study my daughter's cat that she toted home in a plastic bag.

Today is **Make Up Your Own Holiday Day.** May you enjoy your very own special day. It is also **Live Long and Prosper Day**, as well as **Solitude Day.** Hopefully, the latter can influence the former. I do enjoy my solitude. I also enjoy reading history. In 47 BCE (Before Christian Era), Cleopatra was re-instated as co-ruler of Egypt with her brother, Ptolemy XIV. Centuries later, the signing of a peace treaty between Egypt and Israel took place with Anwar Sadat and Menachem Begin in 1979, mediated by President Jimmy Carter at the presidential retreat at Camp David.

Persons born today were Robert Frost (1874), American poet; Tennessee Williams (1911), American dramatist; Sarah Vaughn (1924), African American singer and pianist; Sandra Day O'Connor (1930), first woman to become a U.S. Supreme Court Justice; Diana Ross (1944), African American member of the Supremes; and Mariah Carey (1970), African American singer.

## March 27, 2024

Good morning, all 251. This is **National Scribble Day, Little Red Wagon Day, American Red Cross Giving Day, Manatee Appreciation Day, National Spanish Paella Day,** and **National Joe Day.** For the newcomers to my list, each day may have several celebrations, and I share those that have meaning to me personally. I begin with scribbling. I have many pieces of paper scribbled with telephone numbers, e-mail addresses, and any other *thing* I want to remember for a short while. No one can read my left-handed scribbling but me, just like the signatures of some physicians.

Continuing celebrations, a cousin four years younger than I had a little red wagon, like many young boys had. I don't think my girls had one, as it was not lady-like, especially since we wore dresses, never pants. We girls strolled pushing small baby carriages with our favorite dolls. I was my cousin's older companion, and when I was 12 and he was 8, I pulled him in his little red wagon to collect soda bottles from the neighbors and return them to stores for 2 cents each. One time we took all our pennies and treated ourselves to a jar of green olives from *Tobe's* grocery store on Exeter Ave. Then we ate them all. You see, olives were served only on Thanksgiving and Christmas, so they were a special treat. He and I didn't get stomachaches, either. I still love olives, both green with red pimento or the pit, as well as black ones, pitted or not. The Greek ones are too salty for me to eat many.

**Red Cross Giving Day** reminds me of when we kids would be given some change from home to take to school on the Red Cross collection day. We loved receiving a small metal red cross to wear proudly on our clothing. A teacher and a nurse during the *Civil War*, Clara Barton, was the founder of the Red Cross in 1881.

When I was in Naples, FL, I saw streets named after manatees. Sea cows, or manatees, are regarded as tropical marine mammals that migrate to warmer waters during the colder months of the year. In warmer months they're found in Florida's waterways. They may be the inspiration for mermaids by ancient mariners. I love paella with its wonderful variety of sea food. I remember the Portuguese restaurant, *Don Pepe* in Newark, N.J., where my family would go to feast on it. I have not had any since I moved to Virginia, but maybe someone will go to lunch with me to get some.

## March 28, 2024

Good morning, all 251. The history behind planting cherry trees in D.C. originated in 1912 as a gift of friendship to the U.S. from Japan. In stormy, hot, and windy weather they will go more quickly. How beautiful they are in full bloom. During World War II, Americans stopped using the word "Japanese" and began calling them "cherry trees." Thankfully, they were not all cut down during World War II when everything Japanese was hated.

Today is **Barnum and Bailey Day, National Black Forest Cake Day, Major League Baseball Opening Day, Wear a Hat Day,** and **National Weed Appreciation Day.** Also, this is **National Physicians' Week,** as well as **National Cleaning Week.** When I was a kid, a circus would come to town each summer, but not *Barnum and Bailey*. It was much smaller, held outdoors under a large tent. Cotton candy and cracker jacks were always requisites. I loved watching the tightrope performers, trapeze artists, acrobats, as well as the animals. Who knew that some were being abused? I've been to larger circuses, including one at the Madison Square Garden in New York City. There were always elephants, bears, lions, and horses, which is not happening nowadays. All animals have been eliminated.

Thinking about Black Forest cake, I love anything chocolate, the darker the better. As for baseball, my Ed was a fan, so today would have been important to him. Back in the day he loved the Dodgers with Jackie Robinson and Roy Campanella. Speaking of hats, I am not a fan unless the weather is cold outside. Some women look very glamorous in them. I thought I might become a "church hat-lady" when I reached 80, but I still have not graduated to that position.

In terms of edible weeds, I remember when in early spring my Great Aunt Lillie and her sister, Jessie, would comb the Pennsylvania countryside to pick early milk weed leaves to take home to cook. There were also lamb quarters, and dandelions going into the same pot, as well as wild onions which would later be called "chives." Yes, you can safely eat that onion grass growing wildly in your yard. In the South, collards and kale were once considered weeds but later became southern "soul food." Yay for the edible weeds that kept my ancestors alive!

Would you believe that tomatoes were once considered poisonous? Since Italians are huge consumers of tomatoes, it is ironic that the poison legend traces back to a 16th Century Italian herbalist named Pietro Andrae Mattioli. He classified the tomato as part of the deadly "Nightshade" family because it does resemble the belladonna bush with poisonous berries.

Belladonna vines grow wild in our yards and should be destroyed where children play. My father warned me never to touch them. Touching them would not cause any problem but eating them would. Several physicians on this list can celebrate your achievements this week, especially the one with whom my daughter and I spent two weeks of "Selah" in Naples, Florida, at his beautiful home. Thank you, Dear Friend. Today on the Christian calendar is **Maundy Thursday,** when Jesus celebrated the Passover with His 12 disciples. Some churches celebrate it with a foot washing service and taking Communion (the Eucharist).

**March 29, 2024**

Good morning, all 251 on **Good Friday**. It was always a special day for me when I was a child because my Great Aunt Lillie would take me to the three-hour Good Friday service held at one of the larger churches in our hometown. The service was called "The Seven Last Words of Jesus Christ." Seven pastors each preached one of the "Words," and a hymn was sung between each segment, so, people could come and go. *The Old Rugged Cross* might be sung while snacks were served in the fellowship hall. Some people might attend just during the time when their pastor spoke, but others like my Great Aunt Lillie stayed the entire time to hear every pastor, and so did I. Afterwards, we'd hold hands to walk "over town," which is crossing a bridge to the City of Pittston. Some places have a downtown, others an uptown. Ours is "over town" because we must cross over the Susquehanna River to get there.

My family lived in West Pittston a block from the river, and we'd have to cross one of two bridges to reach Main Street in Pittston where all the businesses were located. Aunt Lillie would treat me to a root beer float at a soda fountain there. It's still a favorite treat, and the time spent with my Great Aunt Lillie are precious memories. Years later in 1982 in Montclair, NJ, a joint Good Friday service was held for Catholics and Protestants at Immaculate Conception Church. It was filled with Protestants who had never set foot in a Catholic Church before. I had because I used to attend Mass with a friend at the African American St. Peter Claver Catholic Church in Montclair.

Peter Claver, SJ was a Spanish Jesuit Priest and missionary who became the Patron Saint of enslaved people in the Republic of Colombia, and the ministry to Africans. I don't know if the ecumenical Good Friday service was repeated after I moved to Virginia, but I know it was a memorable one for me. I will attend today's service at my church, where seven dynamic women preachers on staff will be speaking. Two are on this list. However, we will not be worshipping for three hours like when I was young. The day was so revered that all businesses were closed from 12:00 noon to 3:00 p.m. Over the years customs have changed. Be blessed, everyone, on this special day, as we mediate on the meaning of, "*It is finished.*" *John 19:30.* Thanks be to God.

## March 30, 2024

Good morning, all 260. Today is **Take a Walk in the Park Day.** According to the *Washington Post*, it will be a nice day to still enjoy the Japanese cherry blossoms in D.C. This year breaks a record of how long the blossoms have remained on view there. Perhaps a lovely park is in your area for you to stroll in on this lovely day to watch spring unfold.

Today in 1842 Dr. Crawford Long became the first physician to use anesthetic (ether) in surgery. In 1858 a U.S. patent was granted to Hymen Lipman for a pencil with an attached eraser. In 1867 U.S. Secretary of State William Seward purchased Alaska from Russia for $7.2 million in gold. In 1870 the 15th Amendment granted African American men the right to vote. Other birthdays include actor and brother of actress Shirley MacLaine, Warren Beatty (1937), and legendary guitarist Eric Clapton (1945).

The day before Easter was always a busy one in my house when I was a child, and these customs carried over to my adult life when I was rearing a family. Our family ritual was dyeing Easter eggs, and Ed did this with his young grandsons. Each person in my household always had their own basket filled with jellybeans and chocolates. My favorite chocolate egg was fruit and nut, while Ed's was coconut. Many customs are ethnic, like the intricately decorated Ukrainian eggs. One year a student presented me with a lovely one decorated in the fashion of his Orthodox religion. I placed it in my Easter basket each year until it finally cracked. I wonder what the origin of an Easter parade was, remembering the song, *In Your Easter Bonnet.* When I was a kid, ladies wore hats on Easter Sunday, many quite flowery and fancy. Some places like Atlantic City, N.J. would have parades where awards were given for the most beautiful hats. In my small hometown, families visited the local cemetery to decorate the graves of their loved ones. We always visited the *Civil War* grave of my Great Grandfather, Crowder Patience.

The fancy touch to my Easter church attire was a cymbidium corsage that my father gave me when I was a teenager. That custom my Ed carried on with our daughter and me for many years. Some more "seasoned" women might have worn a large orchid. May we each be blessed today as we prepare to celebrate Easter tomorrow while remembering days of yore with loved ones. "*As for me and my household, we will serve the Lord*" (Joshua 24:15).

## March 31, 2024

Good morning, all 260 on Easter morning. Of course, I know its religious meaning, but it has a non-religious connotation of welcoming spring, such as the singing of *In Your Easter Bonnet,* written by Irving Berlin in 1933 when people would promenade in their finery around a town or in a park. In Branch Brook Park in Newark, N.J., many Japanese families gather on Easter Sunday to have photos taken in their native attire, which includes beautiful kimonos. During some years the cherry trees are in full blossom. It is also a day when many families gather for a special meal. So, I searched some of the popular foods that may be served by some of you on this list of friends and family from different ethnicities. Many customs have survived for centuries, coming from the "old countries." Someone asked me last week if I am familiar with hot cross buns. Yes, from my Irish friends from Pennsylvania and NJ. They were served in the faculty cafeteria in the high school where I taught.

Today I remember the wife of my father's first cousin. Her parents were from Ukraine, and every Easter Nina baked delicious poppy-seed rolls, as her mother had done before her. I tried making them, but that was a disastrous experience. To me, Parker House rolls taste better than cake, especially with some grape or berry jam. "Patience" may be my maiden name but not a characteristic I always possess, especially when it comes to dealing with yeast. I have found *Butter Maid Bakery* that makes delicious rolls, walnut rolls, and apricot treats. Yummy! Favorite Easter foods are buns and cheese from Jamaica, difo from Ethiopia, torta pasqualina from Italy, figoli from Malta, fanera from Equador, and white borscht from Poland. May each of us be blessed on this Resurrection Day. "*Up from the grave He arose"!* Thanks be to God.

## April 1, 2024

Good morning, all 260. 'Tis Easter Monday and some Christian groups may observe this day by having outdoor processions and parades and Easter egg hunts. When I was a kid, we students had Good Friday and Easter Monday off from school. Many school systems have incorporated Easter into their spring breaks. The high school where I worked in N.J., however, always gave us the 16$^{th}$ week of the year off, regardless of when Easter fell. I know that because we bought our Florida timeshare to use every year during that particular week.

## April 2, 2024

Good morning, all 260. Yesterday my daughter got me good on **National Tom Foolery Day**. I had forgotten about it and fell right into her trap when she told me that it was snowing in Connecticut. Well, it could have been! Now if my son had told me about snow at his home in California, I don't think I would have fallen for the April Fool's trick. My students tried to fool me on April 1$^{st}$ and sometimes they succeeded.

It is **International Children's' Book Day**, the birthday of Danish author Hans Christian Anderson, a favorite of mine, and the goal of the day is to create in children a love of reading. Born in 1805, he was influenced by the Grimm brothers and William Shakespeare. In the third grade, there was the little library set up in the back of Miss Isobel Thomas' room. After we finished our classwork, we were allowed to choose books from her library. She even allowed us to take them home and of course expected them to be returned.

I have always been an avid reader and usually carry a "real" book with me in my purse, should I have time to spare, like waiting for someone who is shopping. I am not a shopper. Neither has my cellphone become an appendage like it has for many nowadays. Hans Christian Anderson's stories have followed me through my life. I was recently discussing *The Princess and the Pea,* as it relates to someone I know, who found a mattress to be uncomfortable. The story was published in 1835. As for *The Emperor's New Clothes* (1837), many of you on this list should be familiar with that story, as well, or you can *Google* it. He also wrote *The Ugly Duckling* which he said was about himself, and *The Little Mermaid*, which was made into a Disney movie. All of his stories have happy endings.

**April 3, 2024**

Good morning, all 260. Today is **National Walking Day**. Here, violets are popping up all over. Some people call them weeds, but I was taught in my botany class to call them "wildflowers." "Weed" just means they are not welcome in your yard, like the dandelions now dotting green lawns with their bright yellow flowers that will soon release a multitude of seeds. It is also **National Wildlife Week, World Aquatic Animal Day, National Find a Rainbow Day,** and **Independent Artist Day.** All categories are of interest to me, especially the two biological ones. The last one will include many of you who, like me, are multitalented. However, I am not a "master" of anything, just a dabbler in a lot of different things.

As far as wildlife is concerned, many of you know that giraffes and elephants are my favorites. My least favorites are bats, snakes, alligators, and crocodiles. Once a student asked me if his sister could bring snakes to our class for a "show and tell." She was a former student of the high school studying snakes at nearby *Montclair State College*. She brought several baskets of snakes to my 8th period class, all harmless, but scary. She proceeded to wind them around her arms and neck. I did not allow my students to touch them, but one smart-alecky boy dared me. *"You hold one, too, Mrs. Moss."* What was I to do? I let one wrap around my arm. It was unsettling, to say the least. It was going up my sleeve, but I pretended it was not bothering me a bit, even though it was. One time I was with my two young grandsons at a Medieval Festival. A man was there with a boa constrictor. He was allowing kids to hold it. My grandsons refused, but to show how brave I was, I volunteered to let one wrap around my arm. It felt so heavy and indeed was scary. They are not poisonous but can constrict the life from a person.

Famous people born today are Jane Goodall, the famous chimpanzee expert (1934), and actors Marlon Brando (1924), Alex Baldwin (1958), and Eddie Murphy (1961). Fifty years ago, Martin Cooper made the first cell phone call in New York City. And the rest is history. Telephone booths that formerly dotted cities and towns began disappearing around 2000. Are there any left?

**April 4, 2024**

Good morning, all 260. I am choosing not to discuss any of the 22 celebrations today. Someone commented yesterday about my love for giraffes, which I'll explain now. Once in a Human Development course I was taking for my Masters degree, students were asked to answer the following three questions.

**1**. If we could choose a different occupation, what would it be and why? **2.** If we could be a flower, which would it be and why? **3**. If we could be an animal, what would it be and why? For the different career, I would have chosen to become a minister, which was a profession for women almost as scarce as "hen's teeth" in my generation. I knew only one female pastor when growing up—Rev. Christine Giles, who was my Great Aunt Lillie's close friend and member of Rev. Giles' church, St. Mark's A.M.E. (African American Episcopal). I have no idea how Rev. Giles became a minister. She was a married woman with a teen-age son, and since women did not drive back in the day, her husband escorted her everywhere until he passed away. Afterwards she took driving lessons and took herself wherever she needed to go.

No females in my family were drivers, not even my stepmother, Alice, who had the nerve to be a WAC during World War II. She did not learn how to drive, even after my father's death. She walked or took buses, which, fortunately for her, Wilkes-Barre had. Friends with cars would also take her places. Rev. Giles had "intestinal fortitude," and I admired her. Once she drove herself and gutsy Aunt Lillie across the Pennsylvania mountains to get to the Pittsburgh Conference. As a pastor, she was obligated to attend.

Years later, my father and his brothers would have admired Aunt Lillie, when, at age 91, she moved from our hometown to NJ to live with me and my family. West Pittson residents had been used to seeing the whitehaired, short, "Colored" lady who walked over town to Pittston to shop, to the drugstore and grocery store, and to her Congregational Church. All of my uncles had died, and she was on her own. She hadn't wanted to move, but finally she agreed and lived happily with us for twelve more years, watching her favorite Soaps. I'd hurry home at 3:00 p.m. to watch *The Guiding Light* together. At almost 103, the Lord called her home. She had only a brief illness before her heart stopped. Thankfully, no suffering. She just went to sleep and did not wake up.

Responding to the question about the flower I'd be, I choose the daisy, which reminds me of being loved. Some of you, especially country girls, may remember how we could find out if "he" loved us or not by removing the white petals of a daisy one by one. Daisies were plentiful wildflowers in Pennsylvania. The test was for the heart throb of the moment, and the answer was always the same -- he always loved us. We naïve young girls had no idea about the even number of petals on a daisy, which therefore always provided the same positive answer. On a more religious note, the daisy also reminds me of the hymn that tells me, *"Yes, Jesus loves me, for the Bible tells me so."*

Lastly, what animal would I choose to be? I choose the giraffe, the tallest animal in the world, because its long neck allows it to be aloof and not bothered by what goes on below. A giraffe can lift its head up very high and nibble 60 pounds of leaves a day. It can glance down fleetingly and immediately return to its solitude and lofty thoughts. My personality is much like that. *"How great Thou art."* I am in awe of all of God's creations. I am in awe of God's love of diversity. I am in awe of God's biology. I know that many of you are, too.

**April 5, 2024**

Good morning, all 260. Today is **National Carmel Day, National Dandelion Day, National Flash Drive Day, National Self Care Day, Read a Road Map Day,** and **Walk-to-Work Day.** Some of these celebrations interest me, especially the caramels. It is the first piece I take out of a box of assorted chocolates, the darker the better. Dandelions may be of interest to you because they are popping out all over your yards now. They have long taproots that you must dig up if you want to totally get rid of the weeds. I had friends many years ago who made dandelion wine from the yellow flowers. I watched them once. It was a very tedious job. The long-serrated leaves are eaten in salads nowadays.

As for flash drives, many of you have them for storing important information from documents to precious photos. I have several to store my PowerPoint presentations. Some of you younger folks have never seen a road map or have the faintest knowledge about how to read one. It was something I learned to do, even before I learned to drive at age 16. I also learned to read maps in geography class when I was introduced to longitude and latitude. Back in the day, people used road maps to plot directions before getting on the road in an automobile. The maps showed the destination and the number of miles to get there. Today, all you need is your cell phone. Who needs a road map? Well, I do because I like to see where I am going.

The first lesson I learned about maps was that right is left and left is right. meaning that East is on the right side and West on the left. North is at the top and South is at the bottom. Roads that are even numbered generally travel East to West, and roads with uneven numbers travel North to South. I live a block away from Route 1 that goes from Maine to Florida and is parallel to Route 95. Most rivers in the Northern Hemisphere flow South. However, the Niagara River flows North between two Great Lakes—Erie to Ontario. I learned this from experience when I thought we were travelling in the wrong direction because we were following a North-flowing river that I thought was flowing South like the Susquehanna River does near my home. The road map told me differently, as I looked at the names of towns that we were passing on our way North to Ft. Niagara.

A good navigator instructs drivers who never remove their eyes from the road. Ed and I collected road maps from every place we traveled, until they became raggedy from use. We all have GPS, but I do not get the feeling of where I am with one. But then, I can't be the driver listening for *"Redirect"* or *"Make a U-turn."* I was always the navigator for Ed who was always the driver. His first car was a brand new 1952 black and white *Buick*. We'd fill it with his younger brothers and sisters and take off on Sunday afternoons for a trip to the Pocono Mountains surrounding our hometown. Full car and no seat belts!

Three of you may remember our near-tragic accident in the Poconos in 1958. We hit a patch of unpaved road. It was a Sunday afternoon and there were no workmen holding up "Stop" signs and no orange cones. Ed hit the brakes, and the *Buick* made a circle that ended with its hood pointing toward a deep ravine. I was holding my little daughter in my arms in the passenger seat, and my youngest sister-in-law was seated between her brother and me. The other four were crowded together in the back seat, and we were all screaming. Somebody's guardian angel stopped the car. *"For He shall give His angels charge over you… lest you dash your foot on a stone"* (Psalms 91:11-12).

Someone today offered me these words of wisdom: *"Yesterday is history. Tomorrow is a mystery. Today is a gift."* I thank God for delivering us from a fatal accident years ago, and I thank you, Lord, for waking me up this morning and setting me on my way. Thank you for the gift of today. I never drove Ed anywhere until he became ill. By that time, we had a portable Garmin GPS, which was a life saver. I rely now on the GPS that is installed in my van. I'm in the 21st Century with it, but not so much with my cell phone. Still learning.

**April 6, 2024**

Good morning, all 260. Today there's exactly one month 'til my birthday. How can little Juanita Patience with the dark brown pigtails be 92 years old? That little girl who rode her bicycle all around West Pittston, who ran home every day for twelve years for lunch because the public school had no cafeteria, and who placed flowers on her great-grandfather's *Civil War* veteran's grave. I am that Juanita, but with an unruly mop of curly, white hair. I remember the first day of school in September 1938 and the smallpox vaccination we had during the summer before entering first grade. I see my six-year-old self, sitting quietly in a rocking chair, lest I disturb the smallpox vaccination area that was kept uncovered. I remember Mrs. Straiter, an older woman friend of my great aunts. She had a number of ugly scars on her face which she explained to me. I wonder if curious little Juanita had asked her about them directly. One of my cousins said that I was nosey, but I was just curious. Smallpox vaccinations stopped in 1972 after the disease was eradicated in the United States. Today, Juanita forgets where she put her keys. Thankfully, I am still sharp enough to be able to share my stories, and some of you might tell yours too. I focus on the positive things in my life. The negative things are best left forgotten and untold.

Among the special celebrations are **Caramel Popcorn Day, Love Our Children Day, Cherish an Antique Day, National Gardening Day, National Deep-Dish Pizza Day,** and **Burrito Day.** I have a few antiques in my house, not valuable, but sentimental. They belonged to my Great Aunt Lillie. Many of you know that I enjoy gardening. I also enjoy Double Good caramel covered popcorn that is sold for fundraisers. You will hear from the Bennett College Alumnae the next time we sell it. Lastly, a deep-dish square cut piece of pizza is my favorite.

In addition, it is the 51st birthday of African American singer Pharrell Williams, known for his *Happy* song. He was born in Virginia Beach, Virginia, where last summer I saw the beginning of his surfing business called the "Atlantic." His father and brother are also named Pharoah.

**April 7, 2024**

Good morning, all 260. The sun is right on the horizon at 7:00 a.m. and it has awakened me. Birds are chirping. The temperature is 44 degrees. Time to get up and be at it. Someone is waiting to hear from me today. Yesterday I began reading my past musings to determine whether I have duplicated over two years. Also, I want my newest readers to be able to know what I wrote before they had joined my list.

It's countdown to a total eclipse tomorrow. The *Washington Post* published the following article on April 6th *Countdown to the total solar eclipse. How it will unfold, play by play.* It's worth reading, should you be able to Google it. There was another noteworthy article on the 6th. *Earthquake and strong aftershock shake northeast.* I did not feel it here in Virginia, but my daughter did in Connecticut at 6:00 p.m. The *Washington Post* mentions the earthquake that occurred here on August 23, 2011. I was at the National Archives in Washington, D.C. researching for my book, *Forgotten Black Soldiers Who Served in White Regiments During the Civil War.* The need for the research was because historians, archivists and authors had told me there were no Black soldiers serving in White Regiments, but I knew that my Great-grandfather Pvt. Crowder Patience, who had served in the 103rd PA Volunteers, was one. The proof is carved on his Union tombstone in the West Pittston Cemetery. So, I made the hypothesis that if there was one Black soldier who had served in one White regiment, then there were others. There were thousands, and I was the one fated to pore through military records to find their names. I followed clue by clue and published two small books. It is humbling to realize that I was the one chosen to reveal that forgotten fact 150 years later. The news is out now and cannot be taken back.

Back to the earthquake of 2011, only the Archives librarian and I were in the large library at the frightening moment when the earth was suddenly moved in Washington, D.C. It felt as if God were giving the earth a good shake. The librarian and I were wondering what had happened, when another person suddenly burst into the room to announce that we were to evacuate the building immediately. When I got outside, I met a woman from California who told me that the evacuation was all wrong. In California she informed me, people are admonished not to leave buildings during earthquakes because they might be injured by falling pieces of debris. East or west, we must follow the orders being given. And so, I took myself straight to the to the Metro station across the street. I was trusting in the Lord to get me home safely, and He did.

Among others, today is **National Coffee Cake Day, World Health Day, Metric System Day, National No Housework Day, Empowered Women Entrepreneurs' Day,** and **International Beaver Day.** Several mathematicians on this list will be interested in the metric system. It was never up my alley, math not being my strong suit.

Keeping in good health should be a priority for us all. Such as not eating too much coffeecake today. Several women entrepreneurs are among us, including myself as the author of nine books. www.journeyfromthepast.com. This being the Sabbath for many Christians, the "no housework" appeals to me. It has been a lifelong habit of mine not to do any serious housework on Sundays other than cooking a big meal for my family after attending church. Such was taken seriously by my great aunts. Never ever any washing, ironing or cleaning on Sundays.

I'm sure my Great Aunt Florence Glover gathered eggs in the mornings from her coops on her farm, but she might not have churned butter, calling that "work." My Great Uncle Walter had to milk the cow and feed the pigs. A number of their descendants are on this list and will be interested in learning this about their two ancestors whom I remember well.

No one could go shopping at a grocery or department store on Sundays because there were none in existence when I was a child, and the smaller "Mom and Pop" stores were usually closed Sundays. I recall a drug store being open when I was a teen. I could buy a 5-cent ice cream cone at *Dresslers' Drug Store* on Luzerne Ave. and pay 7 cents for two dips. Classmates on this list may remember doing likewise.

'Tis a day of rest, according to Genesis 20: 8-11. The Creator knows how important rest is to our bodies. I have no difficulty napping and waking refreshed. Following the mid-day dinner, Sunday afternoon naps were a habit. You might try turning off your intrusive televisions and other gadgets to take a nap today. "Silence is golden" and a must for the necessary deep sleep that cleanses our brains. Only twenty minutes should do it, but I take an hour from 3 to 4. Then, per my chiropractor, I eat an apple for energy.

## April 8, 2024

Good morning, all 260. Some of you will peer at the total solar eclipse today when the moon passes between earth and the sun. Awesome! *"The heavens declare the glory of God"* (Psalm 19: 1). I will watch it on my television. When my kids were young, we made a contraption out of a cereal box to view the eclipse. Just be careful if you choose to watch the total solar eclipse today.

Today is also **National All is Ours Day, Draw a Picture of a Bird Day, National Zoo Lovers Day,** and **National Pygmy Hippo Day.** I am a zoo lover, as many of you know. When I was teaching biology in N.J. many years ago, I would take my students on field trips to the *Bronx Zoo* in N.Y. Afterwards we'd go to the *Hotel Piccadilly* in Manhattan for a smorgasbord! There actually is a system for eating a smorgasbord. One is not supposed to just pile food on a plate in any old manner. The directions were given to each person. For instance, nuts and cheese were in the last course.

One of my favorite Netflix movies is *The Zookeeper's Wife.* I have watched it several times. It's about a zoo located in Warsaw Poland, during World War II, based on a true story of a Polish couple who owned a zoo and how they helped hundreds of Jews escape from Warsaw before the Nazis killed them all. *Mila 18*, by Leon Uris is a novel written about that same time.

A historical event occurred in 1513, when Juan Ponce de Leon explored the Florida coastline. He first came to the Americas as a "gentleman volunteer" with Christopher Columbus' second expedition in 1493. America is young compared to the rest of the world. Consider Babylon that we read about in the Bible. Nebuchadnezzar's hanging gardens were considered one of the Seven Wonders of the Ancient World. China is an ancient country, too. On April 8, 1974, Hank Aaron of the Atlanta Braves hit his 715th career home run in a game against the Los Angeles Dodgers, breaking Babe Ruth's record of 714.

## April 9, 2024

Good morning, all 260. Some of you watched the total solar eclipse yesterday on your televisions. I watched on mine from Mexico to Maine which were on the Path of Totality. Many people wanted to see it in person and travelled from faraway places. It touched many personally, some even spiritually. Who could not be in awe of the Creator? About 32 million people were in the Path of Totality. Were any of you? The *Washington Post* headlines this morning report, *Screams, tears as eclipse stuns. Americans took in the awe-inspiring view in communities across the 115-mile-wide path of totality.* A delighted 100 couples got married in total darkness in Tiffin, Ohio. Washington, D.C. was not on the direct path and so there was no total darkness here like in other places. During midafternoon, the outside just looked a little bit like dusk.

Today, in 1939 on Easter morning, the magnificent contralto, Marian Anderson, sang at the Lincoln Memorial in Washington, D.C. Because of the color of her skin, she had been refused by the DAR (Daughters of the Revolution) to give a concert at *Constitution Hall*. There was a "White-artist-only" clause printed in every contract issued by the DAR. However, the DAR would not relent. Walter White, Executive Secretary of the NAACP (National Association for the Advancement of Colored People) suggested an outdoor concert at the *Lincoln Memorial*. Since it was a national monument, the logistics for the day fell to the Secretary of the Interior, Harold Ickes, who led the very nervous Marian Anderson onto the stage. Once she began singing "*My Country, 'Tis for thee, Sweet land of liberty, of thee I sing,*" she lost her nervousness and captivated the audience of 75,000. Fortunately, there was no rain, although it was a chilly morning, as is revealed by the artist's fur coat. You can watch the concert on YouTube.

One of the members of the DAR was first lady Eleanor Roosevelt. Outraged by the decision, she sent her letter of resignation and wrote about it in her weekly syndicated column, *My Day*. Those columns revealed much about her personal life such as who she met, what books she read, which plays she attended, where she traveled, and how she handled the pressures of public life as President Franklin Delano Roosevelt's wife. *My Day* documented her daily musings. Both Marian Anderson and Eleanor Roosevelt, are among my "she-roes."

**April 10, 2024**

Good morning, all 260. Today is **National Hug Your Dog Day, Encourage a Young Writer Day, Global Work From Home Day, National Calvin Day, International Safety Pin Day, National Farm Animals Day, National Nana Day,** and **Salvation Army Founders Day.** Several are special to me, especially being a NANA, even though I am called GRANNY by my six grands. My husband's mother was always NANA to her grandchildren.

On **Salvation Army Founders Day,** I'd like to share my knowledge about the organization. I have an interest in it because there was a corps and a church in my hometown when I was a kid. I attended Vacation Bible School there during the summers. To keep from being competitive, all the Protestant churches held *Bible* schools during summer mornings for several hours. Even Catholic kids would attend. I enjoyed them, which made me an ecumenical Christian.

The families of several of my classmates were members of the Salvation Army playing musical instruments in the band that included men and women who wore traditional bonnets with a red band. Every Saturday evening while attired in their navy-blue uniforms, they strolled through our small town, stopping at corners to play favorite hymns like *Onward Christian Soldiers*. Salvation Army history goes back to London and William and Catherine Booth who wanted to help those in need without discrimination against anyone. They began thinking of themselves as "soldiers for Christ," later changing the name to "Salvation Army." Donning uniforms, they govern with a quasi-military vocabulary of "general," "lieutenant," "captain," and "major." The Salvation Army has continued the same ministry to help the poor. And who has not placed a donation in their red Christmas kettles that debuted in San Francisco in 1891?

While researching the Salvation Army in my hometown, I discovered the names of local sponsors, and among them is the family of someone on our list. When I asked her about that, her reply was: *"We deeply believed in the Salvation Army for all the great work they do. Our parents instilled in us the importance of sharing; hence we are quite philanthropic throughout Luzerne and Lackawanna counties and continue to do so."* To my Pennsylvania high school classmate and her family, I say, "Thank you." *By Googling*, I learned that in 2021 it closed its doors after 109 years, and its members have since been absorbed into the Wilkes-Barre Salvation Army Corps.

In 1633 bananas from Bermuda went on sale for the first time in London. In 1849 the safety pin was patented by Walter Hart in the U.S. In 1872 the people of Nebraska celebrated the first Arbor Day by planting more than a million trees. In 1912 the luxury liner *RMS Titanic* embarked on its maiden voyage but sank after striking an iceberg.

Birthdays are American author, F. Scott Fitzgerald (1898), who wrote *The Great Gatsby*, and film actor Omar Sharif (1932), best known for *Lawrence of Arabia* (1962) and *Dr. Zhivago* (1965). I wish a happy day to Calvin on our list, my son's best friend in high school and now.

## April 11, 2024

Good morning, all 260. The *Washington Post* predicts thunderstorms. I'm glad I do not have to be out because I don't like driving in the rain. It's **National Pet Day, World's Parkinson Day, National Poetry Day, National Cheese Fondue Day, National Barber Shop Quartet Day,** and **National Support Teen Literature Day.** I enjoy reading rhyming poetry. A favorite poem I learned in a public speaking class in junior high with Mrs. Hazel was *The House by the Side of the Road.* Students memorized poems and recited them on Fridays in front of our class. The *Pittston Gazette* would feature a poem every day, notably one of Edgar A. Guest's. Students chose one of his poems to recite because the rhymes were easy to remember and were short. Some classmates would wait until Thursday to memorize their poems, and some recited the same poem that had been in Thursday's newspaper. Mrs. Hazel finally forbade any more Edgar A. Guest poems.

Here are today's historical events: (1814) Napoleon exiled to the Island of Elba where he died in 1821 at age 51; (1865) President Abraham Lincoln made his last public speech at the White House; (1919) Geneva, Switzerland was chosen as League of Nations Headquarters; (1947) Jackie Robinson became the first African American major league baseball player; (1965) 48 tornadoes hit the Midwest; (1968) President Lyndon Johnson signed the Civil Rights Act; (2019) thundersnow hit Minnesota, South Dakota and Wisconsin.

Yesterday while driving to Bible Study, I beheld beautiful flowering shrubs and trees. There are deep pink cherry trees in full bloom on this side of the Potomac, maybe a different species from those at the Tidewater Basin in D.C. I also saw dogwoods and azaleas. Yards without squirrels in residence are filled with beautiful varicolored tulips. The spectacular landscape of lovely flowers around my church is a marvelous sight to behold. My time of the year!

*"And the firmament showeth His handiwork"* (Psalm 19:1).

## April 12, 2024

Good morning, all 260. Today is **National Grilled Cheese Sandwich Day, Submarine Day, National Big Wind Day, D.E.A.R. Day, World Hamster Day,** and **National Licorice Day.** The grilled cheese as we know it may have originated in the United States during the 1920's when loaves of bread were inexpensive, and processed cheese had gained popularity. The first machine to slice bread was invented by Otto Rohweder in 1927. After six years following the invention, more sliced bread was sold than unsliced, making the way for grilled cheese sandwiches. Because of its inexpensive ingredients of bread and cheese, grilled cheese remained popular during the Great Depression of the 30s. Before long, it was in schools and in average households where it became a favorite of kids and grown-ups alike, served with a bowl of steaming tomato soup.

My daughter and son may remember his hamster today. It liked to vacate its cage at night, being a nocturnal critter. It made a nest in my daughter's closet after she had gone away to college. She came home on a break and was up in her bedroom when I heard a loud shriek. Sitting in the middle of her bed, she was petrified because "something" had come down the hall and gone into her closet. There we found the hamster who was as surprised as we were. We made sure it would not return to her room again, but to this day she does not like rodents.

**D.E.A.R. Day** will be easy for me to achieve. It is "**Drop Everything and Read Day.**" I have zillions of books, some read and some partially read. I am determined to complete today an interesting one that I began reading when I was on vacation in Naples, Florida. I love licorice, always choosing the black ones first from an assortment of jellybeans. I like the red ones the least.

As for history, the *Civil War* began this day in 1861 when Confederate forces fired on Fort Sumter, S. C. In 1955 the polio vaccine developed by Dr. Jonas Salk was introduced to the public. Polio was eliminated from the U. S. in 1979 and the Western Hemisphere in 1991. It crippled or killed many people, especially children, and it was called "infantile paralysis." Even our 32$^{nd}$ President, Franklin Roosevelt was a victim, something he concealed from the public for years. May we be blessed today. "*The Lord is in His holy temple. Let all the earth keep silence before Him*" (Habakkuk 2:20). He hears our prayers.

**April 14, 2024**

Good morning, all 261. In 1865, President Abraham Lincoln was shot by John Wilkes Booth while attending a Ford's Theater production in Washington, D.C. He died the next morning.

Today is **National Reach As High As You Can Day**. Even though this goal was not expressed in the same manner in my multi-generational family, it has been the unspoken message passed down to my grandchildren's generation. Our story begins with my great-grandfather, a runaway slave from Edenton, NC, who at age 17 joined the Union Army during the Civil War to fight for freedom for himself and his family. Where did his daring come from? After he became free in 1865 and moved to Pennsylvania, he married and had a family, instilling in his children the goal to complete the 8$^{th}$ grade, the highest one could go to in Wyoming Valley when young boys were forced to go to work in the coal mines, and girls worked in mills or became domestics at very early ages, before Child Labor Laws.

My great-grandfather had a good job, and each of his children completed the 8$^{th}$ grade, which was quite an accomplishment in the late 1890s and early 1900s. Only rich kids attended high school, my Great Aunt Lillie told me. After she had completed eighth grade, she took care of her sister Florence's and brother, Harry's children. Harry's wife, my grandmother, died from pneumonia at age 35 and left six young boys. There was a lot of laundry and ironing and meals to prepare, as well as getting kids off to school. One of my Great Aunt Lillie's younger brothers, Chester, graduated from high school in 1910 and attended *Howard University*. He was the first Patience to graduate from high school and college. After graduation, he moved to Richmond, Virginia, where he had a career in the insurance business. Another brother moved to Baltimore, Maryland, and the youngest to Rochester, N.Y. All escaped the drudgery of the anthracite coal mines.

My grandfather Harry, the second child and eldest son, remained home where, at age 17, he began a business carving items from anthracite coal. That was quite an undertaking at that time. He would maintain a lucrative business until he died suddenly from a stroke at the young age of 46. He, too, had reached as high as he could go. My father did likewise, and so did I and my children and grandchildren. And so have many others who are Crowder's descendants, even some on my list. It may be in their genes. Consequently, this topic has touched my heart today.

Great Aunt Lillie married a man who became a minister. She shocked me when she revealed how they had eloped and kept it a secret for a year. Perhaps they would make the announcement when a baby was on the way, but, unfortunately, none ever came. Uncle Edward had had mumps when he was young, and mumps can make men sterile. He took her with him to the *Practical Bible School* in Binghamton, New York, and earned a diploma. Many husbands and wives attended, with the men going into the ministry and the women preparing to become First

Ladies of churches. For eleven years Aunt Lillie was First Lady at several churches until her husband's sudden death following an operation.

In the next generation, which was my father's, each of the six brothers graduated from *West Pittston High School*. Unfortunately, since their father died young, their aspirations to go to college were unmet. The oldest one spent two years at *Wharton Business College* in Philadelphia and became a businessman. My father had hopes of becoming a lawyer but carried on his father's business at home.

The next generation is mine. Ten first cousins lived in West Pittston, the 4th generation to do so. Two attended nursing school in New York City and remained there to work and marry. Four have earned college degrees, two earned master's degrees, and the daughter of a first cousin earned a Doctorate in Physical Therapy. Other relatives on my musing list and in my children's and grandchildren's generations have reached high goals, too. I am proud of each of you. Grandpa Crowder would be proud of his many descendants who have reached as far as they can go, with some still reaching. And so, I say to my younger relatives and friends today, *"Keep on reaching."*

Today is also **National Gardening Day, National Dolphin Day,** and **International Moment of Laugh Day**. I will not comment on these topics today, but you know that I could. Just watching dolphins swimming would make me laugh with delight. Never swam with any. How about you? Thanks for the following response from a younger friend on our list. She makes me very happy.

*"Thank you for ending your emails with scripture. Psalm 121 is my most beloved Psalm and is to be read at my funeral service. When I was in 7th grade at West Pittston High School, the last year as West Pittston School before it became Wyoming Area, I had Miss Francis for Literature class. She taught the Psalms as poetry. I came to love the Psalms because of her class."*

My favorite Psalm is the 23rd, also. *"The Lord is my shepherd. I shall not want...."* I say it nightly before retiring. The last verse is already carved on my mutual tombstone with my Ed who passed away in 2015. "*And I will dwell in the house of the Lord forever."* What a promise! What "blessed assurance."

In history, the 3rd President of the United States, Thomas Jefferson was born in 1743. The *Metropolitan Museum of Art* was founded in 1870 in New York City. New sights yesterday in my garden were the clematis climbing on its trellis and azaleas beginning to bloom.*"I will lift up my eyes unto the hills from whence cometh my help. My help comes from the Lord"* (Psalm 121-1).

## April 15, 2024

Good morning, all 261. wish I could say *"And all is right with the world,"* but I cannot. I can only internalize these words from the hymn that says, *"I trust in God... And I know He watches me....."* Today is the least loved day of the year -- Income Tax Day. I hope you all have done your duty on time. *"Or else,"* says Uncle Sam. For any of you who might wish to purchase some chocolate covered licorice, you can at nuts.com. Enjoy!

As for the honey baked, spiral ham that I like very much, its history goes back to the invention of the spiral slicer by Harry J. Hoenselaar in 1924 in Detroit, Michigan. While these ham slicers were originally limited, the patent ran out in 1981 and now sliced ham is purchased anywhere it is sold. Does anyone remember scoring the ham with whole cloves? I do. It was fun.

## April 16, 2024

Good morning, all 261. I have begun reviewing my musings for the past two years and selecting the most interesting ones to publish. I will include responses from some of you, as well as several anecdotes I wrote in the past. Seems that I have been writing my life story for years. Some of my musings expand my knowledge of a topic that I am retrieving from my cerebrum. I hope it will entertain and/or inform you while broadening your horizons. I am enjoying musing with all of you, as the list has grown. I have learned additional information from some of you on select subjects, also. Thanks to each of you.

Today is **Emancipation Day** in Washington D.C., because on this date President Abraham Lincoln signed an act abolishing slavery in the District of Columbia in 1862. A parade was held in the city this past Sunday to celebrate the 162nd anniversary. It is not so long ago when slavery existed in this country. I would have been someone's slave. Unimaginable!

This is also **National Orchid Day, National Librarian Day, World Elephant Day, Day of the Mushroom, International Volunteer Day,** and **National Health Care Decision Day**. I find orchids to be beautiful, but I have not been successful raising them. For those of you who might know who Dr. John Hope Franklin was, this renowned African American author and historian's hobby was growing orchids. A favorite aunt of someone on this list grew lovely orchids which I got to see once when I visited her niece.

I remember today one of my favorite people whose son is on this list. Dr. Georgetta Campbell was a librarian, and we worked together at Bloomfield High School in N.J. She had worked in school systems for 50 years, while I put in 33. A brilliant woman, she graduated from high school at 15 but had to wait until 16 to enter college. She recently passed away.

I love mushrooms but my Ed did not. He loved slurping down raw oysters on the shell with lemon juice and hot sauce. I do not. I am not volunteering for anything nowadays, after serving many years with children. In Virginia, in addition to teaching Sunday School to children, I had volunteered on *Dr. Suess Day* to read his books at a local elementary school. I even donned a Dr. Suess hat. I also volunteered during that school's annual book fair. The children were enthusiastic about purchasing books of their very own, and my church donated money for the cause.

Lastly, I do keep track of my health checkups. Right now, I am "fine and dandy." Just 20 more days and I will be 92! Imagine that! *"I will praise the Lord at all times"* (Psalm 34:1).

## April 17, 2024

Good morning, all 261. Happy birthday of someone on our list. Yesterday I had a visit from a young Medicare nurse, my first home visit. I was glad to be able to answer *"No"* to all of her questions, especially ones about my mental health. One of the exercises she had me do was to draw a clock. You may not be aware that it is something a person cannot do if they have mental issues. I learned about it when my husband developed Parkinson's. Yesterday I was able to draw a beautiful clock with its hands at 11:10, just as the nurse requested. I am becoming a little forgetful and will need your PATIENCE when you ask me to remember something that you do.

Ed used to call women, "Lady" and men, "Fella" because he always had difficulty remembering names. And that was long before his Parkinson's. I watched an old movie on *Netflix* last evening. What caught my attention were the telephone booths on the streets and in a railroad station. Also, in homes and offices there were black handheld telephones attached to long cords. The scene looked normal to me but would not to the youngsters on this list who cannot exist without their cordless cellphones. The plot of the movie had the main character running late for appointments and not being able to let people know where he was or how long before he got there. I remember many such times before cell phones. Sometimes I forget mine when I go out of the house. Suppose I needed to make an emergency call with no pay phones available? Like getting a flat tire -- I'd need to contact Allstate and my grandson. Would a kind person allow me to use their phone? I don't want to find out. Sometimes now, even with a cell phone, I asked myself what day it is.

Today is **National Banana Day**, **Bat Appreciation Day** and **National Crawfish Day**. I am partial to bananas. Chiquita is the best brand, as far as I am concerned. The first time I saw bananas growing in Puerto Rico, I was surprised to see that they grow upward and do not grow on trees. Trees have woody trunks, but bananas do not. They grow on a large herb from a bulb. Most bananas are grown within 30 degrees on either side of the equator. My Great Aunt Lillie's favorite breakfast was shredded wheat with sliced banana, sugar and milk. Shredded wheat came in a woven biscuit which she soaked first in hot water. It was very popular before Kellogg and Post cereals were available. I think now there is frosted shredded wheat, but I have never eaten it.

I am not appreciative of bats, although I know they have an important job in the food chain. They are soooo ugly and frightening. Special to several of you on my list will be the fact that this is **Ellis Island Family History Day.** On this one day in 1907, thousands of people flooded through the hall and set the record for the most people processed in one day—11,747. Millions more would file through that year and, today, tens of millions of descendants can claim a piece of that history. Ancestors of some of you may have entered the U.S. via Ellis Island. Do you have the records? Sometime the names got changed.

**National Crawfish Day** will be of interest to those with Louisiana roots. I have never eaten crawfish. Biologically, they are crustaceans called crayfish and cousins to lobsters with similar body parts. I do love lobster tails from *Red Lobster*. It is really the abdomen. The tail is at the very end and is not edible. That's your biology lesson for the day. Couldn't help myself because, *"Once a teacher, always a teacher."* That's me to a T.

## April 18, 2023

Good morning, all 261. Yesterday I was corresponding with a young cousin on this list. I sent her an anecdote I had written in 2002 about her great-grandmother who was our Great Aunt Lillie's sister. My Great Aunt Florence lived on a farm in Mt. Zion, located about five miles from town. Interestingly, someone on my list was her neighbor when she and I were classmates.

When I was young, I rode my bicycle to visit Aunt Florence and Uncle Walter for the day. Instructions from my father were to be home before dark, and since I visited the farm in the summertime, I had at least until 8:00 p.m. The information I shared with you yesterday about life before cell phones reminds me of the anecdote I wrote years ago about visiting my Great Aunt Florence's farm when I was a teenager. Here 'tis.

*"One day when I was visiting my Great Aunt Florence on her farm, a thunderstorm arose, and the rain was teaming down. Of course, I could not start out for home on my bicycle. Aunt Florence told me that when her son Nyles came home from work, he would drive me and my bike home. That would be fine, except that I was concerned that Daddy would be really mad if I were not home before dark. Then I'd be grounded <u>forever!</u>*

*As the time passed, I became more worried since there was no way to contact my father. Aunt Florence didn't have electricity, let alone a telephone. Soon we saw car lights coming up the road. They might belong to one of the neighbors, or they might be Nyles'. No, they belonged to my father's car. He had not been worried about me at all because he knew that his Aunt Florence would never have let me ride my bicycle home in the rain."*

I tried calling my father "Dad" as I matured, but he was "Daddy" until he died in 1972. Notable historic events include the construction of St. Peter's Basilica at the Vatican (1506), and Paul Revere's famous midnight ride (1775). Did any of you have to memorize *The Midnight Ride of Paul Revere*? I did but I only remember the first few lines now.

> *"Listen, my children, and you shall hear*
> *Of the midnight ride of Paul Revere....."*

Henry Wadsworth Longfellow wrote the poem in 1860 in which he took some liberties that historians have corrected. Even so, it is a riveting story to me. *"One by land and two by sea."* The "Curious Georges" on my list may want to *Google* to find out what that important code meant. One time I visited Paul Revere's house in Boston on a tour. It was rather small for a family of 16 children. He had two different wives and eighteen mouths to feed!

In 1906 a magnitude 8.3 (Richter Scale) earthquake struck San Francisco at 5:12 a.m. The city was poorly prepared, with its many unreinforced brick buildings and closely spaced wooden Victorian dwellings. I think of this every time I visit my son who lives near San Francisco, but the buildings are now reinforced to withstand earthquakes. My granddaughter works and lives there. In Alexandria, buildings are reinforced to protect them from earthquakes. Old buildings have stars on the ends of poles intended to keep the buildings upright. Quite a few in Old Town are very old. President George Washington and Gen. Robert E. Lee were guests in some of the houses.

Lastly, the *Washington Post*'s FOOD section featured, *You bought it, so eat it.* It was to encourage us to eat what is in our cupboards and refrigerators in saved "doggie bags" before going out to purchase more food. I try not to go to the grocery store until Mother Hubbard's cupboard is almost bare, and no doggie here. This thought made me wonder about the origin of the "doggie bag." During the 1940s food shortages were happening because of World War II. Restaurant owners began asking their customers who were pet owners to take scraps of food home. Later people took food home for themselves. I do it. Now there is another kind of "doggie bag" with which you dog walkers are very familiar. And it has nothing to do with food.

**April 19, 2024**

Good morning, all 262. Yesterday's *Washington Post* had an article called *The house that haunts me. Can you really return to your childhood home*? I have lived in five houses in my lifetime and had driven past each while visiting West Pittston, Wilkes-Barre and Montclair. I requested to go into only two -–the first one and the last. My last home was a 1940s Dutch colonial that Ed and I bought in Montclair, NJ. in 1974. In the empty attic we discovered the portrait of a beautiful White woman. We just let her stay there, since we knew that she did not belong to the person we bought the house from who was not Black.

Years later, a younger White woman rang my bell and told me that she had grown up in the house and wanted to look around. *"Of course,"* I told her as I welcomed her inside. She was about to leave when I remembered the forgotten portrait in the attic. When I retrieved it, she delightfully exclaimed that it was her deceased mother. It had been left behind by successive owners. What joy there was from her daughter! It was the house I sold in 1992. When advertising it for sale, I attached a photo taken when my beautiful azaleas were in bloom. They were at least 50 years old and quite tall. However, it was not the azaleas that had attracted the young buyers because the first thing they did was to cut them down. My heart was crushed the first time I drove by "my" house and saw "my" front yard devoid of "my" beautiful azalea shrubs. When I went by some years later and asked the young new owner why she and her husband had done that, the former New Yorker said that the azaleas were covering the windows and that was dangerous. Also shocking, they had painted my formerly white living room a bright red.

No, you can't go back home again. And no, I would not purchase the same house again that sold for over 1 million dollars last year. I'd use my million for something more modern. That is, if I could afford the taxes in Montclair, which I could not. The town is attracting many well-off New Yorkers because it is a beautiful town and great place to rear a family, and it's a short train ride from the "Big Apple." That's why Ed and I moved there with our three-year-old daughter in 1958. We loved going to NYC. My daughter, son and I still do. There's nothing like the "Big

Apple." The nickname originated in the 1920 in reference to the prizes, or "big apples" rewarded at many horse races. It was officially adopted in 1971. New York is also called "The City that Never Sleeps."

**National Garlic Day** celebrates a fragrant and potent root that has been seasoning dishes for thousands of years. Garlic is native to South Asia, Central Asia and Northeastern Iran and has long been used as a seasoning worldwide. This is also **National Hanging Out Day** that suggests using a drying rack or clothesline to help the environment by using less electricity. I remember when laundry was pinned with wooden clothes pins out-of-doors in everyone's back yards on Mondays only. That is, in my small town. Everybody knows what clothes pins are, right? When I was a kid, ropes were strung across warm kitchens on rainy days and laundry was hung there to dry. There was always a musty odor in the kitchen when the articles did not dry properly, especially towels. I don't insist that my clothes be air dried, but some of you say that it smells fresher. Perhaps so, since I do remember the unpleasant odor of musty smelling towels. *"Give us this day our daily bread"* (Luke 11:3).

## April 20, 2024

Good morning, all 262. April is **National Garden Month, National Poetry Month, National Pickleball Month** and **National Stress Awareness Month**. Among the several celebrations for this day are **National Pineapple Upside Down Cake Day, Volunteer Recognition Day** and **Husband Appreciation Day**. Gentlemen on this list, perhaps your wives will make you a pineapple-upside-down cake today if the ingredients are in the cupboard. Of course, you enlightened 21st Century husbands can bake a cake all by yourselves. If my Ed were alive, then I would bake one for him today. Someone on my list loves playing pickleball, which is a new sport.

## April 21, 2024

Good morning, all 263. The former Choralaires on my list will remember that on each 3rd Sunday you would conduct the service at *St. Mark United Methodist Church* in Montclair, N.J. You did everything but deliver the sermon. You learned to project your voices long before microphones were available. You were taught to speak directly to the large rose window at the rear of the church. No one speaks today without a microphone.

Today, I noticed that my daffodils finished blooming. Peonies are in bud and lily leaves are poking up. I love seeing little patches of violets in my yard. Purple is my favorite color, as you know. Today is the birthdate of John Muir (1838-1914). I visited Muir's Woods once in California. I saw majestic giant redwoods. Some toppled trees had root systems as high as a three-story house. John Muir was a Scottish-born naturalist and early advocate for the preservation of wilderness in the United States.

On a different note, one of my goddaughters asked me where all 263 people on my musing list come from. Believe me when I say this number is just a portion of the many people in my life's "circle." Back in the day, people belonged to social "circles." For instance, women formed "sewing circles" where they stitched quilts together. Being nearly 92 years old and having lived in four different locations, I have met a lot of folks, beginning with my 1950 classmates from West Pittston High School, three of whom are on my musing list.

Although I was not financially able to graduate with the Class of 1954 from *Bennett College*, I have maintained friendships for a lifetime. I have only two friends from *Wilkes University* where I received my Bachelor degree, and they are on the list. Having been the President of the Bennett College's North Jersey Alumnae Chapter and Northern Virginia Alumnae Chapter, I attended many Alumnae Weekends and met Belles from different classes. I compiled three volumes of Bennett College memoirs titled *Tell Me Why Dear Bennett*. In N.J. I had met *Delta Sigma Theta Inc*. Sorors, and when I moved to Virginia, I became a member of the Northern Virginia Chapter. Many Sorors are on my list. Also, I have been a member of three different churches, all having representation on this list of 263.

I have met several of you in interesting places such as *Best Buy*, a bakery, *Staples,* and the supermarket. Just give me 10 minutes and I will find something that connects us. Some connections are just for that moment, but many of you have become friends who have added to my knowledge and challenged my mind, as well. Thank you. For instance, I met someone new just last week at "Senior Saints" Bible Study. We bonded immediately and I asked if she would like to be on my morning musing list. She agreed. After I sent her the day's musing in which I mentioned Montclair, N. J., she wrote that she had relatives living there. As they say, "*Small world.*" I don't know any of her folks, though.

Some of you I personally invited to my list. Others asked to be on it, and I am honored. Others whom I never met were added by friends or relatives. All of you together remind me of a Venn diagram with me in the middle. As for my many relatives, they are paternal, all descendants of Thomas and Hester Lawrence who were the parents of my Great Grandfather Crowder Patience. They lived in Edenton, N.C. before, during, and after the *Civil War*. Their names are found in the 1870 census, which was the first time Blacks were enumerated with a surname.

For anyone interested in how we North Carolina relatives amazingly discovered each other in 2018 on *23andMe,* you must read my 9th book *Deeply Rooted in North Carolina (*website www.journeyfromthepast.com. It is a unique story. Two young brothers, Thomas and Crowder, absconded from slavery under the name "Patience" to join the Union Army. They were never to see each other again. Why that surname, we still do not know. I believe Crowder's descendants are in the 9th generation now. Some have gotten to know each other via *Ancestry.com* and *23andMe* DNA testing, as well as through me. We once had a lovely Zoom call with many cousins.

As for my maternal relatives, I know few because my bi-racial mother was an orphan. I found her birth certificate via *Ancestry.com* with her parents' names on it. She grew up in a Catholic orphanage in Tacoma, Washington. Through our DNA tests, I discovered a relative of hers who is on my musing list. *Ancestry.com* divides relatives by paternal and maternal, but *23and Me* does not. Several of my stepmother's relatives are on list, too. Alice Patterson married my father when I was 16. She "gave" me all her relatives from Wilkes-Barre, and we call each other "Cousin." Several are on this list, all younger than I. One three years younger than I was my youngest bridesmaid in 1952. Some of you are in more than one category. How blessed I am to have each of you in my life. "*Thanks for being my friend,"* from the *Golden Girls*, the favorite television show of one of Alice's cousins on this list.

## April 22, 2023

Good morning, all 263 on this **Earth Day**. This evening begins **Passover** for our Jewish friends. It has been practiced ever since God led them out of their captivity in Egypt. It lasts for eight days, and a Seder is held on the first or second night. It is a meal that lasts for hours as prayers and responses are uttered. The youngest child present is always asked the question, "*Why is this night different from any other night?"* Once I was invited to a student's home as a guest at a Seder. Her family was Orthodox. I also attended a Seder once conducted by Messianic Jews who have converted to Christianity. That Seder was five hours long. It was profound for me because not only did they conduct the meal as is customary as Jews, but they also demonstrated how Christianity and Judaism can be merged. One of the men said that he was "completed."

Today is **In God We Trust Day**. In 1864 a law was passed by the U.S. Congress that the inscription appears on U.S. coins. In 1955, President Dwight Eisenhower signed a bill placing the phrase on all American currency.

<u>HYMN</u>: "MY HEAVENLY FATHER WATCHES OVER ME"
*"I trust in God. I know He cares for me
On mountains high or on the rolling sea.
Though billows roll, He calms my soul.
My Heavenly Father watches me....."*

## April 23, 2024

*Buenos dias, todas* 263. Today is **National Picnic Day** and **Children's Day**. For fun the two might be combined. Pack a basket and head out for a peaceful spot to eat your goodies. Picnics were commonplace before "fast foods." Today's brown bag lunch is not a picnic for me. When was the last time you went on a picnic? It has been many years for me. Not since I moved to Virginia. My family used to tote wicker picnic baskets full of delicious treats to beaches in N.J. We also took thermal containers to keep certain things from spoiling quickly and to keep beverages cool. We ate as soon as we arrived. Then we hit the water. The waves are great at the Jersey shore.

Today is **Copyright Day, National E-Mail Day, National English Muffin Day, Spanish Language Day, English Language Day,** and **National Asparagus Day.** I'd like to share what **Spanish Language Day** means to me. In the high school I attended, we college preparatory students took Latin in the 9$^{th}$ and 10th$^{th}$ grades. We studied vocabulary, how to conjugate verbs and Roman history. I still remember how to conjugate the verb "amor" (to love). It is *amo, amas, amat, amamus, amatis, amant*. In the 11$^{th}$ and 12$^{th}$ grades, we were required to take a "modern" language. Until World War II, the choice had been French or German at West Pittston High School. After, German was not taught. Spanish was proposed, but there were no Spanish-speaking people living in West Pittston at that time.

Mrs. Miriam Harris, a math teacher who also taught us public speaking, volunteered to take enough Spanish during summer and night school at a nearby college to teach the subject. She was ready just when I was entering the 11$^{th}$ grade in 1948. I loved learning the vocabulary and conjugating verbs that were so much like Latin. Mrs. Harris did her best, but it was not enough for me to become proficient in the language. One classmate did become a Spanish teacher. Ever since that time, I have longed to learn to speak Spanish fluently. It was on my "bucket-list" for retirement. Instead, I have written nine books. Since I am only 92 years old, maybe there is hope for me yet. There are several fluent friends on my list who patiently try to help me. Thank you. One of my goddaughters and her sister speak Spanish fluently. Both are on my list.

Shirley Temple Black (1928) was a child movie star. Her movies were the only ones I was allowed to see as a child, except for *Bambi*. Later in life, she was named United States Ambassador to Ghana and Czechoslovakia and served as Chief of Protocol of the United States.

## April 24, 2024

*Buenos dias, todas 263*. "*Este es el dia que hizo el Señor.*" "*This is the day that the Lord hath made*" (Psalm 118: 24). Today are **Denim Day, Stop Food Waste Day, American Quilters Society Day,** and **Help Animals Day.** I know that several of you are quilters. Learning how to be one was on my retirement "bucket list," along with learning to speak Spanish fluently, do oil painting, and play an organ, none of which I have done after having been retired for 34 years. I have not been idle, though, having written nine books.

Because today is **Denim Day**, I am sharing information about that popular fabric worn by many. Once considered solely work clothing, it's now high fashion. Spun from white and indigo yarn, denim at one time was used exclusively for workwear for mechanics, miners, farmers, and cowboys that required the toughest materials. I remember that my Great Uncle Pete, Great Aunt Rosie's husband, when working in his large garden, always wore denim overalls that had a bib and suspenders. That was the common work outfit for men during my youth, but not for women.

Slacks, pants or trousers were off limits to women for much of recorded history. They wore cotton "house dresses" that they often sewed themselves. In the United States, not until 1923 did the Attorney General of the U.S. declare it was okay for women to wear trousers in public. None of my great aunts ever did. My Great Aunt Lillie bragged that she never wore a bathing suit or trousers. I wonder what she would think of panty hose. Levi Strauss is credited with the invention of blue jeans, and tailor Jacob Davis added reinforcing copper rivets to the pants. They were so strong that it came to clothe nearly all-American laborers by the 1930s. By the time I was a teenager in the late 40s, blue jeans had become popular for girls to wear, although we had to purchase them at the Army and Navy store that was only for men. Our rolled-up jeans bought from there, always held up by a belt, did not fit us well. They were never worn to high school. Jeans used to be called "dungarees."

Historical facts include the Greeks entered Troy using the Trojan Horse (1184 BC); the Library of Congress was established in Washington, D.C. (1800), America's oldest federal cultural institution and the world's largest library; the Spanish American War (1898).

When I was a little girl, on each Memorial Day a parade was held in my hometown. When I came along, there were no *Civil War* veterans left to march or ride in automobiles to the cemetery for the blasting of cannons in honor of dead veterans, but there were some Spanish-American ones still able to march behind the American Legion band. One of them was a family friend who lived in Wilkes-Barre and always came to West Pittston to march with his comrades. attired in their uniforms. "Uncle" George Johnson would wave to this excited little girl standing on the sidelines. Back in the day, "Uncle" and "Aunt" were names respectfully bestowed on older family friends. Pope Benedict XVI (Joseph Ratzinger), successor to John Paul II, became the new leader of the Roman Catholic Church during a mass in St. Peter's Square in Vatican City (2006).

Birthdays are Barbara Joan Streisand (1942), singer, actress, songwriter, producer, and director. With a career span of over six decades, she has achieved success across multiple fields of entertainment, being among the first performers awarded an Emmy, Grammy, Oscar, and Tony. I love her rendition of *People*. *"People who need people are the luckiest people in the world….."* Also, Kelly Clarkson (1982), singer, songwriter and television personality who rose to fame after winning the first season of *American Idol* in 2002 and earning a record deal with RCA Records.

**April 25, 2024**

*Buenos dias,* all 266. Yesterday's responses included one stating that, *"Cone Mills here in Greensboro manufactures the majority of the world's denim."* Another reminded me that yesterday was **Administrative Professionals Day**. A very kind and generous lawyer friend on my list offered, *"So important to recognize the folks who make the rest of us look great in offices around the country."* She always recognizes those professionals in her office. There was a response about *Wolferman's Bakery* selling great English Muffins. **National English Muffins Day** was on Tuesday.

This is **National DNA Day**. It is of great interest to me, being my family's griot—the teller of stories. It may be of interest to some of you who have taken DNA tests to learn about your ancestry, and like me, happily have met new relatives. In 1953 scientists Watson and Crick introduced the double helix, which is the description of the DNA molecule. It looks like a twisted ladder. It was introduced to the public on the front cover of *Life Magazine* in 1958. I had just begun my teaching career in biology, and the student texts did not have the double helix in them. I had to learn about DNA before new biology books were issued to students. I had to teach DNA to myself before I could teach it to my students. What a fascinating study to know that every living thing is composed of the same DNA (deoxyribonucleic acid) on the cellular level, from an amoeba to a blue whale and a giant redwood tree. That DNA is like beads strung by the Creator, the number of which and the order in which they are dictates the long neck of a giraffe, the trunk of an elephant, the feathers of birds, the horns of a bull, and my premature white hair like my father and my son.

Now I have given you the first lesson in DNA 101. *"And God created great sea monsters, and every living creature that moveth, which waters brought forth abundantly, after their kind, and every winged fowl after its kind, and God saw that it was good"* (Genesis 1:21).

**April 26, 2024**

Good morning all 266. Today **is National Audubon Day, National Arbor Day, National Pretzel Day,** and **Your First Kiss Day**, each one interesting to me. **Arbor Day** got its start in Nebraska with the journalist Julius Sterling Morton proposing that Nebraskans plant trees to show appreciation for nature and the environment. The first **Arbor Day** was celebrated in 1872. I remember discussing this day in my high school. We never planted any trees, though.

As for **National Pretzel Day**, a popular story about the origin of the pretzel is that in 610, an Italian monk decided to create a special treat to motivate his distracted students. After rolling out ropes of dough and then twisting them to resemble hands crossed on the chest in prayer, he baked them.

The important historical event was that in 1608, 104 English colonists went ashore at present-day Cape Henry, Virginia, on an expedition to establish the first permanent English settlement in the Western Hemisphere. It would become Jamestown. The birthday celebration belongs to comedian, singer and dancer Carol Burnett (91 today). I enjoyed her television show *The Carol Burnett Show* on CBS from 1967 to 1978.

**April 27, 2024**

*Buenos días, todos 266 amigos and amigas el viente seite de abril* 2024. *Esta dia es sabado.* "*Sabado*" comes from the Hebrew word "sabbath," meaning a day of rest. In Jewish and Christian traditions, God rested on the seventh day of creation, which is Saturday. Today is **National First Ladies Day, Babe Ruth Day, National Pool Opening Day, National Marconi Day,** and **National Kiss of Hope Day.** Several caught my fancy enough to discuss.

**Marconi Day** celebrates the career of the Italian wireless communications pioneer, Guglielmo Marconi. The event takes place each year on the Saturday closest to Marconi's birthday on April 25, 1874. Besides being an inventor, he was an electrical engineer known for his work on long-distance radio transmission, as well as the development of a radio telegraph system.

In 1947 the New York Yankees hosted "**Babe Ruth Day,**" which was celebrated in every ballpark in organized baseball in the U.S. and Japan to honor the man who made the country fall in love with baseball. In 2016 Leslie's Swimming Pool Supplies founded **National Pool Opening Day** to celebrate that first cool dip of that season. It also encourages everyone to make sure their pools are clean and safe. Lastly, each year on this last Saturday in April, **National Kiss of Hope Day,** encourages couples and parents to express their love for one another. *"Blessed are the peacemakers, for they shall be called the children of God"* (Matthew 5:9).

**April 28, 2024**

*Buenos días, todos* 269. This is **Global Pay It Forward Day**. This could be dropping a dollar into the jar of a homeless person or complimenting someone's choice of wardrobe. It only takes a moment to brighten someone's day.

This reminds me of my 90th birthday when some of my close friends joined me for lunch at the *Waterfront* in Old Town, Alexandria. It was a lovely Sunday afternoon when ten women sat outdoors under a canopy to avoid contracting COVID. Everyone sang *Happy Birthday* to me. Other diners sitting nearby who did not even know me joyfully joined in. When it was time for me to pay my bill, I was told that it had been paid by someone in the crowd. Not until he was leaving would I learn which handsome, young stranger had paid my bill. He waved to me as he was leaving the area. I never knew his name but will always remember his kindness. May the young man be blessed, wherever he is, even now as I think about him.

This is also **Great Poetry Reading Day** which is a celebration of poetry as a literary form and a recognition of its enduring role in human expression and storytelling. I enjoy poetry, especially when it rhymes. I like reading it aloud. In history, Maryland became the seventh state to ratify the Constitution of the United States (1788). **Save the Frogs Day** causes me to chuckle. How many frogs (*Rana pipiens*) did I and my students dissect in my 33 years of teaching biology? They were preserved in formaldehyde. Three of my students are on this list and probably remember the fun year they spent with me in Room 406. Others of you may remember the frogs you dissected at the high schools you attended. Do you remember your teachers' names? Many of my students affectionately called me "Mother Moss." A student once made for me a plaque with those words in his Metal Shop class. I was honored. It hung above my classroom door for many years until I retired in 1992. I have it near my computer now.

Another student carved a plaque in his Wood Shop class. It said, *"Boss Moss."* My son has it hanging on a wall in his office in California.

Before I matriculated to *Wilkes College* in 1950, I had never dissected a frog or an earthworm. My 9th grade biology class was strictly a memorization one. The teacher was Miss Doris Wiley who would be quite surprised that I had become a biology teacher because I had little interest in the subject in 1947. The only thing I remember is that I drew a fish which was a perch.

**April 29, 2024**

*Buenos días, todos* 270. This is **Intergenerational Week, National Shrimp Scampi Day, National Zipper Day, World Wish Day, International Dancing Day, National Small Business Week,** and **American Camp Day.** Today, I choose to discuss zippers. Can you imagine life without them? They were not invented; they evolved. In 1913 a Swedish American scientist and inventor, Gideon Sundback, received a patent for a curious contraption he called a "hook-less fastener." Even though similar inventions had been around since 1850, his version is considered the first modern zipper. The name "zipper" became used for a pair of rubber boots on which this fastener was used in 1923. Marketed as "galoshes" fastened with a single zip of the hand, and mirroring the sound that the fastener makes, "zipper" emerged and has stuck for a century.

In history, George Washington was inaugurated on April 29th in Federal Hall in New York City (1789). That was the first national Capitol under the new Constitution.

Birthdays include Edward Kennedy "Duke" Ellington (1899), and singer and guitarist Willie Nelson (1933). My favorite song of his is *Always on My Mind*. In 1964 he became a member of *The Grand Ole Opry*. When I was a kid, I'd listen to that radio program on Saturday nights with the hilarious "Cousin" Minnie Pearl. I don't think I knew that she always wore a price tag for $1.98 on her hats until *The Grand Ole Opry* was on television. Another birthday is Jerry Seinfeld (1954), whose television show *Seinfeld* was a landmark of American pop culture. He was one of Ed's favorites. Other birthdays are Sir Daniel Michael Day-Lewis (1957) and Michelle Pfeiffer (1957).

**April 30, 2024**

*Buenos días, todos* 270. A roaring airplane awakened me to "*rise and shine and give God the glory*" which I am going to do right now. My morning prayer is, "*Thank you, Lord, for waking me up one more day to make merry with my friends and family members.*"

Celebrations are **World Jazz Day, National Tie-Dye Day, National Honesty Day, Day of the Child, National Bugs Bunny Day, National Raisin Day, National Oatmeal Cookie Day,** and **National Animal Advocacy Day. World Jazz Day** is observed to honor the origins of jazz, referred to as "America's classical music" that originated in New Orleans more than a century ago.

As for **National Tie-Dye Day**, I've never tie-dyed anything but think the art form is quite interesting. The roots of tie-dye go back to ancient days, with the earliest known examples originating from Africa, Asia and current-day Peru. Many cultures create beautiful fabrics with tie-dying.

**Day of the Child Day** (*Dia de los niños*) can be a really big deal for those who celebrate in Mexico and other Spanish-speaking places. **National Bugs Bunny Day** commemorates the date when the famous Looney Tunes bunny first appeared in a short film in 1938, named *What's up, Doc?* He became a favorite when a cartoon was part of the movie fare along with a news story and a "short" which was an interesting episode, later called a documentary. All for 25 cents! **National Raisin** and **National Oatmeal Cookie Days** go hand-in-hand for me because I always include raisins in my Oatmeal cookies along with walnuts.

Recognizing history, the United States purchased the Louisiana Territory from France (1803) for 60 million francs, the equivalent of about 15 million dollars. Louisiana became the 18th state of the Union (1812). The New York's World's Fair opened (1939). My father and his youngest brother, Harold, displayed a piece of Patience anthracite coal art there, called the "Trylon and Perisphere," which was the theme of the New York's Fair. They were two tall modernistic structures in the Theme Center.

I don't know the size of the Patience replica, but I remember seeing it in my father's office until it collapsed one day. Thankfully, someone had taken a photograph that will last forever. A photo is in the book I wrote about my father's work. Anthracite coal is not hard like marble. It fractures easily and needs museum conditions for it to last, but there were no museums in Wyoming Valley in 1939. Many of my father's pieces now are safely stored in museums, including the *Anthracite Heritage Museum* in Scranton, Pennsylvania. I've already shared the website for more information on p.69.

**Anthracite Coal Heart Carved by Charles Edgar Patience**

**May 1, 2024**

Good morning, all 270. If my younger brother, Harry were still living, he would celebrate his 90th birthday today. When he was a little boy, he thought he was older than I because his birthday was six days before mine. I'm thanking and loving his five children and several grandchildren who are on this list.

This is **International Workers' Day, National Interpreter Appreciation Day, National Black Barber Shop Appreciation Day, Skilled Trades Day,** and **May Day,** one of the most important holidays in Communist countries. For that reason, the popular May pole festivities in the United States were discontinued. When I attended *Bennett College* in 1951, there was still a May pole event. Do any of my younger Bennett sisters recall one when you were students?

Historical events include Christopher Columbus presenting to Spanish Queen Isabela I his plans for a western route to the Indies (1486); Swedish botanist Carl Linnaeus introducing the study of taxonomy which gave every plant a Latin or Greek name (1763). Animals are also classified in that manner, such as *Homo sapiens*. In 1807 the *Slave Trade Act* abolished the slave trade within the British Empire. In 1930 Pluto was named. In 1931 the *Empire State Building* was dedicated. In 1971 *Amtrak* took over U.S. passenger rail service. In 2011 Pope John Paul II was beautified by his successor Pope Benedict XVI.

Birthdays begin with George Inniss, landscape artist, as well as a well-known abolitionist and labor reform advocate (1825), because Montclairians on this list will recognize one of the schools named for him. Kate Smith (1907) was referred to as "The First Lady of Radio" and known for her rendition of *God Bless America*. I would listen to her every day when I ran home for lunch. She introduced her program with *When the Moon Comes Over the Mountain*. I can hear her contralto voice in my memory still. *Ma Perkins* came on at 12:15 p.m., sponsored by *Crisco*, and news was at 12:30 p.m. Gwyllyn Samuel Newton "Glen" Ford (1916) was a Canadian who became an American actor during Hollywood's Golden Age, and he was one of the biggest box-office draws of the 40s, 50s and 60s. He often portrayed ordinary men in unusual circumstances such as in 1955 when he starred with Sidney Poitier in *Blackboard Jungle*.

There was a *Washington Post* article entitled, *Small diet changes add up in big ways*. My only health issue is that when I sit to relax, I conk out. The article suggests adding protein, so I'll add an egg and cheese to my oatmeal breakfast. Who has a recipe for white beans? The article suggests eating nuts, too. I sometimes drink a chocolate *Boost* as was suggested by Ed's oncologist.

**May 2, 2024**

Good morning, all 270. My rosebush and clematis are climbing their shared trellis. My pink peonies are opening, too. Today is **National Day of Prayer, National Life Insurance Day, World Tuna Day, Baby Day, National Password Day, National Brothers and Sisters Day,** and **National Physical Education and Sport Week.** The **National Day of Prayer** was designated by the U. S. Congress. The President signs a proclamation on the first Thursday of May to encourage all Americans to pray, and people turn to God in prayer and meditation. The 2024 theme is "*For you are my lamp, Oh Lord and my God, lightens my darkness*" (II Samuel 22:29).

In history, the first recognized Negro National League (NNL) baseball game was played (1920). The league was founded by African American Rube Foster, who excelled on the diamond as manager and executive and was called the "father of Black baseball." Segregated baseball continued until Jackie Robinson broke the color barrier with the Brooklyn Dodgers (1947). My Ed was an avid Dodgers' fan until they abandoned Brooklyn for California. In 1939, New York Yankee Lou "Iron Horse" Gehrig ended his streak for consecutive baseball games played (2,130), setting a record until Cal Ripken, Jr. (1995). In 1963, 1,000 Black children peacefully protested against racial segregation in Birmingham, Alabama, as part of the Children's Crusade. Through television we saw the police brutality that spurred Civil Rights advances. Dwayne Douglas Johnson (1972) was an African American actor, businessman, and professional wrestler called "The Rock."

**May 4, 2024**

Good morning, all 270. Today is **Star Wars Day** and **National Self-Employed Day.** I am self-employed because I sell the books I've written, but thankfully, I am not dependent upon what I make. I do not have the ambitious spirit of an entrepreneur but admire those of you who do.

In history, 1776 Rhode Island became the 1st American colony to renounce allegiance to King George III (1776); President Abraham Lincoln was buried in Springfield, Illinois (1865); The U.S. officially acquired the Panama Canal and took over its construction (1904); Belgium-American actress Audrey Hepburn was born (1929); first Annual Grammy Awards were held (1954); Ella Fitzgerald became the first Black woman to win a Grammy Award (1959); first Freedom Ride departed from Washington, D.C. (1961); African American Willie Mays broke the National League's home run record (1966); Margaret Thatcher became the first woman Prime Minister of England (1979); the Channel Tunnel linking the United Kingdom with France was opened (1994).

**May 6, 2024**

Good morning, all 271 on my 92nd birthday! *"The Lord is blessing me right now. He woke me up this morning and set me on my way....."* In 1937, the German zeppelin Hindenburg disaster occurred at Lakehurst, N.J., and thirty-six persons died. In 1940 John Steinbeck was awarded the Pulitzer Prize for *The Grapes of Wrath.*

**May 9, 2024**

Good morning, all 275. I had a wonderful "Selah" (rest) from musing, but not from praying for each of you and myself and loved ones who need prayer. My birthday week has been wonderful. I received many greetings and well wishes, plus gifts including three green gardens in pots and three beautiful floral arrangements. I have been taken to a Spanish restaurant in Washington, D.C. for paella, a Greek one for a Reuben, and my favorite "soul food" one for wings, and a Thai restaurant for Pad Thai. I have several "doggy bags" in my fridge for later nibbling.

On Tuesday when I came home from a trip to the *Phillips Art Gallery* that was recommended to me by someone on this list, I beheld a large UPS box sitting in my driveway. It was quite heavy, with the word "bagels" on it. The return address was New York City so I knew they would be REAL bagels. Inside were bagels, lox, and cream cheese, my favorites! Thanks, Dear Niece in Idaho. I also received three boxes of chocolates from across the country.

I like pizza, too, especially with pepperoni and lots of cheese, but I get to eat that often. I used to eat a lot of Chinese food, but since discovering Thai food, I prefer the latter, especially shrimp Pad Thai. Once upon a time in N.J., my favorite Chinese dish was Lobster Cantonese. Today I will have "surf and turf" at *Outback Steak House* with someone on this list.

Moving from food, my biology students used to dissect crayfish in the lab. Their bodies are similar to lobsters. They are crustaceans called "crawfish" in Louisiana.

Thanks to each of you dear ones from the bottom of my heart, for making my 92$^{nd}$ birthday a memorable one. I am already planning the 95th party for May 6, 2027. Please plan to come to Virginia. There is plenty to see and do in D.C. I will be away from May 14$^{th}$ to May 22$^{nd}$, travelling by train to *Bennett College* in Greensboro, N.C., for my 70$^{th}$ class reunion. Years ago, an older friend celebrated her emerald year in person while sitting in a wheelchair pushed by her daughter, also a *Bennett College* graduate. So, I may be able to celebrate my 75$^{th}$, hopefully not in a wheelchair. I will enjoy my 70$^{th}$ with the several of us who are able to attend.

**May 10, 2024**

Good morning, all 275. Today is **National Shrimp Day, National Day Calendar, National Public Gardens Day, National Small Business Day, Trust Your Intuition Day,** and **One Day Without Shoes.** I am going to share **National Washington Day** with you today because my mother was born in Tacoma, Washington and for years lived in Seattle after she and my father divorced.

**My Mother Cora Richley Johnson**

Several family members on this list reside in the state of Washington now, while still others have visited the beautiful "Evergreen" state. I did only once. Also born in Tacoma, Washington, was Bing Crosby in 1903, one of the radio and screen's most beloved crooners during my twenties. His velvet voice earned him roles in many musical films as well as receiving numerous awards. My favorite movie of his was *Going My Way*.

Changing topics, according to my computer May is important for Moms in Mexico, too, just like in the U.S. However, **Mother's Day** in Mexico is always celebrated every May 10th. Several family members on my list who have Mexican ancestry may be celebrating this special holiday today.

In 1908 after gaining financial backing from Philadelphia department store owner John Wanamaker, Anna Jarvis organized the first official **Mother's Day** celebration in the U. S. at St. George's Methodist Episcopal Church in Grafton, West Virginia. In 1865 Confederate President Jefferson Davis was captured by Union forces at Irwinsville, Georgia; in 1869 the first coast-to-coast railroad was completed. The Central Pacific and the Union Pacific railroad systems were joined at Promontory Summit in Utah, using a "Golden Spike" that is housed in the Cantor Arts Museum at Stanford University. 1994 saw the inauguration of South Africa's first Black President, Nelson Mandela in Pretoria, attended by politicians and dignitaries from more than 140 countries.

### HYMN –"MY HEAVENLY FATHER WATCHES OVER ME"
*"I trust in God, I know He cares for me,*
*On mountain bleak or on the stormy sea;*
*Though billows roll, He keeps my soul,*
*My heavenly Father watches over me...."*

**May 11, 2024**

Good morning, all 276. It's **National Technology Day, National Windmill Day, World Fair Trade Day, National Train Day, National Twilight Zone Day, Screen Free Week,** and **National Nurse's Week.**

I saw large windmills in Holland that look nothing like those in the United States. I'd like to introduce you to the amazing Arctic Tern, with the longest migrations of any bird species on the planet. Mating for life, Arctic terns breed in Arctic breeding grounds and certain locations in the United Kingdom during summer months and travel all the way to Antarctica in the winter. The yearly migration can range from 44,000 miles to 59,000 miles. In its life span, one Arctic tern typically flies a distance that is equivalent to three round trips to the moon. *Awesome!*

I remember my first train ride which was taken when I was thirteen years old. It was to Philadelphia to visit an aunt and uncle during my spring break from school. During that time, President Franklin Delano Roosevelt died on April 12, 1945, while serving a fourth term in office. It was because of him that the U.S. Presidential term was reduced to two consecutive terms.

I remember that trip well because I had become ill. The weekend before when I was in the backyard hanging some clothes on the line, I had stepped on a nail while I was wearing a pair of moccasins.

I remembered that my health teacher had told us that if we stepped on a rusty nail that we should see a doctor right away because we could get tetanus. I showed my foot to my father who told me to put some alcohol on it since it was not bleeding. Several days later when I was on the train with my two great aunts, Lillian and Jessie, I was not feeling well. I remember being dizzy.

When we got to Philadelphia my aunt there looked at me and knew something was wrong. She said she would call her doctor to make a house call which was done back then. Unfortunately, he was out of town. Another doctor was to come by in the morning.

In the middle of the night, my guardian angel awakened me to tell me that I might have tetanus due to stepping on a rusty nail. When the doctor came in the morning I was able to tell him that. My aunts didn't even know about the nail. I had not told them, I suppose, thinking that they might not have taken me on the trip. I was thirteen years old and had been looking forward to travelling on a train to visit Philadelphia. The doctor gave me some medicine and told my aunts to watch me carefully, lest I swallow my tongue. Tetanus is called "lock jaw," in case you don't know that. It can be fatal. In two days, I was feeling much better and even attended a neighbor's birthday party. A good time was had by my great aunts and me, alike. Thanks be to God.

Historical events were that in 1858, Minnesota was the 32$^{nd}$ State in the Union; the Academy of Motion Picture Arts and Sciences was founded (1927); the Rural Electrification Administration was created as one of President Franklin D. Roosevelt's New Deal programs (1935).

Birthdays included dancer Martha Graham (1894), whose technique reshaped American dance; Salvadore Dali (1904), a surrealist artist renowned for his technical skill, precise draftsmanship and bizarre images; songwriter Irving Berlin was born (1888), giving us *White Christmas, Easter Parade* and *God Bless America*. A *TIME* magazine article in 2001 suggested that he wrote 1,250 tunes with 25 reaching #1 on the pop charts.

**May 12, 2024**

Good morning, all 278 on this **Mother's Day**. Wishing all you "Moms" a lovely day. I remember my Great Aunt Lillian Mariah Patience Cuff today, along with other women who, though they had no children, were "Moms" to many. Some who might have influenced you, too are a grandmother, aunt, sister, cousin, or even a family friend or neighbor. Several on my list will remember my Great Aunt Lillie because she was a fixture in our extended family. Some of you attended her 100$^{th}$ birthday party at my home in N.J. She lived to be close to 103 years old. I hope I inherited that longevity gene. We both have a premature white hair gene.

Ladies, when you were young, did you wear a carnation to church to honor your Mom? That was the custom in my church. Red was in the honor of a living mother and white a deceased one. Since I had a living mother and a stepmother, I wore a pink carnation in honor of them both.

The church was always filled on Mother's Day, with folding chairs in the aisles for the overflow. Today churches have overflow rooms with large TV screens. Mine does.

I received a lovely photo from a niece after my Washington State musing. It shows *Mount Ranier* in the distance and was taken near the Space Needle that was created for the 1962 World's Fair. My mother and other Seattle residents were excited by it because it had a rotating restaurant on the top floor. Unfortunately, she passed away in October 1971 at only 58 before I had the chance to have a meal with her there. My family had been making plans to visit her in 1972.

**May 14, 2024**

Good morning, all 278. Today is **National Buttermilk Biscuit Day, Bond With Your Dog Day, International Chihuahua Appreciation Day, Online Romance Day,** and **National Decency Day.** As for **Buttermilk Biscuit Day**, I wonder how many of you know what buttermilk is. It's a fermented dairy drink from when butter was churned from cultured cream, as my Great Aunt Florence did. The liquid left behind is called "buttermilk." It can be drunk or used in making biscuits, etc. For **Online Romance Day,** send a heartfelt message to a friend or family member, or connect with a long-distance friend over a video call. It's the perfect opportunity to remind those dear to you how much you care about them. **National Decency Day** celebrates the basic standard of civility that every American deserves. Every day should be one for decency.

'Tis my last musing until the 21$^{st}$. I'm off to my 70$^{th}$ reunion at *Bennett College* in Greensboro, N.C. tomorrow via AMTRAK. I thought you might like to see the following response I received yesterday from a person 104 years old who is on our list. He wrote:

*"I became interested while reading today's message, about the postage stamp issue. I enjoyed seeing the illustration of the 3-cent stamp. It brought back cherished memories. I remember them well. However, I go a little farther back in the postage issue. I remember the penny and one-half stamp. Yes, the regular postage for a one-ounce letter was associated with the 3-cent stamp. However, during that era unsealed letter envelopes would be delivered with the one-and-a-half-cent stamp. Our family was overjoyed during the Christmas season. What a saving!"*

I, too, remember unsealed envelopes being mailed at a lower price. We tucked them carefully so what was inside would not fall out.

In 1796, the first smallpox vaccination was administered by British physician, Edward Jenner. The basis for vaccination began when the doctor noticed that milkmaids who had gotten cowpox from the cows they milked were protected from smallpox. Dr. Jenner took material from a cowpox sore and inoculated it into the arm of the 8-year-old son of Jenner's gardener. Months later, Jenner exposed him several times to the variola virus, and the boy never developed smallpox. To enter the first grade in 1938, I had to be vaccinated for smallpox. It was a badge of honor to have a smallpox scar on my arm. After 1972, smallpox vaccinations were no longer given to children in the U.S.

In 1804, Captain Meriwether Lewis, Lieutenant William Clark and crew departed on the "Corps of Discovery," heading west into the new lands of the Louisiana Purchase and were the first Americans to reach the Pacific Ocean. In 1878 Robert August Chesebrough trademarked Vaseline petroleum jelly. In 1904 St. Louis, Missouri, hosted the first Olympic games in the USA. In 1973 NASA launched the first U.S. space station, *Kylab*.

In 1944, George Lucas was born. He was an American filmmaker and philanthropist who created the *Star Wars* franchise when much of the technology didn't exist to produce it.

**May 21, 2024**

Good morning, all 280. I returned home to my musings after a short "Selah" (a rest). On the 15th, I took an *Amtrak* train from Alexandria to Greensboro, which took seven hours. I read, slept, and ate a peanut butter sandwich for lunch. I was met by a Belle who took me to her home. When I travel North to Connecticut, I enjoy the Quiet car where people keep their voices low. There is not one on trains going South, so I needed earplugs to avoid the noise.

Naturally, the train ride would remind me of when I travelled South for the first time in 1951 on a segregated train, my first-time experiencing separate "everything." When I reached Washington, D.C., I had to exit the coach I had been on from Wilkes-Barre, Pennsylvania, where the seats were comfortable leather. In D.C., though, I had to lug my heavy suitcase to the "Colored" coach with its uncomfortable wooded benches, and where I was not allowed to eat in the dining car. In 1951, I was eighteen and travelling from Pennsylvania to North Carolina with my trunk and suitcase. When I took my daughter to college 22 years later, our station wagon was filled with her necessities, including an electric typewriter and a refrigerator. I had neither. I had only my electric radio with an alarm clock to make sure I got to breakfast and classes on time.

I don't remember how many hours my first North Carolina trip took, but it was overnight, and the next morning, girls from the campus met the train in a taxi to transport me to the campus. Two other girls on my train were going to *Bennett College*, but I didn't know that until we disembarked from the train. We were all dressed up in our hat, suit, stockings, and heels -- the usual attire for Bennett women, as older Belles will attest. We could not wear any "trousers."

I had a wonderful time at my 70th reunion. I thought I'd be the oldest Belle there, but two from the Class of 1950 had attended. Some Belles go every year just to enjoy the alumnae events. I saw many old friends and met a lot of younger Belles. Only four of us from the Class of 1954 were at the President's tea and none from the Class of 1949. That **was the class** that triggered me to compile three volumes of *Bennett College* memoirs because our classes were always in reunion together. So, I decided to gather Belle memoirs and publish them in the *Tell Me Why Dear Bennett* trilogy. Sadly, most Belles who contributed to Volume I are deceased, but they are reflections of the history of the United States of America.

Today is **National Eat More Fruits and Vegetables Day, World Day of Cultural Diversity, International Tea Day, National Strawberries and Cream Day, National Memo Day,** and **National Waiters and Waitresses Day**.

Here are important events: Clara Barton founded the American Red Cross (1881), the first bicycles were introduced in NYC (1819), with Karl von Drais developing the "swift walker" that had no pedals and two wooden wheels with iron rims and leather-covered tires; the *Greyhound Bus Co.* began in Minnesota (1914); the U.S. House of Representatives passed an amendment allowing women to vote (1918); Charles Lindberg in his plane the "Spirit of St. Louis," landed in Paris after the first solo air crossing of the Atlantic Ocean (1921); the Pulitzer Prize was awarded to Eugene O'Neill for *Anna Christie* (1922); Amelia Earhart landed in Northern Ireland, (1932), after flying seventeen hours from Newfoundland in Canada, becoming the first transatlantic solo flight by a woman. In 1960 Leontyne Price became the first African American to sing the lead in the opera *Aida* in Milan, Italy.

I returned home to see my pink peonies in bloom and my hydrangea beginning to bloom. Purple spider wort is taking over my garden. They are early morning and late afternoon bloomers that can take over a garden if not controlled. I love purple and blue flowers. The pansies I planted in November are still smiling happily. Soon I will plant red and white vinca in my circular flower bed, and they'll last until the frost hits. Everything in its own time, programmed by DNA and the Creator.

**May 22, 2024**

Good morning, all 280. Today is **International Day for Biological Diversity, National Solitaire Day, National Vanilla Pudding Day, Sherlock Holmes Day, National Numeracy Day,** and **Buy a Musical Instrument Day**. Of course, the topic of most interest to me as a biology teacher for 33 years is **Biological Diversity**. The world is filled with diversity in plants and animals, including my favorite, the giraffe and second favorite, the elephant.

In many places in the U.S., trees still have their full foliage and can be identified by their leaves. This is my favorite time of the year. Later this morning, I will plant some annuals. Someone on my list will be helping me. She is a wonderful landscaper. Thanks for your help.

As for its being **National Numeracy Day**, it is a time for me to pay more attention to the numbers in my life, such as balancing my checkbook. I did not care for algebra in high school but liked geometry. Trigonometry was difficult for me, but I passed the course at Wilkes College. I think my distaste for math might be Miss Burrows' fault when I was in the third grade. She was getting ready to retire and taught my class very little that year. I just know that she was old and sat at her desk a lot. I was on my feet all of the time as a teacher.

Today in 1843, 1000 pioneers headed West as part of the Great Migration. That is only 181 years ago, making us realize how young our nation is—this experiment in democracy. I visited an old building in England once, and our guide said that the new section had been put on in the 1200s. This is also **Sherlock Holmes Day** because creator Sir Arthur Conan Doyle was born in 1859.

**May 23, 2024**

Good morning, all 280. A cousin on this list who lives in North Carolina told me that she is about to plant her petunias. I have not been successful with petunias, but maybe they will do well in the hanging baskets I'm thinking about. I also received a response from someone whose husband plays a harmonica, and another who has a giraffe collection, and another who sent information on how I can hear different bird songs on my computer. I will ask my grandson or my favorite young neighbor who is on this list to help me find it. I am barely in the 21$^{st}$ century.

Yesterday's *Washington Post* showed photographs of the destruction in Iowa from 20 tornadoes. Considering the six feet of snow in 1882 on May 23$^{rd}$, I wouldn't choose to live there.

Today I am thinking about a deceased high school classmate whom I saw last at our 50$^{th}$ reunion in 2000, and we reconnected and kept in touch until her death. She told me that she and her husband were *Red Cross* volunteers who travelled many places to help people just like those in Iowa today.

'Tis **Brother's Day, Don't Fry Day, National Scavenger Hunt Day, National Road Trip Day,** and **National Smile Month.** Blessed are you who have brothers, and blessed are you who are brothers. If your brothers are living, I hope you have good relationships. If not, then *you* be the one to do something about it. *"Blessed are the peacemakers for they shall be called the children of Go"* (Matthew 5:9). I wish I could say, "Good morning" to my two deceased brothers.

Most of you can relate to **National Road Trip Day**. Road trips have been around ever since vehicles were driven for any distance. The first record of a road trip happened when Horatio Nelson Jackson drove from San Francisco to New York in 1903 for 63-days with his dog and his mechanic. Route 66 opened here in the 1930s, after which road trips became more prevalent. With memories like loading the car with kids (no seat belts), packing a picnic, singing songs, playing the license plate game, and "cows," and riding backwards in the "way-back" seat of a station wagon like my first one, road trips brought great joy and made wonderful memories for many Americans, especially my family. Our longest road trips were Canada to the North, North Carolina to the South, Indiana to the West, and lots of places in between, but we always returned home to Pennsylvania for Thanksgiving, Christmas, birthdays, and other occasions to be with parents and Ed's siblings. We were happy when Route 80 was completed ca. 1972 because it took less time to get to NYC.

A long family trip we four took was to Niagara Falls and then Canada. Ed and I made trips to Mashpee, Massachusetts when we left the kids with Nana in Pennsylvania. During other summers, I drove myself to graduate courses at Buzzard Bay, Massachusetts. After I began researching my ancestry ca. 2000, Ed escorted me several times to North Carolina. Maybe the longest trip was when Ed drove me to and from Fort Wayne, Indiana, where I taught a 5-week summer course in English to inner city students. I needed my van to get around.

Scavenger hunts were something that my youth group at church had for entertainment when I was a teenager. We were given a sheet of paper with items we had to collect within a given amount of time. We had to run home first, then run to neighbors, relatives or friends' homes to get what was on the list. The person who collected the most was the winner. It was a lot of fun. Can you imagine letting your kids do that nowadays? No way! To show how much times have changed, we were out and about running in the streets after the streetlights came on. When we were younger, we had to be home before that. If I were preparing a scavenger hunt list for today, I would include a thimble, a shoehorn, a crochet needle, a whisk broom, a hankie, a pair of cuff links, a grapefruit spoon, a hat pin, a hand can opener, a fountain pen, a potato masher, a 3-cent stamp, a penny post card, a clock key for winding, an ice pick, and a 1950 penny. Do you have any of these?

In 1883 a brilliant feat of 19th Century engineering was the official opening of the *Brooklyn Bridge*, spanning the East River from Brooklyn to Manhattan, designed by John Augustus Roebling. In 1844 Samuel Morse sent the first telegraph message from Washington to Baltimore, which read, "*What God hath wrought?*" In 1949 NATO (North Atlantic Treaty Organization) was officially established and its first headquarters was in Washington, D.C.

For birthdays, Queen Victoria of Great Britain was born (1819), along with Hollywood actor John Wayne (1907) and American singer-songwriter Bob Dylan (1941).

**May 25, 2024**

Good morning, all 280. 'Tis **Towel Day, National Brown Bag-It Day, National Tap Dance Day, National Italian Beef Day, National Sing Out Day, World Fish Migration Day, Global African Day,** and **Greek Pride Day.** I can't sing beautifully, and I can't tap dance. When I was a little girl and Shirley Temple was a child star, little girls across the country took tap dance lessons. They wanted to dance just like her while wearing Shirley Temple curls. I wore them to church on Sundays. For the rest of the week, I was in two pigtails with bows at the ends. There have been many famous tappers, including Bill Robinson, Fred Astaire, Gene Kelly, Eleanor Powell, Ginger Rogers, the Nicholas Brothers, Ann Miller, Gregory Hines, John Bubbles, and Savion Glover who was a tap prodigy. He made his Broadway debut at eleven and I had the privilege of seeing him perform. He was amazing then and still is even now.

There were a number of historical events. In 1521 Emperor Charles IV's Edict of Worms outlawed Martin Luther and his followers for initiating the Protestant Reformation. In 1787, the Constitutional Convention opened in Philadelphia, where 55 state delegates, initially charged with amending the Articles of Confederation, drafted the Constitution of the United States. In 1793 Father Stephen Theodore was the first U.S. Roman Catholic priest ordained. In 1935 Babe Ruth hit his last home run. In 1961 President John F. Kennedy asked Congress to support the space program. In 1962 Wand Records released The Isley Brothers' single *Twist & Shout* which became their first top 20 hit. In 1977 the Chinese government removed the ban on Shakespeare.

One of you on my list gave me a spiritual word of encouragement yesterday. **PUSH** -- *"Pray Until Something Happens."* I like that and I will. Thank you.

**May 26, 2024**

Good morning, all 282. 'Tis **Memorial Day,** my favorite time of year. Today we honor our veterans. One of my cousins on this list remembers her *Revolutionary War* ancestor and his two sons who served during the *Civil War*. I remember my great-grandfather and his brother who served in the *Civil War*, my stepmother, a WAC during *World War II*, my uncle, wounded at Anzio beachhead, Italy, my 2$^{nd}$ cousin, suffering from the malaria he contracted in the South Pacific, my husband, who was in the Army during peacetime between *World War II* and the *Korean War*, and my brother, who served in the *Korean War*. Several high school classmates served during that war, and one became an Admiral. John Jenkins had been the Valedictorian of our class. We always knew he was destined for greatness.

**WAC Sgt. Alice Patterson Patience WW II**

Memorial Day was the first day when folk planted annuals in their Pennsylvania and New Jersey gardens. We planted pansies, but also edibles like green peppers and tomatoes plants for transplanting what had been started earlier in glass covered "hot houses," also called "greenhouses." We had several Italian neighbors like Mr. Manganiello, who lived across the street, and Mr. Ciampi, who lived next door. My great aunts purchased their plants from them.

In later years, I lived in New Jersey where it was "cook-out" time for family and friends on the patio in the back yard. Hot dogs and hamburgers were cooked on a small hibachi grill with charcoal for fuel. Potato salad, coleslaw and baked beans would be the usual sides. Yellow and chocolate cakes were the desserts served with vanilla ice cream. It was too early for corn on the cob and watermelon. My father used to get me up really early to drive to a farmer's stand several miles away to get corn that had just been plucked. The sugar in the corn kernels will convert very quickly to starch. I like mine crunchy and sweet, boiled for only five minutes. And vine-ripened summer tomatoes are the best tasting.

Memorial Day is one of eleven federal holidays celebrated on a Monday. Originally called "Decoration Day," the name was changed in 1971. On May 30, 1868, Maj. Gen. John A. Logan established "Decoration Day" as a way for the nation to honor veterans with flowers on the graves of those who had died during the *Civil War*. Ohio Rep. James A. Garfield, former general and future U.S. president, addressed a crowd of 5,000 gathered at *Arlington National Cemetery*. Afterwards, the visitors placed flowers on tens of thousands of graves in the newly formed cemetery. The land was formerly an estate of Mary Custis Lee (great-granddaughter of Martha Washington), who was married to her distant cousin, Confederate Army General Robert E. Lee. Today the Arlington House, situated on the property, honors Robert E. Lee for his role in promoting peace and reunion after the Civil War. He lived five years after the war and died at 63.

Memorial Day has become a day of remembrance to military personnel who served in all wars, including World War II, the Vietnam War, the Korean War, and the wars in Iraq and Afghanistan. We owe a debt of gratitude to those who have fought and died for our freedoms.

**80-year-old Crowder Patience, A Civil War Soldier in 103rd PA Infantry**

In 1923 Henry Kissinger was born, later serving as Secretary of State and National Security Advisor in the 1970s. He was awarded the *Nobel Peace Prize* and died at the age of 100 in 2023.

In 1935 Lee Meriwether, American actress, model, and Miss America in 1955, was born. Ramsey Emanuel Lewis II (1935) was an African American jazz composer, pianist and radio personality who recorded over 80 albums and received five gold records and three Grammy Awards; Louis Gossett Jr. (1936) was the first Black man to receive an Oscar for the Best Supporting Actor in *An Officer and a Gentleman*; Dee Dee Bridgewater (1950) is an African American jazz singer and actress and a triple Grammy winner; Dondre Terrell Whitfield (1969) is an African American actor on *The Cosby Show* and the ABC daytime soap opera *All My Children*.

**May 28, 2024**

Good morning, all 282. The compilation of Crowder Patience I included yesterday is the work of Delantha Joseph Mills Jr., a *Bowie State University* art student in Maryland. My publicist introduced us in 2009 after he had mentioned that he wanted to win a college art contest and needed something unique. He used my great-grandfather's photograph and created a compilation of his photograph, discharge record and America flag. He won! Sadly, Joe passed away in 2012 from diabetes. He had been photographer and digital printmaker, skilled in ceramics and sculpture, and a very kind young man.

The photo of Grandpa Crowder is precious to his descendants because it is the only one in existence, as far as I know. It was in Great Aunt Lillian's photograph album with photos of the Patience family at the turn of the 20th Century. Someone had a *Brownie* camera and took photos at family gatherings at the Patience homestead. From the three children who remained in West Pittston, 20 grandchildren were born, and I have many black and white photos of them.

In 1431, Joan of Arc was accused of heresy and executed. In 1521 Pope Leo X signed a treaty with Holy Roman Emperor Charles V. In 1742 the first indoor swimming pool opened in London. In 1811 "Walk-in-the Water" was launched as the first steam vessel to sail Lake Erie. In 1830 President Andrew Jackson signed the *Indian Removal Act* allowing the Army to force out Cherokee, Chickasaw, Choctaw, Creek, and Seminole tribes from Georgia and surrounding states. This Cherokee *Trail of Tears* was a horrible blight on American history.

In 1863 the first Black Regiment, the 54th Massachusetts, departed for the Civil War, marching through Boston and loading onto the transport DeMolay to "glory," after which the movie *Glory* was named. In 1892 the Sierra Club was founded by John Muir to conserving nature, and I visited Muir Woods giant redwood trees. In 1929 the first all-color, talking picture *On With The Show* was released. Ethel Waters, African American actress, performed in it. In 1934 the Dionne quintuplets were born, the first known quintuplets to survive infancy. Two of the Dionne's 14 children are still living at age 90! Imagine that!

Young girls of my day played with paper dolls. I spent many hours playing with them and creating dolls' clothing of my own. At age 10, I was going into clothing design, but God had other plans for this child.

Birthdays include Jim Thorpe (1887), American Olympic gold medalist and first Native American to win a gold medal for the United States; Gladys Knight (1944), African American singer. I love her rendition of *Midnight Train to Georgia.*

**May 29, 2024**

Good morning, all 282. Today is **World Tiger Nut Day,** which has nothing to do with nuts! Interested? Just *Google* it and be surprised like I was. In 1798 the U.S. Congress empowered President John Adams to recruit a standing American Army of 10,000 volunteers. In 1848 Wisconsin became the 30th State in the Union. In 1900 a total solar eclipse occurred. In 1923 U.S. Attorney General Harry Daugherty said it was legal for women to wear trousers anywhere. In 1942 Bing Crosby recorded *White Christmas*. He starred in seven *The Road to*— movies released from 1940-1962 with Bob Hope and Dorothy Lamour. In 1953 Edmund Hillary and Tenzing Norgay became the first to surmount Mount Everest, a height of almost 29,000 feet and the tallest mountain in the world. In 1996 Benjamin Netanyahu became Israel's Prime minister and still is. In 2008 multiple tornadoes touched down in Nebraska and Kansas. Someone of you added Oklahoma.

Birthdays include Charles II of England (1630); "*Give me liberty or give me death*" Revolutionary lawyer and politician Patrick Henry (1736); Leslie Townes "Bob" Hope (1903), whose career spanned nearly 80 years in vaudeville, network radio and television, plus 57 tours for the USO entertaining military personnel in WW II, Korean War, Vietnam War, and Persian Gulf War. He appeared in more than 70 short and feature films and starred in 54, dying in 2003 at age 100. In 1917 President John F. Kennedy was born.

## HYMN: "I WILL TRUST IN THE LORD"
*"I will trust in the Lord, I will trust in the Lord,
I will trust in the Lord, Til I die...."*

**May 30, 2024**

Good morning, all 282. I received a response concerning the tiger nut I mentioned on Tuesday. It is a small tuber that grows on the roots of a plant called the "yellow nutsedge," a pest growing in the yards of people living in Smithville, N.J., according to someone on my list.

For my Catholic, Anglican and Lutheran friends and family members, today is **Corpus Christi Day,** celebrating the **Eucharist**. It is also **National Creativity Day, World Multiple Sclerosis Day, National Water a Flower Day, International Hug Your Cat Day, International Day of the Potato, National Hole in My Bucket Day,** and **E-Bike Day.**

In case you don't know, white potatoes are not roots but tubers that grow roots. You can grow a lovely indoor plant from rooting a sweet potato. The white potato originated in Peru and first introduced in China in the 17$^{th}$ Century. There are more than 200 varieties of potatoes in the United States: russet, red, white, yellow, blue/purple, fingerling, and petite.

In 1498 Christopher Columbus departed with six ships for his third trip to America. In 1539 Spanish explorer Hernando De Soto arrived in Florida with ten ships and 700 men. In 1868 "Decoration Day," later called Memorial Day, was observed in Northern U.S. In 1897, 92 degrees was the highest temperature ever recorded in May in Cleveland, Ohio. In 1906 Hershey Park near Harrisburg, PA was founded by Milton S. Hershey for the exclusive use of its employees. I visited Hershey Park with my kids several times and families love it. In 1908 a Federal Workman Compensation Law was approved, and also the first passenger rode in an airplane. In 1922 the completed Lincoln Memorial was dedicated by U.S. Chief William Howard Taft in front of 50,000 persons. In 1964 the Beatles had a #1 hit *I Want to Hold Your Hand*. In 1965 Vivian Malone became the first Black to graduate from the University of Alabama. In 1967 motorcycle daredevil Robert "Evil" Knieval's motorcycle jumped 16 automobiles in Gardena, California. My son remembers my coming home to find him and his reckless young buddies playing "Evil" Knieval on their bicycles in my long driveway. I sent his friends home. In 1980 the first papal visit since 1814 was made to France.

Birthdays include bandleader Benny David Goodman (1909), American clarinetist and bandleader known as "King of Swing;" Mel Blanc (1908), voice for most Warner Brothers' *Looney Tunes* and *Merry Melodies* cartoon characters.

## HYMN: "SHOWERS OF BLESSINGS"
*"Showers of blessings.
Shower of blessings we need.
Mercy drops round us are falling,
But for the showers we plead....."*

**May 31, 2024**

Good morning, all 282. Today's celebrations are **Macaroon Day, European Neighbors Day, National Fisherfolk Day, National Save Your Hearing Day, National Smile Day, National Speak in Complete Sentences Day, Web Design Day, World No Tobacco Day, World Parrot Day, What You Think Upon Grows Day,** and **National Heat Awareness Day.**

**What You Think Upon Grows Day** celebrations leave us feeling better than we were., named for Norman Vincent Peale, a clergyman who served as a pastor in Marble Collegiate Church, New York, and was an author. I heard him speak several times and I was always moved by his encouraging words. As for **National Smile Day,** I remember my Department Chairman at

Bloomfield High School greeting me with, "*Here comes the lady with the smile.*" I hope I smile more often than I frown. I am smiling as I think of each of you. "*Thank you for being my friend*" from *Golden Girls*.

In 1859 the Great Clock Big Ben in London started keeping time and is still doing so. I saw and heard it when I visited London in 1988. In 1961 South Africa became an independent republic.

Birthdays include Walt Whitman (1819), poet, journalist, and essayist who wrote *Oh, Captain, My Captain* written in 1865 about Abraham Lincoln; Pius XI (1857), Pope from 1922-1939; Fred Allen (1894), humorist influencer of radio and television performers; Norman Vicent Peale (1898), American religious leader; Don Ameche (1908), actor; Patricia Roberts Harris (1924), first Black woman to serve as ambassador, Dean of Howard Law School, and in a President Jimmy Carter's Cabinet. I was so happy when I learned that my lawyer daughter's photo would one day hang near hers, too. I am so proud of my little girl and so was her Dad.

Some words of wisdom from Dr. Norman Vincent Peale: "*The way to happiness: keep your heart free from hate, your mind from worry. Live simply, expect little, give much. Fill your life with love. Scatter sunshine.*"

### HYMN: "I'LL BE A SUNBEAM FOR JESUS"
"*Jesus wants me for a sunbeam,*
*To shine for Him each day;*
*In every way try to please Him,*
*At home, at school, at play ...* "

**June 1, 2024**

Good morning, all 282. Today is **World Milk Day, Wear a Dress Day, Say Something Nice Day,** and **Stand for Children's Day.**

My astilbe and lilies are in bloom. I planted a beautiful blue hydrangea across the yard from one that is now a lovely pink. If the blue one is pink next year, then it will need a chemical to make it blue. Remember the chemistry formula: *Acids turn blue litmus red*. Perhaps I need some fertilizer that is basic. *Que sera sera.*

A dear colleague passed away 20 years ago soon after her retirement. Her mother had named her "June." I wonder if she had been born on the day before, would she have been "May?" Dr. June Bohannon Powell was a beloved African American French teacher at Bloomfield High School with me for many years.

Someone on my list said bears have been sighted in Maryland, Virginia and Washington, D.C. I never met any up close, but someone remembers one visiting her home in the Poconos.

Among the events today were the Beatles' release of *Sgt. Pepper's Lonely Hearts Club Band* (1967), for years considered by many to be the greatest rock 'n' roll album of all time; Ted Turner's *Cable News Network* (CNN) (1980), with 24-hour live news broadcasts gaining worldwide attention in 1991 for its around-the-clock coverage of the Persian Gulf War.

Birthdays were Jacques Marquette (1637), who explored the upper Mississippi River with Louis Jolliet; Marilyn Monroe (1926), model and actress before her tragic death at age 36; Andy Griffith (1926), actor, singer, comedian, television producer and writer for seven decades; Pat Boone (1934), singer, actor, television personality, and composer selling nearly 50 million records and 38 top hits; Morgan Freeman (1937), African American actor, producer and narrator.

### SONG: FROM THE MUSICAL *CAROUSEL*
"*June is bustin' out all over!*
*All over the meadow and the hill,*

*Buds're bustin' outa bushes,*
*And the rompin' river pushes*
*Ev'ry little wheel that wheels beside a mill......"*

**June 2, 2024**

Good morning, all 282. Today is **National Cancer Survivor's Day, National Child's Day, Gun Violence Awareness Day,** and **National Stepparents' Week.** During **Stepparents' Week**, I give honor to my stepmother, Alice Patterson Patience, who after she married my father in 1948 when I was sixteen years old, became a beacon for me to have a successful and happy life. She encouraged me to attend college, as she had done in 1936. She had earned her B. A. Degree at Bennett College in Greensboro, N.C. in 1940, was a WAC during World War II, and earned her M. A. at Scranton University in 1954. A brilliant woman, she became the first Black manager at Blue Cross/Blue Shield in northeastern Pennsylvania. Unfortunately, seven years before her death in 2000, she became blind from glaucoma, a family curse. She spoke her musings into a tape recorder I gave her, and I transcribed them without edits. The result is two small tomes called "Bittersweet Memories of Home," published by the Wilkes University Press. My B. S. Degree in 1958 is from *Wilkes College.*

Historical events today include Felix Mendelssohn's (1847) *Wedding March* used for the first time in Tiverton, England. What we recognize as *Wedding March* was originally for an 1842 production of Shakespeare's *A Midsummer Night's Dream.* In 1924, President Calvin Coolidge signed the Indian Citizenship Act, granting citizenship to all Native Americans born within the territorial limits of the United States. In 1979 Pope John Paul II became the first pontiff to visit Poland -- a Communist country.

Another of Dr. Norman Vincent Peale's, insightful quotes Is: Today's is: *"Four things for success: work and pray, think and believe."* May each of us be blessed today by those four verbs.

### HYMN: "I BELIEVE"
*"I believe for every drop of rain that falls, a flower grows*
*I believe that somewhere in the darkest night, a candle glows.*
*I believe for everyone who goes astray, someone will come to show the way.*
*I believe, I believe.*
*I believe above the storm the smallest prayer will still be heard.*
*I believe that someone in the Great Somewhere hears every word.*
*Every time I hear a newborn baby cry, or touch a leaf or see the sky,*
*Then I know why I believe!"*

**June 3, 2024**

Good morning, all 282. Today is **Love Conquers All Day, National Respect Day,** and **National Leave the Office Early Day.** Yesterday, the graduating high school seniors at my church were proudly wearing attire from the colleges they will attend. It reminded me of the New Jersey teenage Choralaires, some of whom are on this list. I would say, *"Good-bye"* for 17 consecutive years, praying for the best for each of you. I am grateful that my musings are uniting us once again. My choir jacket is still in good condition. Your mothers and others got together in the church kitchen to prepare platters to sell to raise money for those jackets, and Dads contributed by delivering orders to homes. Proverbs 22:6 says, *"Train up a child in the way he should go: and when he is old, he will not depart from it."* May God bless those of you who presently are training the youth of today in many capacities. I am very grateful for my early childhood training. It kept me out of trouble when my peers were getting into it, some experiencing lasting negative consequences.

In 1492, Martin Behaim introduced his terrestrial globe called *Erdapfel* or *"Earth Globe."* It is in a darkened room in a museum in Nuremberg, Germany. In 1889 the Canadian Pacific Railway was completed coast to coast. In 1937 the Duke of Windsor married Wallis Warfield Simpson in Monts, France. My stepmother, Alice, was a student at Bennett College when that happened, and she told how the King of England spoke via BBC radio: *"I have found it impossible to carry on the heavy burden of responsibility and to discharge the duties of King, as I would wish to do, without the help and support of the woman I love."* On December 11, 1936, Edward VIII shocked the world with his decision to abdicate the throne. Alice and some of her Bennett College classmates boo-hooed throughout the historical announcement as they gathered around someone's radio in a dormitory room. *"Such a beautiful love,"* those romantic young freshmen were fantasizing.

Charles Richard Drew (1904) was an African American surgeon and researcher of blood transfusions, improving techniques for blood storage and blood banks early in World War II. Although he was named medical director of the American Red Cross-National Blood Collection program in 1941, Dr. Drew was unable to donate to the very program he oversaw. Not until 1948 would the Red Cross discontinue segregating blood.

African American and French singer and actress, Josephine Baker (1906) was a world-renowned performer, World War II spy and an activist; Jill Tracy Jacobs Biden (1951), educator and U. S. First since 2021 and Second Lady from 2009 to 2017. Anderson Cooper (1967) is a broadcast journalist and political commentator on CNN.

**June 4, 2024**

Good morning, all 280, including the island of Tortola in the Caribbean. We are expecting an unusually hot summer. What did people do without electricity? Well, they got up at the crack of dawn and did their work in the mornings. Spanish-speaking countries are known for taking siestas in the middle of the day. I was surprised when taking Caribbean cruises that during midday most businesses closed on many of the islands for several hours.

When I was a child, window shades and drapes were kept tightly closed during the heat of the day, especially in the parlor, which was an extra room for guests and also where dead family members were "laid out." Rugs were pulled up and hung on outside and beat with rug beaters before being rolled up in moth balls for storage over the summer. During the night, windows were kept open by small removeable screens to "catch a breeze." I used them until I had my first portable window air conditioner in 1960. Homes with screened-in porches allowed people to sleep outside on very hot nights. Women canned foods for the winter. Thank God that freezers were invented by the time I got married in 1952, and I had one at the bottom of my refrigerator.

'Tis **National Cheese Day, Audacity to Hope Day, International Day of Innocent Children Victims of Aggression, National Christian T-Shirt Day** and **Shopping Cart Day.** Back in the day there were no shopping carts or supermarkets, just small "Mom and Pop" grocery stores. One opened in my hometown as a butcher shop that expanded to sell groceries. My chores included carrying a shopping list to a store for an item my great aunt liked. Three of them would send me to grocers to purchase meat from Bonfanti's, ground beef from Denti's, and bread from Morgantini's or Berti's.

Prior to World War II, shopping changed considerably due to the "war effort." Meat, coffee, sugar, and butter were rationed, and families went to the police station to get ration stamps. One person on my list, age 104, knows about rationing during World War II. I am blessed to know him.

Historic events included the Montgolfier brothers (1783) who demonstrated the first hot air balloon; In 1812, the U.S. House of Representatives approved a declaration of war against

Britain -- the War of 1812; the first Pulitzer Prize was awarded (1917); the 19th Amendment granted women the right to vote (1919); **Bruce Springsteen released** *Born in the U.S.A.* (1984).

**June 5, 2024**

Good morning, all 282. 'Tis **National Ketchup Day, Word Environment Day, National Tailor's Day,** and **Sausage Roll Day.** In 1876, H. J. Heinz Company produced catsup, soon to be called "ketchup."

I remember Great Aunt Lillian's "from scratch" gingerbread served with hot lemon sauce. Speaking of "from scratch," most of you on this list won't remember when there were no cake mixes in boxes. I never have made a cake from scratch. My daughter has her Aunt Marian's oven pound cake recipe. Aunt Marian baked my daughter's four-tiered wedding cake in 1982.

There was a time when a tailor raised hems in trousers, took out seams to make jackets larger, and took in seams to make them smaller. By the time I was a teenager, the only tailor in town had an establishment for male and female customers. Two of my great aunts were seamstresses. Some wealthy women were among my great aunts' clientele. Many homes had a bust sitting in a corner somewhere because most female clothing was made by the women of the house.

Today's birthday is Kenneth Bruce Gorelick, "Kenny G" (1956), jazz saxophonist, composer and producer., whose 1986 album *Duotones* made him one of the best artists of all time.

**June 6, 2024**

Good morning, all 283. I received a gift in the mail this morning but have no idea who the beautiful blue and white kaftan is from. If it is one of you, please let me thank you. Today is **National Gardening Day, National Eyewear Day,** and **Queensland Day.** Considering eyewear, I got my first pair of glasses when I was 10 years old. Eyes were not checked for children in schools back in the day. My great aunts weren't unaware that I could not see distances, and I always got A's and B's. Following my cataract operation 15 years ago, I am now far-sighted and need glasses only for reading, with a special pair for the computer and piano.

Since this is **Queensland Day**, named after Queen Victoria of England, I'll tell you about my trip to Australia. I visited a deep cave when I was touring with a group of U.S. teachers. The tour guide told us that the acoustics were magnificent in the cave in which we were standing and asked if anyone would like to sing. I suggested that we sing *Amazing Grace*. When our voices harmonized, it was super marvelous. Everyone was so uplifted.

Later today I'll see my trusty chiropractor in celebration of **National Gardening Day.** He is among our numbers. My back is calling to him after my leaning over to garden for several days., but my flowers look beautiful from the effort.

Historically, in 1844, the YMCA (Young Men's Christian Association) was founded in England. The first "Y" in the U.S. was in Boston, Massachusetts. "YWCA" came in 1870. Two YMCAs were in Wilkes-Barre, Pennsylvania when I was young, both segregated. One was for White men only and had a swimming pool. The other was for Black men and women and did not have a swimming pool. Black girls were finally given permission to swim in the pool at the YWCA. My stepmother, Alice, was a teen in the mid-1930s requesting to swim there. They were allowed in the pool on Wednesday evenings, after which the pool was emptied and refilled for Thursday mornings. When I moved to Montclair, N.J. in 1958, there was a YWCA for Black women, the only Black one in America. By the way, New Jersey was the last northern state to give up slavery and had segregated beaches, housing, movie theaters, and schools, even in 1958!

In 1876, the Transcontinental Express train arrived in San Francisco after completing its journey from New York City in just 83 hours and 39 minutes. In 1998 *Sex in the City* began airing on HBO and became one of the most popular television series of the time. In 2008, Phylicia Rashad became the first African American to win a Tony Award for best actress in *A Raisin in the Sun*.

This was **Prince Rogers Nelson (1958), "Prince's" birthday. He was an African** American singer, songwriter, multi-instrumentalist, record producer, and actor.

**June 7, 2024**

Good day, all 283. I am late with my musing today because I had to rise at 5:30 a.m. to go to the DeMatha Catholic High School graduation of my young cousin in Washington, D.C. He's a member of the National Honor Society., and his proud parents are on my morning musing list.

The *Washington Post* today had an enlightening article about why D-Day (yesterday) was important during World War II: *Almost terrifying to contemplate: Why D-Day nearly didn't happen.* The *Post* also ran an article called *The Fight Over Jackie Robinson.* Both worth googling.

'Tis also **National Chocolate Ice Cream Day,** and **National VCR Day.** The video cassette recorder (VCR) (1953) was one of the most famous innovations in the history of technology because there was a time when nearly every household in the U.S. owned one. How wonderful it was to go to Blockbusters to rent a favorite movie from the past. Presently, I am spoiled by the quality of the film on Netflix.

In 1712, Pennsylvania's colonial assembly voted to ban the further importation of enslaved people. Slavery ended – was declared over -- in the U.S. in 1865. In 1929 Vatican City became an independent state.

Birthdays include Dean Martin (1917), singer, actor and comedian, nicknamed "The King of Cool." He gained his career breakthrough with comedian Jerry Lewis, billed *Martin and Lewis*, in 1946. In 1940 Welsh singer Sir Tom Jones was born in the United Kingdom. Yesterday, he gave a stunning performance at the 80$^{th}$ D-Day memorial in Normandy, France. In 1952, Liam Neeson was born in the United Kingdom and received Academy Award nominations. In 1959 Mike Pence, 48$^{th}$ Vice President of the U.S., was born.

### HYMN: "THE LORD IS BLESSING ME RIGHT NOW"
*"The Lord is blessing me right now, right now.*
*He woke me up this morning and set me on my way….."*

**June 8, 2024**

Good morning, all 283. Happy birthday to two people on our list. Someone asked me what a "cruller" was. It is a heavy, uniced cake-like donut, round or long, great for dunking.

'Tis **National Best Friend Day,** and **U.S.S. Liberty Remembrance Day.** Once my young daughter asked me who my best friend was. I replied that I had friends for different occasions because all my friends did not like to do the same thing. My best friend in high school and I went to the movies every Monday, sometimes with other friends. She and I did many other things together, like roller skating at the indoor rink on Saturdays, ice skating on ponds in winter, bicycling and mountain climbing in spring, summer and fall. After our high school graduation in 1950, I went to N.C. to college, and she became a nun which was a big surprise for me. Sister Marguerite and I renewed our friendship via letters. I visited her at the schools where she taught Spanish, and she attended one of my presentations in Scranton, Pennsylvania. She always prayed for me, and sadly, she is deceased. Thank you, Sister Marguerite, for your prayers throughout the years.

In 1789, James Madison, once the most vocal opponent of the Bill of Rights, introduced amendments to the Constitution and hounded his colleagues to get it passed. **In 1864 Abraham**

Lincoln was nominated for another term as President. In 1949, George Orwell wrote *1984,* a novel warning against totalitarianism. I read it in college freshman English in 1950, and when that year came, much of what was predicted in the novel did not happen. I have not seen any mention of it in the newspapers, but I will not be surprised if I do, with politics in 2024. In 1953, the U.S. Supreme Court ruled unanimously that restaurants in the District of Columbia could not refuse to serve Blacks.

Frank Lloyd Wright (1867) was an American architect, designer, writer, and educator who designed more than 1,000 structures over 70 years. Ed and I went once to see Frank Lloyd Wright's Fallingwater in Pennsylvania. It is spectacular. Barbara Bush (1925) was the first lady of the United States from 1989 to 1993 as the wife of George H. W. Bush, the 41st President. She was second lady from 1981 to 1989 and founded the Barbara Bush Foundation for Family Literacy. Joan Rivers (1933) was a comedian, actress, producer, writer, and television host. Gabrielle Giffords (1970) is a retired politician and gun control activist who served as a member of the U. S. House of Representatives from Arizona's 8th Congressional District. She is married to astronaut Mark Kelly.

**June 9, 2024**

Good morning, all 283. Today is **National Children's Day** which was created by Rev. Dr. Charles Leonard in 1856. In church, the second Sunday of June was Children's Day. A talented teen might recite James Weldon Johnson's *Creation*.

### POEM: CREATION

*"And God stepped out on space,*
*And He looked around and said:*
*I'm lonely— I'll make me a world....."*

Friday's *Washington Post* had an article -- *Creating the golden age of friendship.* Thanks for being my friend. Today is also **Coral Triangle Day,** and **Georgia Blueberry Day.** Being a retired biology teacher, I am very interested in the **Coral Triangle**. I love strawberry rhubarb pie. My Great Aunt Lillie grew rhubarb in her garden, which is a very tart red stalk. You use a lot of sugar to be able to eat it and it must be cooked. Strawberries add sweetness. Aunt Lillie also concocted a compote of rhubarb and strawberries without a crust.

In 1934 Disney introduced Donald Duck to the world. In 1983 Margaret Thatcher was easily reelected to a second term as Prime Minister in England. Les Paul (1915) was a guitarist, songwriter and inventor. John Christopher Depp II (1963) is an actor and musician. In 1981 Natalie Portman (1981) is an Israeli American actress. Michael J. Fox (1961) is an actor and activist. He has suffered from Parkinson's Disease for many years. This hymn makes me admire Michael J. Fox's remarkable life of overcoming adversary.

### HYMN: "BRIGHTEN THE CORNER WHERE YOU ARE"

*"Do not wait until some deed of greatness you may do*
*Do not wait to shed your light afar*
*To the many duties ever near you now be true*
*Brighten the corner where you are....."*

**June 10, 2024**

Good morning, all 283. Today is **National Ballpoint Pen Day, National Herbs and Spices Day,** and **National Egg Roll Day.** When I was a child, I wrote everything in pencil. My left hand would get smudged from the graphite (not lead) in pencils, but when I entered Wilkes College in 1950, Professor Dr. Charles Reif insisted that our diagrams be completed in India ink that came in a small bottle. I had to purchase it, as well as a wooden pen holder and points to dip into the India ink. My left hand smeared the ink. I decided to draw the diagram in pencil first and then add the ink from right to left like Hebrew and Chinese. Success!

When I went to Bloomfield, N.J., to teach biology, I took my brilliant idea for left-handed students. My students' diagrams had to be completed in India ink, just like Dr. Reif demanded at Wilkes College. This went on for several years until a student brought me a ballpoint pen that made great diagrams. The India ink became history, and two former students on this list can attest to this.

Judy Garland (1922) was an actress, singer and dancer attaining international stardom. Who can forget her in the *Wizard of Oz* (1939)? In 1963 the U.S. Equal Pay Act was signed into law by President John F. Kennedy. In 1977 Apple Computer shipped its first Apple II computers.

**June 11, 2024**

Good morning, all 283. Today is **National Call Your Doctor Day**, and **National Making Life Beautiful Day**. Thanking each of you for adding beauty to my life by reading my musings. I remember when I had scarlet fever, I spent my $10^{th}$ birthday in bed and was quarantined in my home. My father gave me an easel, and I drew a lot of pictures. Thought I was going to take up oil painting in retirement, but instead, I am working on this, my $10^{th}$ book. I was one of the taller girls in the $7^{th}$ grade, but one of the shorter ones in $12^{th}$ grade.

Interesting to you animal lovers may be the bobcat, the most adaptable of the lynx species in North America. Bobcats, also known as wildcats, are smaller than mountain lions which are their closest relatives. Negative interactions with humans are extremely rare.

**June 14, 2024**

Good morning, all 290. Today is **Flag Day**. Congress created our national flag 246 years ago by commemorating Betsy Ross' creation. Since then, there have been 27 variations of the flag as the colonies grew into 50 states. 74 years ago, I graduated from West Pittston High School with three others on my list. The night before on Sunday there had been a Baccalaureate service. It was ecumenical and religious leaders in town were invited to represent the graduates. A fun Class Night was on the Friday before. I played the piano for a dance number by several female classmates. The music was the lively *Hoop-Dee-Do* that was introduced in 1950 by singer Perry Como. A cousin made me a lovely white eyelet dress to wear under my black Commencement robe. We graduated in black robes, which was the first of four black academic robes I would don in my lifetime. A pleasant surprise was that I was awarded an art award. I had been the art editor of our 1950 *Caravan* yearbook. Also, in our high school yearbook certain books were chosen to describe our character. For me it was *For Whom the Bell Tolls* because I was always late for activities and for school.

Later, two large high schools were formed, one with Pittston on the east side of the Susquehanna River and the one with our town on the west. We got an excellent education, and when I attended *Wilkes College*, I was in classes with students from a private school who were no smarter than I was. I am planning to attend our All-Classes reunion in October 2024, hoping to see some of my old classmates again. A respectable number showed up at our $50^{th}$ reunion in 2000 with spouses, but after that, just a few loyalists have remained true friends, the ones I hope to see in October.

<u>**POEM**</u>**: "MAKE NEW FRIENDS"**
*"Make new friends but keep the old.*
*One is silver, the other is gold.*
*A circle is round, It has no end.*
*That's how long I will be your friend."*

**June 15, 2024**

Good morning, all 290. Today is **Native American Citizenship Day, National Photography Day,** and **World Elder Abuse Awareness Day.** I will be attending a Juneteenth event in a nearby park. On June 19th I will explain in my musing what Juneteenth is for those who may not know. May and June have brought several graduations to my family. A master's for one granddaughter and a bachelor's for another. High school diplomas were given to two male cousins and a female great niece. Several proud parents are on my musing list, as well as proud grandparents. Congratulations to all. We are so proud of each one.

Smile today in hopes that your smile will make another person smile who makes another person smile. When we smile at someone, we acknowledge their value and worth in our smiles.

<u>**SONG**</u>: **SUNG BY FRANK SINATRA "WHEN YOU SMILING"**
*"Oh, when you smilin', when you smilin'*
*The whole world smiles with you.*
*Yes, when you laughin', when you laughin'*

My personal thought about smiling is something I told my grandsons when they were little. From my imagination, I said that when God created animals, the only one to whom He gave a smile was humankind. Some animals may grimace like monkeys do, but only humans can truly smile. Maybe God gave us the smile to make others happy. It is a choice. Give it a try.

In 1215, King John put his seal on the *Magna Carta*, signifying that **the king and his government were not above the law. In 1776 George** Washington was named Commander-in-Chief of the colonies by the Continental Congress. In 1846 the United States and Britain signed the *Oregon Treaty* in Washington D.C., establishing the border between Canada and the United States. In 1924 President Calvin Coolidge signed the *Indian Citizenship Act*, which ended a long debate over birthright citizenship for American Indians. It is shameful that it took so long. Did God create us differently to test us? I love Him and His diversity in nature, including in *Homo sapiens*.

*"If a man say, I love God, and hateth his brother, he is a liar for he that loveth not his brother whom he hath seen, how can he love God whom he hath not seen?"* **1 John 4:20 KJV**

**June 16, 2024**

Good morning, all 290. May each father on this list be blessed today. I am thanking God for my son who is a #1 father, and also for my son-in-law, who is, too. I recently saw someone wearing seer-sucker slacks. Now I might be able to find a pair. My Ed always owned a blue and white seer-sucker suit for the summer and for cruising. Perhaps some gentlemen on my list have worn it, too. In yesterday's *Washington Post* was an article called *The Senate lightens up.* On **National Seer-Sucker Day** many senators wore that fabric to work.

Another article was *Several comedians walk into the Vatican.* Pope Francis shook hands with Jimmy Fallon and Chris Rock, who were among more than 100 comedians invited to the Vatican. The Pope stressed to the comedians the value of humor. Whoopie Goldberg was among them. Many of you may have enjoyed her performances in *Sister Act I and II.* I enjoyed both movies.

**June 17, 2024**

Good morning, all 290. It's **National Stewart's Root Beer Day, National Apple Strudel Day,** and **National Eat Your Vegetables Day.** On Saturday I had a surprising *"It's such a small world"* episode. It will be of special interest to the West Pittstonians on my list. I was introduced to a woman close to my age who was attending the same community event here in northern

Virginia. When she was introduced to me, I did not catch her surname. Later, I asked her surname, which was Lithuanian and was her husband's. I asked where her husband was from, and she replied, *"Pennsylvania." "Wyoming,"* she responded, adding *"His father had been a coal miner there."* Wyoming is a neighboring town to the one where I grew up. Our football teams were rivals. Her deceased husband and I may have attended the same football games in the late 40s. Few, except for those in the Wyoming Valley area of Pennsylvania, would know about Wyoming and West Pittston. What a pleasant surprise. Small world, indeed.

When I began teaching, teachers were served apple strudel for dessert on Mondays. New Jerseyans on this list may know about *Stewart's Root Beer* in Bloomfield, N.J. The glasses were iced before the root beer was poured into them. The Choralaires would sometimes go there for a special treat following choir rehearsal. *Stewart's* was a nostalgic soda fountain, originated as the Stewart's Restaurants, a chain started in 1924 by Frank Stewart in Mansfield, Ohio. After the *Statue of Liberty* was presented to the U.S. Minister to France on July 4, 1884, in Paris, it was disassembled and shipped to the United States on June 17, 1885. Barry Manilow (1943) is a singer, pianist and songwriter with a career spanning seven decades. Hit recordings include *Could It Be Magic, Looks Like We Made It,* and *I Write the Songs.*

### SONG: "I WRITE THE SONGS"
*"I've been alive forever*
*And I wrote the very first song*
*I put the words and the melodies together*
*I am music, and I write the songs....."*

## June 18, 2024

Good morning, all 290. 'Tis **International Day for Countering Hate Speech, International Sushi Day,** and **National Wanna Get Away Day**. I am going to discuss only **International Sushi Day**. My introduction was years ago at an International Foods event sponsored by several United Methodist churches. Everyone contributed their specialties for others to partake. I chose some sushi from the Japanese station. Wasabi is the spicy horseradish condiment that accompanies sushi. My Ed tasted some but did not know what the green stuff (wasabi) was and ate too much. He was miserable for a while but learned his lesson. He never became fond of sushi, though.

**National Wanna Get Away Day** reminds me of when several of us teenagers from my Presbyterian Church went to the Montrose Bible Conference for two weeks in the summertime. We had religious classes in the morning but were free in the afternoons. Nerlene**,** Harold and I walked to the nearby Montrose Lake and rented a rowboat. We couldn't swim but had fun rowing to the middle of the lake and back. Our guardian angels must have been present.

In 2006 Prelate Katharine Jefferts Schori was **elected Bishop of the Episcopal Church in the U.S.A.** She was the first woman churchwide leader in the 400-year history of the Anglican Communion. Sir James Paul McCartney (1942) was an English singer, songwriter and musician with the Beatles. Blake Shelton (1976) is a country singer and television personality.

## June 19, 2024

Good morning, all 279 on **Juneteenth.** When I was a child there was no Juneteenth The *Juneteenth National Independence Day Act* was passed by Congress recently and signed by President Joseph Biden on June 17, 2021, commemorating the day when 250,000 slaves in the state of Texas learned they were free. The name is a blend of "June" and "nineteenth," since it was on June 19, 1865, when Major General Gordon Granger ordered the final enforcement of the *Emancipation Proclamation* in Texas at the end of the Civil War. President Lincoln had decreed that slavery ended when he signed the *Emancipation Proclamation* in 1863, but he could not enforce that law until the Confederacy surrendered on April 9, 1865. I share this with you because of the gumption of my great-grandfather Crowder Patience, who at age 17 joined the Union Army with his older brother Thomas. Three of Thomas' descendants are on this list with their youngest brother, Joe. Unfortunately, Grandpa died two years before I was born. Otherwise, I could have said that I sat in the lap of a freed slave. After the war Grandpa traveled to Pennsylvania with his regiment (103rd PA) to be mustered out of the Army, and he settled in northeastern Pennsylvania in West Pittston where our family was the only Black one three generations later.

### HYMN: "BATTLE HYMN OF THE REPUBLIC" CHORUS
*"Glory, glory, Hallelujah,Glory, glory, Hallelujah,*
*Glory, glory Hallelujah, His truth is marching on...."*

There was a controversy over *The Battle Hymn of the Republic* when it was written in 1861, because one verse, "let us die to make men free" meant to fight to end slavery. Those words angered southerners because it claimed that God was on the North's side. Seems that He was. Thank you, Lord, for freedom from slavery. Unimaginable to us today—to be owned by someone else for life. But it was only 159 years since the Civil War ended three generations before me.

Last night I saw Opal Lee, age 97, being interviewed on CNN. An African American retired teacher, counselor and activist in the *Civil Rights Movement*, she worked to make Juneteenth a federally recognized holiday. She is described as the "grandmother of Juneteenth." Today, I will don my Juneteenth tee shirt and go with one of you to the neighborhood Farmer's Market.

**June 20, 2024**

Good morning, all 279. Today is **American Eagle Day.** Reminds of me of one of my favorite Bible verses that has helped me along my 92 years. It is Isaiah 40:31. The Chinese would say 93 years because they count one's actual birthday as one year old. Makes sense to me.

Today is also **National Seashell Day.** One of my favorite topics to teach was on seashells. I have a bowl of seashells in my living room. One of my favorite seashell gifts from a student was a sand dollar decorated to become a Christmas ornament. I wear it on a gold chain at Christmastime. It was from the daughter of one of my favorite students who is on this list.

Other celebrations are **National Daylight Appreciation Day, Tall Girl Appreciation Day,** and **World Peace and Prayer Day.** Today is the first day of Summer 2024, with the longest period of sunlight in 2024. The Summer Solstice occurs in each hemisphere annually when one of the earth's poles has maximum tilt toward the sun. A miracle occurs each time the earth reverses its tilt. Otherwise, it's all over for us! Proves God is still in charge of His universe. Tomorrow the number of hours here will be equal to yesterday's as we head towards fall and the autumnal equinox. How faithful is the Creator! Man cannot change His schedule even with global warming that is destroying some of our earth, thanks to humans and the *Industrial Revolution* which began in Britain in the 18th Century. It had replaced the Age of Agriculture.

Guiness World Records reports that Rumeysa Gelgi of Turkey is the tallest living woman, at 7 feet 0.7 inches tall. In 1782 Congress approved the Great Seal of the United States, featuring the bald eagle. In 1863 West Virginia became the 35th state. I went to the Farmer's Market for ingredients to make ratatouille, bedecked in my Juneteenth tee.

**June 21, 2024**

Good morning, all 279. Today is **National Take Your Dog to Work Day, Wagyu Day, National Dachshund Day,** and **World Music Day.** When I was teaching, the most important period of the day was lunch. I always went to the teachers' lunchroom and got to know many of my colleagues over my 33 years. I am gregarious, as many of you on this list already know. Would you believe I even integrated the lunchroom? Not racially since I was the only Black teacher in 1958. No, it was the male table. One day, I said mischievously to a friend, "Let's go sit at the men's table." At first the guys were shocked but soon got used to it.

We owned a dog named Missie, who went to school with my son when students were allowed to bring pets. My Great Aunt Lillie and Missie developed a special bond. Missie's mother was a Dachshund named Heidi and today is **National Dachshund Day.** Missie was a beautiful long-haired light brown dog whose daddy could have been any neighbor's pet who caught Heidi's fancy.

In 1675, the foundation stone for St. Paul's, one of the most famous cathedrals in the world, was laid. In 1788, New Hampshire became the ninth and last necessary state to ratify the **Constitution** of the United States, thereby making the document the law of the land. In 1893, the first Ferris Wheel premiered at Chicago's Columbian Exposition and could hold up to 2000 people in 36 cars and was 264 feet tall. It was a 15-minute ride. Presently, the Ferris Wheel in nearby Maryland at the National Harbor is only 180 feet high, has 42 climate-controlled gondolas for round the year comfort, and can carry 336 persons maximum. I went up with my son and his wife for a 12-minute ride. In 1913, the first successful parachute jump was made from an airplane by Georgia Broadwick, age 18, over Griffith Field, Los Angeles, California.

**June 22, 2024**

Good morning, all 279. Today is **Be Kinder Day, National Chocolate Éclair Day,** and **National Limoncello Day. National Limoncello Day** suggests that even the most difficult situations may be turned into positive experiences. May we pray for each other who have experienced some recent lemons in our lives. Speaking of lemons, my son in California has a lemon tree in his backyard where he picks them right off the tree and cleans his garbage disposal with it. **Be Kinder Day** should be every day. Onion rings are not healthy, but I do love chocolate éclairs. I miss being kissed by my Hubby who has been gone now for 9 years. *Tempus fugit.*

In 1633, Galileo who was a philosopher, astronomer, mathematician, discoverer of the four largest moons of Jupiter, was found guilty of heresy and spent the rest of his life under house arrest rather than be imprisoned. He was one of many scientists who were not believed at first. In 1939 Princess and future Queen Elizabeth met her future husband—Philip of Greece. In 1940 the first Dairy Queen opened in Joliet, Illinois. In 1947, twelve feet of rain fell in twelve minutes in Holt, Missouri. In 1949, President Franklin Delano Roosevelt signed the GI Bill of Rights (Servicemen's Readjustment Act). When I entered Wilkes College in 1950, many older World War II veterans were attending under the GI Bill before it was discontinued. With it, my stepmother Alice, who had been a WAC during World War II, earned her master's at *Scranton University*. In 1970, President Richard Nixon signed the extension of the 1955 *Voting Rights Act* that requires the voting age at 18 in all federal state and local elections.

Dianne Feinstein (1933) was a politician who served as Senator from California from 1992 until her death in 2023. A member of the Democratic Party, she served as Mayor of San Francisco from 1978 to 1988. Kris Kristofferson (1936) was a retired country singer, songwriter and actor. Some songs were *Me and Bobby McGee, For the Good Times, Sunday Mornin' Comin' Down,* and *Help Me Make It Through the Night.* Danny Glover (1946) is an African American actor, producer and political activist. He received the Jean Hersholt Humanitarian Award, Academy of Motion Picture Arts and Sciences, the NAACP's President's Award, as well as nominations for five Emmy Awards and four Grammy Awards. I met him once at a Bennett College event.

**Danny Glover and Dr. Juanita Moss at *Bennett College***

Finally, Merryl Streep (1949) is an actress known for versatility, described as "the best actress of her generation."

**June 23, 2024**

Good morning, all 279. Today is **National Typewriter Day, Pink Flamingo Day, National Fatherless Children Day,** and **International Pink Day.** *"What's a typewriter?"* a youngster might ask. It would be hard to explain, as would shorthand and office machines. I asked someone on our list who is Detroit-born about Detroit pizza. *"I like their combination of cheeses, and they had a buttery crust."* I ate pepperoni pizza and drank my favorite soda with it called Rock 'n Rye. It was stronger than Coke and also a Detroit-based "pop" (soda to Virginians and Pennsylvanians). Porridge originated in Scotland, even though the following rhyme comes from England. The rhyme refers to pease pudding or pease pottage. "Pease Porridge Hot" is a riddle in John Newbery's *Mother Goose's Melody* circa. 1760.

*"Pease porridge hot, Pease porridge cold. Pease porridge in the pot Nine days old......"*

The **International Day of Pink** is a day against bullying and discrimination everywhere.

In 930, Iceland's first Parliament and the oldest recorded legislative body, the Althing, was established. In 1314, was the Battle of Bannockburn, where Scots defeated English, regained their independence under Robert I. In 1868, American inventor Christopher Latham Sholes and two others were granted a patent for a typewriter. In 1961, the Antarctic Treaty was enacted, reserving the entire continent for free and nonpolitical scientific investigation. No country owns Antarctica. Instead, it is governed by a group of nations in a unique international partnership. One person on our list cruised there to observe penguins. It was during January, which was its summer.

June Carter Cash (1929) was a county singer and actress married to singer Johnnie Cash. She played guitar, harmonica, and autoharp, and was inducted into the Christian Music Hall of

Fame in 2009. In 1940 African American sprinter, Wilma Rudolph, was the first woman to win three track-and-field gold medals in a single Olympics. She had overcome childhood polio and went on to become a world-record-holding Olympic champion and international sports icon in track and field following her successes in the 1956 and 1960 Olympic Games. Ted Shackelford (1946) was an actor in *Dallas* and *Knots Landing* which were two of my favorite evening shows during the 70s. Clarence Thomas (1948) is the second Black justice to serve on the Supreme Court, Thurgood Marshall being the first.

The two Sunday meals used to have distinguishing names in different households. I eat dinner every day, but supper was for our Sunday 6:00 p.m. meal. I got a very good religious education, which is where I played the piano.

**June 24, 2024**

Good morning, all 279. **Today is National Pralines Day, St. John's Day,** and **Swim a Lap Day.** I recently ate some pralines from New Orleans. They are very sweet. A praline in French confectionery is a cooked mixture of sugar, nuts, and vanilla, often ground to a paste for uses as a pastry or candy filling, analogous to marzipan. **International St. John's Day** has been celebrated on June 24 since the 4th Century. It was created by the Catholic Church to honor John the Baptist. In 1922 the American Professional Football Association was renamed the National Football League.

**June 25, 2024**

Good morning, all 292. Today is **Leon Day**, an unofficial holiday marking the halfway mark to Christmas. "Leon" is "Noel" spelled backwards a day when some crafters begin making homemade gifts and decorations. It is **Color TV Day, National Catfish Day** and **National Strawberry Day.** In 1954 the first RCA color television set, the CT-100, was produced with a 12-inch screen and a cost of $1,000. Only rich people could afford one. Not until the 60s, would color television become profitable and reasonable. We had a black and white television set for years to watch Tennessee Ernie Ford, Jackie Gleason, Lucille Ball, and Ed Sullivan. I was perfectly satisfied until I saw something broadcasted in color. Then I had to have a color television set, too. At first the color was dim but much improved through the years. Netflix is a joy to watch. I like black and white *Turner Classics*, with my favorite movie being *Random Harvest*.

As for catfish, I enjoy it. We did not eat fish in my household when I was young, but a neighbor went fishing and brought me some catfish. Ed enjoyed catfish, and so I began purchasing raw nuggets to prepare for him. Quite tasty. I have not had any in recent years.

In 1788, Virginia was the 10th state to ratify the Constitution and join the union. In 1913 Civil War veterans began arriving at the Great Reunion in Gettysburg, Pennsylvania. The gathering of 53,407 veterans (including 8,750 Confederates) was the largest Civil War veteran reunion. All honorably discharged veterans in the Grand Army of the Republic and the United Confederate Veterans were invited, and veterans from 46 of the 48 states attended (none from Nevada and Wyoming). In 1947 the *Diary of Anne Frank* was published. In 1950 the Korean War began when North Korea invaded South Korea. I had graduated from high school eleven days before, and several young men from my class were drafted into the military. The *Korean War* draft called up men between 18 and 35 for two-year terms of duty. In 1951 the *Universal Military Training and Service Act* was passed, requiring males between 18 and 26 to register. These were my classmates. The U.S. does not currently have a draft. In 1953, Jacqueline Bouvier and Massachusetts Senator John F. Kennedy announced their engagement.

June Lockhart (1926), aged 98, is an actress in *A Christmas Carol* and *Meet Me in St. Louis*. Carly Simon (1943) is a musician, singer, songwriter, memoirist, and children's author. Jimmie

Walker (1947) is an African American actor and comedian who portrayed James Evans Jr. in the CBS television series *Good Times*. He was nominated twice for a *Golden Globe* Award.

**June 26, 2024**

Good morning, all 292. This is a very important day to my family, for on it, God gave Ed and me a beautiful baby daughter in 1955, who is on this list. Happy Birthday, Daughter Dear. You arrived during a time when we did not know the sex of babies until their birth. You were so beautiful and still are. On the advice of my mother-in-law who had nine children, I put you in a diaper and set your carriage outside on the shaded back porch.

Today is **World Refrigeration Day,** and **National Beautician Day.** When I was a kid, the local iceman made rounds for people to purchase chunks of ice. A clock-like sign hung on the front door so he would know what size chunk to cut and place in the corrugated tin iceboxes that sat on back porches. He'd delight us neighborhood kids with the slivers of ice he would chop off with his sharp pick. Once, I asked my Great Aunt Lillie where the ice came from in the summer. She told me that it was harvested from nearby clean lakes during winter and stored by icemen in underground cellars or caves, usually insulated with sawdust. In the 1860s, tin iceboxes were introduced to middle class homes. Electric refrigerator came in the late 1930s.

Cabbage, potatoes, carrots, and onions were stored in holes dug in the ground for "root cellars" lined with straw. That was where all the canned food got stored for over the winter. Another interesting foodstuff I remember was murky-looking vinegar forming in a large pot that sat on the top of the cellar steps.

This is also **National Beautician Day.** My first trip to a beautician was when I had my two pigtails cut. It was a rite of passage to get a grown-up hair style before junior high school. My braids are in a small box. Otherwise, I would not remember the color of my hair because it has been white since college. I inherited the premature white gene from my father and passed it to my son, but not to my daughter. I colored my hair until I was 44. Then I cut it short and let the white show. So, I've looked basically the same for the past 48 years.

In 684, St. Benedict II began his reign as Catholic Pope; in 1945, the United Nations Charter was signed, establishing the United Nations to promote peace and cooperation worldwide; in 1959, President Dwight D. Eisenhower and Queen Elizabeth II, opened the St. Lawrence Seaway, creating a navigational channel from the Atlantic Ocean to all of the Great Lakes; in 1974, at a supermarket in Troy, Ohio, a pack of Wrigley's Juicy Fruit chewing gum became the first grocery item scanned with a Universal Product Code, or UPC.

**June 27, 2024**

Good morning, all 292. Today is **Industrial Workers of the World Day, National Bingo Day, National Sunglasses Day,** and **National Pineapple Day**. I am an occasional BINGO player. Once when Ed and I were on a cruise, we played BINGO, and I won the game where the whole card got covered! The pineapple is one of my favorite fruits. Canned pineapple juice was around for a long time because when I had scarlet fever at age 10, the sulfa pill I couldn't swallow was crushed into a glass of pineapple juice for me to get it down. For years I could not drink it without remembering the taste of the sulfa medicine. Sulfa preceded penicillin that wasn't used until post-World War II. Have any of you seen pineapples growing in fields? They do not grow on trees! When pineapples are harvested, they are ready to eat, so, you don't need to pick them over like watermelons.

In 1956, *Moby Dick* premiered in New Bedford, Massachusetts, known as the "whaling city." The historical heritage of the city is within the Seaport Cultural District filled with stories of whaling days, the Underground Railroad, and the African American abolitionist and orator

Frederick Douglass, as well as the legendary white whale, which inspired Herman Melville to write *Moby Dick*.

**June 28, 2024**

Good morning, all 292. 'Tis **National Calendar Day,** and **Happy Heart and Hugs Day.** In 2017 the **National Day Calendar** celebrated Alaska as the 49th state of the Union. Regarding **National Calendar Day**, in the U.S., holidays are created by federal and state law. Congress or states and/or the President may create national observances by resolution (not law). Only 25 new submissions are chosen a year out of 20,000 requests.

In 1870, Congress created federal holidays (New Year's Day, Independence Day, Thanksgiving Day, and Christmas Day), initially applicable to federal employees; in 1874, the Freedmen's Bank closed; in 1904, Helen Keller, deaf and blind since 19 months old, graduated *cum laude* from Radcliffe College and was the first Deaf Blind person to earn a bachelor's degree; on May 21, 1927, Charles A. Lindberg completed the first solo, nonstop transatlantic flight from Long Island, New York, to Paris, France in his Spirit of St. Louis.

**The birthday to be recognized was** Leon Panetta (1938), retired politician and government official who served as Defense Secretary, CIA Director, White House Chief of Staff, and U.S. Representative from California.

**June 29, 2024**

Good morning, all 292. I had a wonderful time yesterday with a bevy of cousins—young and old. We were all the descendants of three of my great grandparents' children—Florence, Harry and Percy. My musing list includes many more cousins. It gives me much joy to be your griot. A response from one of you concerning ripening avocados is to place them in a closed paper bag. I do that with green tomatoes in the fall, too.

'Tis **International Asteroid Day,** and **Lightening Safety Awareness Day.** When my grandsons frequented a swimming pool here in Alexandria, as soon as lightning came, the pool was closed for the rest of the day. My Great Grandmother, Elsie, was struck by lightning once when she was peeling potatoes. According to my Great Aunt Lillie, her daughter, the shoes were pulled off her mother's feet. Aunt Lillie would shut off all electricity and wait out storms. Our dog, Missie, didn't like lightning either, so the two of them would go into hiding until the storm was over. I would be sitting in a chair waiting for the lightning to go away.

In 1859, daredevil Jean Francois Gravelet-Blondin, the "Great Blondin," was the first to cross Niagara Falls on a tightrope. In 1905, Albert Einstein published his groundbreaking Theory of Relativity. In 1936, *Gone with The Wind* was published, and she received the Pulitzer Prize for Fiction in 1937. The film in 1939 received the Academy Award for Best Picture. I took my teenage daughter to see it, and the technicolor and special effects were outstanding. But there were also protests from Daughters of Union Veterans, and the NAACP objected to the treatment of Black characters. Hattie McDaniel was the first African American actress to win an Oscar for her role as Mammy, but she was barred from the Atlanta premiere due to segregation laws.

Mike Tyson (1966) is an African American professional boxer from 1985 to 2005. Michael Phelps (1985) is a former competitive swimmer, the most decorated Olympian with 28 medals.

**July 1, 2024**

Good morning, all 292. It is **National Zip Code Day, National U.S. Postage Stamp Day, National Postal Workers Day, National Television Heritage Day,** and **National Deep Fried Clams Day,** Happy Day to the postal worker on our list.

In 1840, the first adhesive postage stamp was issued in the United Kingdom. The first in the U.S. went on sale in New York City in 1847. Benjamin Franklin was on the 5-cent stamp, and George Washington on the ten-cent stamp. On July 14th, the FOREVER postage stamp will cost 73 cents. I remember when a stamp cost 3 cents and a postcard a penny. My wages were $40.00 a week at the factory where I worked. My proud husband told me, *"No wife of mine is going to work."* I defied him and got a job in a dress factory, taking home $32.00. Our rent was $35.00 per month. I hated Mondays because working in the factory was the only job a Black woman could get in Wilkes-Barre in 1955, except for domestic work. The machines sounded like 100 dentists' drills. That's when I told Ed that I wanted to return to Wilkes College to get my bachelor's degree and a job as a teacher. In 1958 I became the first Black woman to graduate from Wilkes College and the second Black ever!

I applied for a job in Islip, N.Y. but was told that Islip was not ready for a Black teacher. Bloomfield, N.J. hired me, and I stayed 33 years. The ZIP in ZIP Code stands for Zone Improvement Plan, introduced in 1963, as part of a plan to improve the speed of mail delivery.

**National Deep Fried Clams Day** reminds me of the orange-roofed *Howard Johnson* restaurants that were popular until fast food chains beat them out. I enjoyed their fried clams served with tartar sauce. Delicious! How I long for some today.

One person on our list resides in Tortola, British West Indies, best known for its picturesque beaches, turquoise water, coral reefs, and lush mountainous landscape. I've been invited. **American Zoo Day** reminds me that two **giant pandas have safely arrived at their new home at the San Diego Zoo. The iconic bears are the first to come to the U.S. in 21 years, marking a renewed panda diplomacy between China and Washington, D.C.** Celebrate **National Television Heritage Day** with a Classic TV Show Marathon, with shows like *I Love Lucy, The Twilight Zone* or *Alfred Hitchcock Presents*.

In 1863, the pivotal three-day Civil War Battle of Gettysburg, resulting in a Union victory, began in Pennsylvania. In 1867, Canada became a self-governing dominion of Great Britain with the British North America Act. **In 1960, Ghana became a republic, breaking ties with Britain and electing Kwame Nkrumah as its first President.** In 1966, the Medicare federal insurance program went into effect.

Daniel Edward Aykroyd (1952) is a Canadian American actor, comedian, screenwriter, and producer, member of the *Not Ready for Prime-Time Players* and *Saturday Night Live* from its inception in 1975 until in 1979. Princess Diana (1961) was born in England. Frederick Carlton Lewis (1961) is a former African American track and field athlete who won nine Olympic gold medals, one silver, and ten World Championships medals, including eight gold.

**July 2, 2024**

Good morning, all 293. Today is **I Forgot Day, World Tutors' Day,** and **Special Recreation for the Disabled Day.** I went to a Bob and Ethel's Diner with two of my Bennett sisters for brunch. In 1872 Walter Scott sold food out of a horse-pulled wagon to the employees of the *Providence Journal* in Rhode Island. His was the first diner to have walk-up service with windows on each side of the wagon. The first stationary diner (1913) had a design modeled after the chrome look of a train's dining car. Soon diners were sprouting all over the United States.

I like licorice, so I will treat myself to a box of *Good & Plenty* when I go food shopping. I also love iced Italian anisette cookies at Christmastime, called "knots." A school cafeteria worker whose son I had taught presented me with anisette cookies. I asked her for her recipe and have made them.

**I Forgot Day** is definitely for me. I write more notes to myself and don't rely on memory any longer. My cerebrum is overloaded, which is why I remember walking to school with Elaine Oliver (deceased) in 1938 but not where I put my keys. Throughout our 12 years together in school, I always sat behind Elaine whenever we were seated in alphabetical order.

In 1937, aviator Amelia Earhart and her navigator, Fred Noonan, were heard from for the last time before disappearing. In 1964, President Lyndon Johnson signed into law the *Civil Rights Act* in a nationally televised ceremony at the White House. In 2001, the world's first self-contained artificial heart transplant was performed. Thoroughgood "Thurgood" Marshall (1908) was the Supreme Court's first African American Justice, serving as Associate Justice of the U. S. Supreme Court from 1967 to 1991. Imelda Marcos (1928) was a Filipino politician and First Lady of the Philippines (1965-86), best remembered for her 3,000 pairs of shoes.

### July 3, 2024

Good morning, all 293. 'Tis **Disobedience Day,** and **National Compliment Your Mirror Day. Disobedience Day** has biblical, legal, and domestic implications. 2020-25 Dietary Guidelines for Americans recommends 1-3 cups of beans, peas and lentils per week.

In 1839, Africans on the Cuban schooner *Amistad* rose up against their captors and seized control of the ship transporting them to chattel slavery. John Quincy Adams represented the Mende Africans before the Supreme Court, being academically qualified and abhorring slavery. In 1841, it ruled that the Mende people had been illegally transported as slaves and rebelled in self-defense. On November 25, 1841, 35 former slaves returned to West Africa. A statue of the *Amistad* story stands outside the government building where my daughter worked as a lawyer for the Justice Department in New Haven, Connecticut.

In 1844, the last known pair of Great Auks, flightless birds, were killed off the coast of Iceland at the request of a collector. The fancy women's hats of that day were covered with feathers, the more the merrier among the wealthy. In 1863, following intense fighting and more than 50,000 casualties, the *Battle of Gettysburg* ended with a Union victory and was seen as a turning point in the *Civil War*. My great grandfather enlisted in the Union Army at Plymouth, N.C. in 1864. He's buried in the West Pittston Cemetery beneath a Union tombstone, GAR (Grand Army of the Republic) stanchion and an American flag that is replaced every Memorial Day. In 1940 the first *Walmart* store, then called *Wal-Mart*, opened in Rogers, Arkansas.

Montel Brian Anthony Williams (1956) an African American television host, actor and motivational speaker hosting *The Montel Williams Show* from 1991 to 2008 and currently hosting *Military Makeover: Operation Career on Lifetime*. Audra Ann McDonald (1970) is an African American singer and actress who won six Tony Awards, more performance wins than any other actor and is the only person to win in all four acting categories.

### July 4, 2024

Good morning, all 293. When I was a little girl with dark brown pigtails, my father would light sparklers and let me run around the yard with them. Years later when living in New Jersey, I took my kids to see the fireworks at *Woodman's Field* where the high school football games were played. The kids enjoyed being with their friends and everyone enjoyed the fireworks. The only downside was the mosquitoes. Here in Virginia, firework stands are set up in parking lots or along roadsides. In New Jersey, my small family enjoyed a midday meal in the back yard with loved ones now all gone to be with Lord. Their memories bring tears to my eyes.

Yesterday's article in the FOOD section of the *Washington Post* reminds me of happy holiday meals. *Hot dogs! Get your hot dogs* has pictures of ways they are served with **different toppings** (Sonoran, New York, Carolina, Coney Island, Detroit, Chicago, and Seattle). My son-in-law, born in Chicago, swears that Chicago's are the best. My favorite hot dog is the New York Kosher beef one served with sauerkraut and yellow mustard. However, my all-time favorite is with raw onions and the special chili sauce from *Dominick Nardone's* in West Pittston.

In 1776, the Declaration of Independence was adopted. Most delegates to the Second Continental Congress signed on July 2, 1776, putting their names on that paper and risking everything if the British had won the American Revolution. In 1802 the United States Military Academy opened at West Point, New York. In 1803 the Louisiana Purchase was bought from France. In 1817, in Rome, New York, construction was begun on the Erie Canal. In 1818, the U.S. Flag Act of 1818 created a 13 stripe flag with a star for each state. New stars were added on July 4 after a new state had been admitted. In 1827 slavery was abolished in New York State. In 1831, Samuel Francis Smith wrote *My Country, 'Tis of Thee*. In 1885 Walt Whitman published *Leaves of Grass*. In 1876 Susan B. Anthony addressed Congress on suffrage. In 1888, France presented the Statue of Liberty to the United States. In 1895, *America the Beautiful* was published and later set to music. In 1909 Washington, D.C. celebrated Independence Day on the National Mall for the first time. In 1927 the "Lockheed Vega," Amelia Earhart's plane, debuted in Los Angeles. In 1950, Radio Free Europe broadcasted for the first time. In 1966, President Lyndon B. Johnson signed the Freedom of Information Act. In 1997, NASA's Pathfinder probe landed on Mars.

Nathaniel Hawthorne (1801) wrote *Scarlet Letter* and *The House of the Seven Gables*. Calvin Coolidge (1872) was the 30th President of the United States from 1923 to 1929. Eva Marie Saint (1924), at age 99, is a retired actress of film, theatre, radio, and television. Marvin Neil Simon (1927) was playwright, screenwriter and author, with more than 30 plays including *Odd Couple*. Willian "Bill" Harrison Withers, Jr. (1938) was an African American singer and songwriter, including, *Ain't No Sunshine, Grandma's Hands, Use Me, Lean on Me, Lovely Day,* and *Just the Two of Us*. Geraldo Rivera (1943) is a journalist, attorney, author, and political commentator at the Fox News from 2001 to 2023. He hosted the *Geraldo* from 1987 to 1998 and became better known with the 1986 television special *The Mystery of Al Capone's Vaults*. Thomas "Tom" Cruise Mapother, IV (1962) is an actor and producer. Malia Obama (1998) is first daughter of President Barack Obama and Michelle. A *Harvard University* graduate, she is writer and director known for *The Heart* (2023), *Swarm* (2023) and *West Wing Week* (2010).

Please pray for our country so that freedom will continue for all of us who are citizens and for others who want to be. The English in 1776 predicted it would not last. America was called a "social experiment," because it would be governed "by the people." An article in the *Washington Post* STYLE section, yesterday, *How will America fete 250?* refers to just two years from now.

**July 5, 2024**

Good morning, all 263. Today is **National Hawaii Day,** which recognizes the 50th state in the U. S. in 1959. I have been to Hawaii twice, once with my family on a boat ride around the west side of Kawaii where there are no roads. One beautiful and surprising sight was a lagoon of emerald water. Green foliage covers the mountains, making them look like accordions with their fluted sides. They are volcanic, having emerged from the sea eons of years ago.

I saw Mount Waialae, touted as the wettest place on Earth with an average of around 450 inches per year. In 1982, the mountain experienced an unimaginable 683 inches of rain, the highest ever recorded there. I was also in Tahiti, Hawaii was on my way back from Australia. I was amazed by the complicated branching of the banyan trees, which are actually native to India and brought to the Hawaiian Islands in 1873 by missionaries. I had the pleasure of visiting a high school classmate on Oahu who had moved there years ago where he had a business and reared his family. He is now deceased, but Ronald Darby is being remembered by our classmates on this musing list.

In 1811, Venezuela declared independence from Spain. I twice visited Caracas, Venezuela, on cruise ships. It was there where I first saw geraniums and marigolds growing as shrubs. The Caribbean Ocean was filled with jellyfish. In 1975, Cape Verde gained independence from Portugal. **In 1947, Larry Doby became the first Black player to play in the American League.** In 1954, record producer Sam Phillips recorded an unrehearsed performance by an unknown young truck driver named Elvis Presley. It's regarded as the beginning of the rock-and-roll revolution. In 1975, Arthur Ashe defeated the heavily favored Jimmy Connors to become the first Black man ever to win Wimbledon. In 1996, the world's first live cloned mammal was born. It was a sheep named Dolly.

Phineas Taylor (P.T.) Barnum (1810) was a showman, politician and businessman remembered for the Barnum & Bailey Circus. Jumbo, Tufts University's official mascot, was a male African elephant owned by P. T. Barnum, a Tufts trustee and benefactor. Jumbo was the largest elephant known at the time, standing approximately 12 feet tall weighing six tons. Barnum donated his stuffed hide to the college in 1889 when the pachyderm became the Tufts mascot. I saw Jumbo in 1973 when my daughter became a student at Tufts. Edie Falco (1963) is an actress who received four Primetime Emmy Awards, two Golden Globes, five Screen Actors Guild Awards, and a Tony Award nomination, best known in *The Sopranos*.

**July 6, 2024**

Good morning, all 293. Today is **National Fried Chicken Day,** and **Umbrella Cover Day.** The only Umbrella Cover Museum is in Peaks Island, Maine. It opened in 1996 when founder and curator Nancy Hoffman was not sure what to do with her leftover umbrella covers. Nancy opened her museum by finding others willing to donate their umbrella covers.

In 1785, the Continental Congress of the United States authorized the issuance of the U.S. dollar. The "dollar" had been in usage since the Colonial period when it referred to the Spanish dollar valued for its high silver content. The first 1,758 silver dollars were coined in 1794 and immediately delivered to the Mint Director for distribution to dignitaries for souvenirs. In 1853, William Wells Brown published "Clotel: The President's Daughter," first novel by an African American. He was an abolitionist, novelist, playwright, and historian born into slavery, who, at the age of 19, escaped to Ohio and later Boston where he became a prolific writer. In 1885, Louis Pasteur injected the first rabbit spinal cord suspensions containing progressively inactivated rabies virus into a 9-year-old boy. The boy survived and lived to age 64. In 1942, Anne Frank and her family went into hiding in Amsterdam, Holland. She wrote *The Diary of Anne Frank*. When in Amsterdam thirty years ago, I walked past the house. In 1957, African American Althea Gibson became the first Black tennis player to win the Wimbledon singles championship. In 1969, no-fault divorce was first legalized in California in 1969 by then-Governor Ronald Reagan, the first U.S. president who had been divorced. By 2010, every state had legalized no-fault divorce. In 1957, Paul McCartney met John Lennon for the first time at a church event in Liverpool, England, where the latter's band was performing. The duo would later form the Beatles. In 2009, African American tennis player Serena Williams defeated her older sister **Venus** to win her first **Wimbledon** singles title.

Nancy Davis Reagan (1921) was a film actress and U. S. First Lady from 1981 to 1989. Bill Haley (1925) was an African American singer and songwriter, considered the father of rock and roll, thanks to his 1955 hit *Rock Around the Clock*. Jeanette Helen Morrison "Janet Leigh" (1927) was an actress with a career spanning five decades. She and Tony Curtis are parents to actress Jamie Lee Curtis. George Walker Bush (1946) was a politician, businessman, and 43rd

President of the United States from 2001 to 2009. Sylvester Gardenzio Stallone (1946) is an actor and filmmaker.

**July 7, 2024**

Good morning, all 293. Today is **Global Forgiveness Day.** It is time to let go of the burden of grudges and anger and to forgive those who have wronged us. It is also **National Day of Rock 'n Roll,** and **National Koi Day.** Koi are colored varieties of carp fish kept for decorative purposes in outdoor ponds. My son has a small pond with them in northern California. For those interested in reviewing Moses' Ten Commandments to make sure you are keeping them all, they are found in Exodus 20: 2-17. I learned them as a child because they were recited as the Decalogue (meaning 10) in the *A.M.E. (African American Episcopal)* church my family attended.

Two people on my list responded about Maine. One told me it was too chilly in the summertime for swimming. The other, a former student, had visited the unique Umbrella Cover Museum in Maine and sent a video of her having fun with the owner. In 1928 the world celebrated the introduction of sliced bread. Some people living today are older than sliced bread. What bakers in the early 20th Century thought would be a passing fad became a staple in kitchens across the world. Otto Frederick Rohwedder invented the first bread slicing machine that cut a whole loaf at a time. But during World War II, the U.S. government stopped the sale of sliced bread because the slicers were made of steel and the bread was wrapped in waxed paper, both being necessary for the war effort. In 1958 President Dwight D. Eisenhower signed Alaska into statehood. In 1981 Sandra Day O'Connor was appointed to the U.S. Supreme Court by President Ronald Reagan. She was the first woman to be appointed.

Charles Tindley (1851) was an African American gospel music composer and minister in Philadelphia. I once toured his church called *Tindley Temple United Methodist Church*, named for its founder, Rev. Dr. Charles Albert Tindley. *We'll Understand It Better By and By* was written by him in 1905 and it is one of my favorites.

### HYMN: "WE'LL UNDERSTAND IT BY AND BY"

*"By and by, when the morning comes*
*All the saints of God are gathered home*
*We will tell the story how we've overcome*
*And we'll understand it better by and by....."*

**July 8, 2024**

Good morning, all 293. 'Tis **One Of Us Is Missing Day**, which memorializes our departed loved ones. My Great Grandmother, Elsie died in 1940 and hers was the first funeral I attended. I sorely miss my husband, Ed, to whom I was married for 62 years. He would be 97 on August 1st if he were alive. Addressed as "Chazzie," "Ed," "Edward," "Mr. Ed," "Mr. Moss," "Dad," "Pop," "Brother," and "Uncle Buddy" has been gone for nine years now and is missed by all who knew him.

In 951 A.D., the City of Paris was founded. The "Left Bank" was the intellectual district, while the Right Bank was known for business. In 1497, Vasco da Gama sailed from Lisbon and opened a sea route from western Europe to India by way of the Cape of Good Hope. In 1776, the first public reading of the Declaration of Independence was done by Colonel John Nixon in Philadelphia. That was the nation's Capital from May 10, 1775, until December 12, 1776. In 1889, the first *Wall Street Journal* was published. In 1918 Ernest Hemingway, an 18-year-old ambulance driver for American Red Cross, was struck by a mortar shell while serving on the Italian front during **World War I. 1914.** He became a novelist, short story writer and journalist best known for

*The Old Man and the Sea, The Sun Also Rises, A Farewell to Arms, For Whom The Bell Tolls,* all of which I have read. In 2000, Venus Williams won at Wimbledon for the first time, becoming the first Black female Wimbledon champion since Althea Gibson in 1957 and 1958.

John D. Rockefeller (1839) was one of the most influential figures in American business, as co-founder of *Standard Oil Company*. His innovative and ruthless business practices revolutionized the petroleum industry and established him as a leading figure in the American Industrial Era. Angelica Huston (1951), daughter of actor John Huston, is an actress, director and model known for portraying eccentric characters. She received an Academy Award and a Golden Globe Award, with nominations for three British Academy Film Awards and six Primetime Emmy Awards. Kevin Norwood Bacon (1958) is an actor who received a Golden Globe Award, a Screen Actors Guild Award, and a nomination for a Primetime Emmy Award.

**July 9, 2024**

Good morning, all 293. This day is **Black Women's Equal Pay Day,** and **Call of the Horizon Day.** I can relate to **Call of the Horizon Day,** having watched many sunrises and sunsets. I especially loved St. Petersburg Beach in Florida, where the sun drops into the Gulf of Mexico, sometimes with a green glow. It's Earth's moving away from the sun.

In 1777 the Declaration of Independence was read to Gen. George Washington's troops in New York. In 1937, a fire at 20th Century Fox's storage facility in Little Ferry, New Jersey destroyed most of the studio's silent films.

Thomas "Tom" Jeffrey Hanks (1956) is an actor and filmmaker known for comedic and dramatic roles and is regarded as an American cultural icon.

My guardian angel woke me in the night to ask me what number was stuck on the windshield of my car. Suddenly, I remembered that the number must be changed annually. When I checked in the morning, it was # 6, and this is the 7$^{th}$ month! Oops! I didn't want to be stopped by Virginia police, so, now # 7 is stuck on my windshield. *"For He shall give His angels charge over thee, to keep thee in all thy ways. They shall bear thee up in their hands, lest thou dash thy foot against a stone"* Psalms 91:11-12.

**July 10, 2024**

Good morning, all 293. A response to my Tuesday's message about sunrises and sunsets came from the oldest sage on this list. The 104-year-older wrote, *"the sun and everything in existence, planets, stars, galaxies, universes, - visible or invisible are on the move. Everything is on the move."* A cousin on this list asked me yesterday why the sticker with a number must be placed on my windshield. It is to be able to park our vehicles in the state of Virginia. Our vehicles must be inspected annually in order to get the sticker.

Today is **National Day of Prayer and Thanksgiving,** which stands as a call to humbly come before God to seek His guidance for our leaders and His grace to us as a people. My simplest prayer is, *"Please Lord."* And then turn it over to Him. That's all I can do. My worrying won't change a thing.

In yesterday's *Washington Post* was an obituary for Romay Johnson Davis, age 104 and a surviving member of the only Black unit of the Women's Army Corps (WAC) to serve overseas during World War II, diligently delivering mountains of mail from home. It was the 6888$^{th}$ Battalion about which a movie will be released on *Netflix* in January 2025. My stepmother, Alice Patterson Patience, was a member of the WACs. In her autobiography *Bittersweet Memories of Home*, she detailed her experiences in the segregated army which was not integrated until 1949.

In 1893, the trailblazing physician Daniel Hale Williams successfully performed one of the world's first open-heart surgeries at Provident Hospital in Chicago. He was one of three African

American physicians allowed to practice in Chicago at a time when many white-run hospitals refused to treat Black patients, much less hire Black doctors. In 1925, in Tennessee, the "Scopes Monkey Trial" began with John Thomas Scopes, a young high school science teacher, being accused of teaching evolution in violation of a Tennessee state law. In 1962, the U. S. Patent Office issued the Swedish engineer Nils Bohlin a patent for his three-point automobile safety belt "for use in vehicles, especially road vehicles." In 1973, the Bahamas gained independence from Britain within the Commonwealth. In 2019, the final Volkswagen Beetle, a coupe clad in Denim Blue paint, rolled off the assembly line in Puebla,

Mary McLeod Bethune (1875) was an educator who was active in national Black affairs and a special adviser to President Franklin D. Roosevelt. She was also a close friend of Eleanor Roosevelt, wife of the President.

**July 11, 2024**

Good morning, all 293. 'Tis **National Swimming Pool Day,** and **World Population Day.** Those fortunate enough to have access to a swimming pool, enjoy it today. As for blueberry muffins, I like anything made with blueberries.

When I visited the Public Library, I would carry home several books and read them before they were due. I never had a summer job. If I had been a boy, my father would have had me working in his shop with him, but it was far too dirty a business for a girl. I could have gotten myself killed one hot summer day when I disobeyed my father who had told me never to go on the railroad bridge near our house. It went over the Susquehanna River and several trains crossed it daily. Kids liked to cross it from the West Pittston side for fun. One day my neighbor and her friend decided to take a walk. I was expected to go home but didn't. When I asked to join them, they said, *"No, you'll be a chicken."* The bridge was built over blocks of cement called piles. My friend told me that if a train came on the bridge while we were on it, we'd have to jump down on the nearest pile. A train came barreling onto the bridge and we jumped onto a pile and watched it rumble overhead. I did not tell my father I had been on that bridge until I was a grown woman.

In 1804, Aaron Burr shot Alexander Hamilton to death in a duel. Vice President Burr was indicted but not arrested. Same 'ole politics. In 1848, John Quincy Adams, 6th U. S. President and son of 2nd President John Adams, was the first to be photographed. In 1914, Babe Ruth was sold to the Red Sox. He was an outstanding pitcher who hit long home runs, a feat unusual for any player in "the dead-ball era," which was the time from 1900 to Babe Ruth's emergence in Major League Baseball in 1919. In 1960, *To Kill a Mockingbird* by Harper Lee was published and became instantly successful.

John Quincy Adams (1797) was born. I am related to him on my mother's father's side, which I learned from my favorite genealogist who is on this list. I am a distant cousin. As I watch the politics in our nation, I am reminded of a Negro spiritual by the Bennett Choir when I was a member in 1951. It was made famous by great Gospel singer, Mahalia Jackson.

### HYMN: "HOLD ON"
*Hold on Hold on*
*Keep-a your hand on the plow, hold on.*
*Heard the voice of Jesus say Come unto me, I am the way.*
*Keep-a your hand on the plow, hold on.*
*When my way gets dark as night, I know the Lord will be my light.*
*Keep-a your hand on the plow, hold on....."*

**July 12, 2024**

Good morning, all 293. 'Tis **National French Fry Day,** and **New Conversation Day.** The *Washington Post* published yesterday something about "flounder" houses. In 1770 when people were purchasing property here, a house had to be built on it within two years. Some people did not have enough money, so, they built only half a house that would be sufficient to claim their property. Some of those half-built flounder houses remained the same for decades. Their roofs look like half a flat flounder fish's head, hence the name. Yesterday's *Post* article in the LOCAL LIVING section is *One of the last 'flounder' houses in Old Town*, which is what Alexandria, Virginia is called.

In 1862, President Abraham Lincoln signed a bill authorizing the Army Medal of Honor. In 1957, the first President to fly in a helicopter was Dwight D. Eisenhower. Also, the U.S. Surgeon General Leroy Burney connected smoking with lung cancer. In 1984, Walter Mondale chose Representative Geraldine Ferraro as his Presidential running mate. She was the first female candidate to represent a major political party. In 1987, in one of his most famous Cold War speeches, President Ronald Reagan challenged Soviet Leader Mikhail Gorbachev to "tear down" the Berlin Wall, a symbol of the repressive Communist era in a divided Germany. It finally got torn down.

Josiah Wedgewood (1730) was a potter who produced a ceramic medallion in support of the abolition of the slave trade. In 1759 he founded the *Wedgwood Company* which produces fine jewelry and china. I purchased a lovely blue brooch when I visited London. Henry David Thoreau (1819) was leading Transcendentalist, best known for *Walden*, a reflection upon living simply in natural surroundings. I have a copy of it. Milton Berle (Mendel Berlinger) (1908) was an iconic comedian and actor, hosting NBC's *Texaco Star Theater* and appearing in 75 television shows and 7 Broadway plays. Beulah Elizabeth Richardson (1920), known professionally as "Bea Richards," was an African American actress of stage, screen and television, and a poet, playwright, author, and activist. Harvey Lavan "Van" Cliburn Jr. (1934) was a pianist who, at age 23, achieved worldwide recognition when he won the inaugural International Tchaikovsky Competition in Moscow in 1958 during the Cold War. Denise Donna Nicholas (1944) is an African American actress in the ABC comedy-drama *Room 222* and in the NBC/CBS drama series *In the Heat of the Night*. Rolonda Watts (1959), my older brother's daughter, is an African American actress, producer, and television and radio talk show host, presently working in New York City. Finally, Lauren Brooke Baldwin (1979) is a journalist, television host, and author who was at CNN from 2008 to 2021, hosting CNN *Newsroom with Brooke Baldwin*.

**July 13, 2024**

Good morning, all 293. Today is **National Barbershop Music Appreciation Day, International Rock Day,** and **Embrace your Geekiness Day.** Embrace our geekiness today. The four-part harmony barbershop quartets are called so because in England and the U.S., barbershops served as social gathering places for men and making music. Once confined to males, in 1945 *Sweet Adelines* began as a small group of women who loved to sing, but it has evolved into an organization that spans the globe connecting singers around the world in song. I enjoy male barbershop singing, especially the basses.

In 1930, France defeated Mexico 4-1, and the United States defeated Belgium 3-0 in the first World Cup football matches played simultaneously in Montevideo, Uruguay. The World Cup has since become the world's most watched sporting event. In 1939, backed by trumpeter Harry James, Frank Sinatra recorded his first single, *From the Bottom of My Heart*. Ed's favorite Sinatra song was *My Way*. In 1949, the Vatican released its "Decree Against Communism." Pope Pius XII issued the Cold-war edict that excommunicated all communist

Catholics. In 1960, John F. Kennedy named Senator Lyndon B. Johnson as his running mate. On November 8, 1960, they defeated incumbent Vice President Richard Nixon and United Nations Ambassador Henry Cabot Lodge, Jr. In 1985 at Wembley Stadium in London, Prince Charles and Princess Diana opened *Live Aid*, a worldwide rock concert organized to raise money for the relief of famine-stricken Africans.

**July 14, 2024**

Good morning, all 294. 'Tis **National Mac and Cheese Day,** and **Pandemonium Day.** The word "pandemonium" first came about in the 17th Century in the poem *Paradise Lost* by John Milton, re-telling the biblical story of Adam and Eve's temptation in the garden by Satan. A long strip of cloth or paper marked in inches or centimeters came into general use around 1820, which was helpful to women responsible for sewing the family's clothing. I use it to hem a pair of slacks or jeans that are too long.

In 1798, the first direct U.S. federal tax on states was enacted to finance military build-up. Dwellings, land and slaves were subject to tariff. In 1853, the Exhibition of the Industry of All Nations opened at Crystal Palace in New York City. President Franklin Pierce attended the opening, which was the first World's Fair hosted in the United States. In 1933, all German political parties, except the Nazi Party, were outlawed. In 1946, Dr. Spock published *The Common Sense Book of Baby and Child Care.* In 1968, Atlanta Braves slugger Henry "Hank" Aaron hit his 500th home run in a 4-2 win over the San Francisco Giants. On April 13, 1954, Aaron became the last Negro League player to make his debut in the major leagues. In 1980, the Republican national convention opened in Detroit, where nominee-apparent Ronald Reagan said he would "make America great again." Sound familiar?

American folk singer-songwriter Woody Guthrie (1912) was famous for writing *This Land is Your Land*. Gerald Rudolph Ford, Jr. (1913) was the 38th U. S. President from 1974 to 1977 and the 40th Vice President under Richard Nixon from 1973 to 1974. John "Jack" Joseph Nicholson (1937) is widely regarded as one of the greatest actors of the 20th Century.

**July 15, 2024**

Good morning, all 294. Today is **Global Hug Your Kid Day, World Youth Skills Day, National Be A Dork Day,** and **I love Horses Day.** My Great Aunt Lillie had some currant bushes in her garden. The British include currants in their delicious scones which I love. I ate them for the first time at *Harrad's* in London where my daughter and I had "Tea" at 4:00 p.m. Brought home a green shopping bag which showed off that I had been there.

In 1090 during the first Crusade, Jerusalem was plundered by Christian forces. In 1805 Zebulon Pike led an exploring party in search of the source of the Mississippi River, reaching Colorado, where he spotted the famous mountain later named Pike's Peak. In 1955 eighteen Nobel laureates signed the Mainau Declaration against nuclear weapons which was later co-signed by 34 more. In 2006 the San Francisco-based podcasting company Odeo officially released Twttr —later changed to *Twitter*, which is a short messaging service (SMS).

Remembering today the words of wisdom from Dr. Norman Vincent Peale: *"The way to happiness: keep your heart free from hate, your mind from worry. Live simply, expect little, give much. Fill your life with love. Scatter sunshine."*

**July 16, 2024**

Good morning, all 294. Here are two responses to yesterday's musing for sharing with you. Thank you for telling me that you enjoy my musings. *"Mention of Pike's Peak brings back pleasant memories for I have driven, solo, up to Pike's Peak following a business trip in Vail, Colorado. It was a little scary, being so close to the edge of a road in such a steep area. I bought a souvenir magnet which proclaimed I'd visited Pike's Peak."* The response about currants *is from one of my former students:*

*"I use currents when I make Irish Soda Bread around St. Patrick's Day. I especially enjoy it with my black coffee with no sugar."* A fritter is anything which has been battered or breaded and deep fried. I enjoy them with maple syrup. Fritters were once a popular fare for families to stretch food.

In 1935 the world's first parking meters were installed in Oklahoma City, designed by Carl C. Magee. In 1941 American baseball player Joe DiMaggio set a Major League Baseball record for most consecutive games (56) with a hit. In 1945 the U.S. tested the first atomic bomb near Alamogordo, New Mexico, and the following month dropped atomic bombs on Hiroshima and Nagasaki, Japan, hastening the end of World War II.

In 1979 Saddam Hussein became president of Iraq. His brutal rule lasted 24 years and was marked by costly and unsuccessful wars with neighboring countries, as well as atrocities against the Iraqi people. What makes people so evil? Evil is everywhere when people allow it.

Birthdays included Ida B. Wells-Barnett (1862), African American journalist who led a crusade against lynching. Barbara Stanwyck (1907) was a film and television star, and when my Great Aunt Jessie (Great Aunt Lillie's younger sister) took me to see my first "grown-up" movie for my 13th birthday, it was *Double Indemnity* with Barbara Stanwyck and Fred McMurray. My 1st cousin, Jane came too, because her 14th birthday was a week later. Our Great Aunt Lillie would bake a cake for us.

## July 17, 2024

Good morning, all 294. 'Tis **National Hot Dog Day** and **Send an Electronic Greeting Card Day.** In 1955 Disneyland Park in Anaheim, California, opened and ran out of food and drinks early. Counterfeit tickets led to unexpectedly large crowds. In 1984 Rev. Jesse Jackson delivered his Rainbow Coalition speech at the Democratic National Convention.

Birthdays included John Jacob Astor (1763), an American real estate mogul and investor who made his fortune investing in real estate in New York City. He was the first multi-millionaire in the U.S., and he perished on the Titanic in 1912. Camilla Parker Bowles (1947) is Queen of the United Kingdom and wife of King Charles III. Angela Dorothea Merkel (1954) is the retired German Chancellor who served from 2005 to 2021 and was the first woman to hold that office. Marcenia Lyle Stone "Toni Stone" (1921) was the granddaughter of someone on this list. She was an African American professional baseball player who played in predominantly male leagues. In 1953, she played with a major-level professional baseball team, the Indianapolis Clowns, in the previously all-male Negro leagues.

## July 18, 2024

Good morning, all 294. This is **Insurance Nerd Day, Nelson Mandela International Day, National Caviar Day, Black Leaders Awareness Day,** and **National Sour Candy Day. Nelson Mandela International Day** was declared by the United Nations in November 2009. Nelson Rolihlahla Mandela (1918) was the country's first Black Head of State and first elected in a fully representative democratic election. He was an extremely brave South African anti-apartheid activist, politician and worthy statesman who served as the first president of South Africa from 1994 to 1999.

Today I scoured my pitiful looking tea kettle that sits on my stove through all kinds of cooking. "Curious George" is wondering if young homemakers know what "scouring" is. Looking for some responses.

Franklin Delano Roosevelt (1940), 32nd President, was nominated for an unprecedented third term, and later a fourth, after which Congress made the length of a U.S. presidency no more than two terms. James Brolin (1940) was an actor who received a star on the Hollywood Walk of Fame in 1998. He is the father of actor Josh Brolin and husband of Barbra Streisand, whose music I love, such as the beautiful song *People*. I became a fan of James Brolin when he played Steven Kiley on *Marcus Welby, M.D.* (1969–1976). Ed and I were faithful viewers.

Keeping each of you and our nation in prayer. There is no era in American history that I want to go back to. My simplest prayer is, *"Please, God, we need a sign from you."* And so, I wait.

**July 19, 2024**

Good morning, all 294. It is **Stick Out Your Tongue Day, National Football Day,** and **National Karaoke Day.** I cannot stick out my tongue because of my childhood upbringing. That and thumbing one's nose would be the same as a middle finger gesture nowadays. My Great Aunt Lillie didn't even like me to chew gum. *"Teachers do not chew gum,"* she reprimanded. Ladies didn't either, according to her. I'm of the opinion that we should not when in church. 'Tis just one of my idiosyncrasies.

Historical events were the great fire of Rome (64 BC), which destroyed much of the city, and the Women's Suffrage Movement (1848) to gain rights for women, notably the right to vote.

Birthdays were Edgar Degas (1834), French Impressionist artist famous for his pastel drawings and oil paintings. More than half his works depict exquisite ballerinas. My daughter and I are aficionados of impressionist painters. Percy Spencer (1894) was the inventor of the microwave oven. I bought my first one soon after my Great Aunt Lillie passed away in 1983. I thought about how much she would have liked it for warming leftovers.

**July 20, 2024**

Good morning, all 295. 'Tis **National Pennsylvania Day, National Woodie Wagon Day,** and **International Chess Day.** Pennsylvania was the second state to join the Union. During my first year at Wilkes College, freshmen had to take a Pennsylvania history class with that fact included. **National Woodie Wagon Day** honors the "woodie wagon, made from wood at a time when steel was needed for World War II. It remains one of the favorites of vintage car collectors. Buick's 1953 Super Estate Wagon and Roadmaster Estate Wagon were the last to retain real wood construction. I had several station wagons for toting my kids and their friends, but never a "Woodie." I have a van for toting my books when giving presentations or driving with *Bennett College* sisters to alumnae reunions in Greensboro, N.C. "Blue Belle" gets me around to church and the supermarket.

Historical events included Astronauts Neil Armstrong and Edwin "Buzz" Aldrin becoming the first men to walk on the moon after reaching its surface in their Apollo 11 lunar module in 1969, and America's robot spacecraft, the Viking I, successfully landed on Mars in 1976.

Alexander the Great (356 BC) created one of the largest empires in history, stretching from Greece to northwestern India. He claimed, *"I have no more worlds to conquer."* Humans have always been fighting. They want to take what other people have. Such is the story of the United States of America. How long had indigenous people lived here before the Europeans arrived and stole their land?

Gregor Mendel (1822) was a Czech biologist, meteorologist, and mathematician who established many of the rules of heredity, now referred to as the Laws of Mendelian Inheritance. I hope my former students on this list will remember my teachings on the genetics of Mendel's garden peas. It was my favorite topic to teach.

Today is my oldest grandchild's birthday. I hope he has a great one.

**July 21, 2024**

Good morning, all 294. 'Tis **National Be Someone Day,** founded by Project Harmony and meant to bring communities together through education and awareness and to help end child abuse.

In 1798 Napoleon's Army of Egypt used a new military tactic to defeat Egyptian forces at the Battle of the Pyramids. When I visited Egypt, in awe I beheld the Sphinx and the Pyramids. How they were built is still a mystery. In 1983 the world's lowest recorded temperature, −128.6 °F (−89.2 °C), was measured at Vostok Station, Antarctica. In 2011 the U.S. space shuttle program ended after 135 missions, as the orbiter *Atlantis* landed at NASA's John F. Kennedy Space Center at Cape Canaveral, Florida. I visited there once.

My publicist's birthday is today. It is also the birthday of my stepmother, Alice (1916), who was her parents' youngest child. Emma Lazarus (1849) was an author of poetry, prose and translations, as well as an activist for Jewish causes. She wrote the sonnet *The New Colossus*, which was inspired by the *Statue of Liberty* in 1883. Ernest Hemingway (1899) is famous for writing *The Old Man and the Sea*, about man's eternal struggle against nature. After he died in 1961, his home in Key West, Florida, became a museum and a home for 50 descendants of his cats, about half of which are polydactyl, that is, having six toes. I visited that museum. Norman Frederick Jewison (1926) was a Canadian American filmmaker who addressed social and political issues. *In the Heat of the Night* was my favorite movie produced by him. I remember the proud words spoken by actor Sidney Poitier when he was asked by the segregationist played by Carroll O'Conner what he was called in Philadelphia. *"They call me Mister Tibbs."*

Finally, Janet Wood Reno (1938) was the first female and 78th U.S. Attorney General from 1993 to 2001. My lawyer daughter had the pleasure of working under her at the Justice Department. Janet Reno was known for her support of women's rights including work life balance issues.

**July 22, 2024**

Good morning, all 294. 'Tis **Pioneer Day,** and **National Marine Weekday.** In 1866, Tennessee became the first state to be readmitted to the Union after the Civil War. In 1911, Yale University history professor Hiram Bingham, III found the Lost City of the Incas, Machu Picchu, in Peru.

Birthdays include Simon Bolivar (1783), who led what are currently the countries of Colombia, Venezuela, Ecuador, Peru, Panama, and Bolivia to independence from the Spanish Empire. I visited his home when I was on a Caribbean cruise, where I first saw geraniums growing as woody shrubs.

Alexander Dumas (1802) was a Haitian-born French novelist and playwright who is one of the most widely read French authors. He was the son of a French nobleman and Marie-Cessette Dumas, an African enslaved woman. Since the early 20th century, his novels have been adapted into nearly 200 films: *"The Count of Monte Cristo," "The Three Musketeers,"* more. Amelia Mary Earhart (1897) was an aviation pioneer who, on July 2, 1937, disappeared over the Pacific Ocean while attempting to become the first female pilot to circumnavigate the world. Jennifer Lynn Lopez Affleck (1969) is an actress, singer, dancer, and businesswoman, known as "J. Lo." She is credited with breaking barriers for Latino Americans in Hollywood and helping propel the Latin pop movement in music. May each of us be blessed today. Sing this song.

<u>**HYMN**</u>: *"Keep your hand in the hand of the Man who stilled the water,*
*Put your hand in the hand of the Man Who calmed the sea....."*

**July 23, 2024**

Good day, all 294. Today is **Peanut Butter and Chocolate Day,** and **National Gorgeous Grandma Day.** I never knew either of my grandmas, but I did know my Great Grandmother Elsie, who passed away at age 83 when I was 10. She was my father's grandmother and wife of the Civil War veteran, my Great Grandfather Crowder Patience. She was beloved by her numerous grandchildren who spent many Sunday afternoons at her home in West Pittston, Pennsylvania, where she loved to bake pies for them.

In 1777 Casimir Pulaski traveled to North America to help in the American Revolutionary War. He saved the life of George Washington at Brandywine. A bridge in Newark, New Jersey, near where I lived for 33 years, is named after him – Pulaski Bridge. In 1829 William Austin Burt patented the first typewriter, a rectangular wooden box with a depressed rotating lever that caused ink to be released onto a sheet of paper. The first practical typewriter was invented in 1873 by Christopher Latham Sholes with the "qwerty" keyboard of letters spread apart to avoid the jamming of the most used "hammers."

In 1872 Elijah McCoy, Canadian-born of African American descent, filed his first patent on the drip cup registered under the title "Improvement for Lubricators in Steam Engines." In 1904 Charles E. Menches conceived the idea of filling a pastry cone with two scoops of ice cream and thereby invented the ice cream cone for the World's Fair in St. Louis, Missouri. Andrew Lloyd Webber (1948) composed 21 musicals, and several of his songs have been widely successful outside of their parent musicals, such *I Don't Know How to Love Him* from *Jesus Christ Superstar*.

**July 25, 2024**

Good morning, all 294. Today is **St. James TG, National Intern Day, National Hire a Veteran Day,** and **National Hot Fudge Sundae Day.** I have learned that the **Feast of St. James the Apostle** is celebrated on July 25th. He and his brother John were the sons of Zebedee and among the first four Apostles chosen by Jesus. In mid-19th-century England, carousels became popular fixtures at fairs. The first steam-powered mechanical "roundabout" (merry-go-round), invented by Thomas Bradshaw, was at the Pot Market Fair in Bolton, Massachusetts in 1861. When I was a kid, there was a carousel at the Rocky Glen Amusement Park near where I lived, and every July our annual Sunday School picnic was there. The last time I was on a carousel was when my daughter was three years old. As I was standing next to her while her horse went up and down, I became very dizzy. Never again!

In 1866 Ulysses S. Grant was named General of the Army of the United States, the first officer to hold the rank. In 1965, at the Newport, Rhode Island Folk Festival, singer and songwriter Bob Dylan eschewed his acoustic guitar to go electric. The controversial performance is considered one of the most pivotal moments in the history of Rock and Roll.

Birthdays include Rosalind Elsie Franklin (1920), whose work was central to understanding the molecular structures of DNA and RNA. Her contributions were unrecognized during her life, since James Watson and Francis Crick took credit for the discovery. Same old story when it comes to women's achievements! Emmett Louis Till (1941) was an African American teenager abducted and lynched in Mississippi in 1955 after being accused of whistling at a white woman in her family's grocery store. Finally, Louise Brown (1978) was the first human to be conceived using in vitro fertilization (IVF).

**July 26, 2024**

Good morning, all 294. 'Tis **National Marine Week, National Bagel Fest Day, National Aunt and Uncle Day,** and **One Voice Only Day.** It is also part of **National Marine Week.** I am thinking of my great aunts and uncles and my father's brothers and their wives. They were all very kind to me when I was growing up. Uncle Bob, my father's oldest brother, is who got me interested in our family history **since he** was. I guess he thought I could follow his lead since I was always asking questions. And I have. He would be pleased.

In 1775 the U.S. Postal Service was established by the Second Continental Congress, and Benjamin Franklin was named the first Postmaster General. In 1943 Los Angeles experienced its first major smog as a "hellish cloud" descending on the city, limiting visibility. In 1948 U.S. President Harry S. Truman signed Executive Order 9981, which finally abolished racial segregation in the U.S. military. In 1990 the Americans with Disabilities Act (ADA) was signed into law by President George H.W. Bush. Finally, in 2016 at the Democratic National Convention, Hillary Clinton was officially nominated for President of the United States, thus becoming the first woman to top the presidential ticket of a major party in the United States.

Birthdays included George Catlin (1796), who was born in Wilkes-Barre, Pennsylvania, where I lived for six years. He specialized in portraits of Native Americans on the American frontier. George Bernard Shaw (1956) was an Irish playwright, critic, polemicist, and political activist whose most financially successful work, *Pygmalion,* was adapted into the popular movie *My Fair Lady* which I loved with Audrey Hepburn. I also saw the Broadway play starring Julie Andrews. Shaw won the Nobel Prize for Literature in 1925. Sandra Annette Bullock (1964) is an actress and film producer who received an Academy Award and a Golden Globe Award. She was the world's highest-paid actress in 2010 and 2014 and was named one of *Time's* 100 most influential people in the world in 2010.

### July 27, 2024

Good morning, all 294. **Today is National Walk on Stilts Day.** The memory for me is the stilt. Near where I grew up on Washington Street lived a red-headed girl named Carol who was the coalman/iceman's daughter. She wore stilts and went walking through the neighborhood on them.

In 1586 Walter Raleigh took the first tobacco from Virginia to England. In 1789 U.S. Congress established the Department of Foreign Affairs, now the State Department. In 1947 New York Yankees catcher Yogi Berra had a 148-game errorless streak. We both lived in Montclair, N.J. at the same time but were not neighbors. In 1954 the classic film *On the Waterfront*, with Marlon Brando's most iconic performance, was released. In 1974 the House Judiciary Committee recommended that President **Nixon** be impeached.

A notable birthday in 1922 was Norman Lear, who produced and wrote over 100 shows, including *All in the Family, Sanford and Son, One Day at a Time, The Jeffersons,* and *Good Times.*

### July 28, 2024

Good morning, all 294. Today is **World Day for Grandparents and the Elderly Day** and **National Parents Day.**

In 1868 the 14th Amendment was adopted, giving citizenship to all persons born in the U.S. including former slaves. It included my great-great grandparents, Thomas and Hester Lawrence. In 1870 they were listed on the U.S. Census with two names, which was the first time Blacks needed a last name.

Birthdays included Jackie Kennedy Onassis (1929), who was the First Lady from 1961 to 1963. Elizabeth Cheney (1966) is an attorney and politician who represented Wyoming in the House of Representatives from 2017 to 2023 and was Chair of the House Republican Conference from 2019 to 2021. Bill Bradley (1943) is a politician and former professional basketball player. He served three terms as Senator from New Jersey. Finally, the U.S. 4x100-meter freestyle relay team earned its first gold medal after holding off Australia by 1.07 seconds.

**July 29, 2024**

Good morning, all 294. 'Tis **National Chicken Wing Day,** and **National Lipstick Day.** The wing is my favorite part of chicken. And I never go outdoors without my lipstick, the redder the better. I enjoy lasagna, but it's too much work for this old lady. The Bengal is my favorite tiger, most likely because it was Bloomfield High School's mascot.

In 1981 Prince Charles and Lady Diana Spencer were wed in St. Paul's Cathedral.

**July 30, 2024**

Good morning, all 294. Today is **National Cheesecake Day**. The Marlboro Bakery near where I lived in N.J. made New York cheesecake. Climbing a mountain is what I remember doing as a teenager on Saturday mornings after my chores had been completed. Several girlfriends and I would ride our bicycles to the bottom of a mountain five miles from West Pittston, and then we'd climb the mountain to the top.

In 1619 in Jamestown, Virginia, the Virginia General Assembly convened for the first time. In 1932, United States Vice President Charles Curtis declared, *"I proclaim open the Olympic Games of Los Angeles, celebrating the tenth Olympiad of the modern era."* A crowd of 100,000 spectators watched 1,332 athletes, representing 37 nations paraded into the stadium. In 1965, President Lyndon Johnson signed Medicare into law. Henry Ford (1863) was founder of Ford Motor Company. His corporation developed and manufactured the Model T for working-class people. Laurence Fishburne (1961) is an African American actor, three-time Emmy Award and Tony Award winner.

**July 31, 2024**

Good morning, all 292. 'Tis **National Raspberry Cake Day, National Jump for Jellybeans Day,** and **Uncommon Instruments Day.** Raspberry cake is my favorite. I first tasted an avocado when my niece introduced me to guacamole and chips in Gilroy, California. She is on this list. Jellybeans are addictive to me. I'll eat the black ones first because I love licorice. Some uncommon instruments are the double contrabass flute, harpsichord, hurdy-gurdy, jaw harp, and auto harp. Many Baroque composers of the 17$^{th}$ & 18$^{th}$ Century played the harpsichord, including Bach and Handel, who used combinations of keyboard and bass instruments.

In 1498 Columbus discovered Trinidad and Tobago, both inhabited by the Arawak Indians who were killed by European settlers. Just another story about man's inhumanity which is the story of the New World that was stolen from its original inhabitants. In 1971 Apollo 15 astronauts James Irwin and David Scott first used the four-wheeled battery-powered Lunar Roving Vehicle to extensively explore the Moon's surface, in particular the Hadley-Apennine site. In 1981, Arnette Hubbard, the first female President of the U.S. National Bar Association, was appointed. The National Bar Association is the nation's oldest and largest global network of predominantly Black American attorneys and judges.

**August 1, 2024**

Good morning, all 292. Today is Ed's 97$^{th}$ birthday. It would be my Great Grandmother Elsie Patience's 168$^{th}$. It's **National Girl Friend Day, National Minority Day,** and **Respect for Parents Day**.

In 1498 Christopher Columbus was the first European to visit Venezuela. In 1774 the element oxygen was discovered. Oxygen is like God, omnipresent. In 1834 slavery was abolished in the British Empire after Parliament passed the Slavery Abolition Act of 1833. In 1876 Colorado became the 38$^{th}$ state to enter the Union, earning it the moniker "Centennial State."

In 1936, during the Olympics in Germany that African American Jesse Owens won his medals and shocked and angered Adolf Hitler. Black Americans were randomly beaten by White Supremist men as a result of Owens' win. 'Twas the first sign of the terrible things to come that became World War II. In 1987 African American boxer Mike Tyson defeated Tony Tucker and was unanimously recognized as heavyweight champion of the world.

Notable birthdays are Herman Melville (1819), author of the classic *Moby-Dick*, and Henrietta Lacks (1920), was an African American woman whose cancer cells are the source of the HeLa cell line, the first immortalized human cell line and one of the most important in medical research.

**August 2, 2024**

Good morning, all 296. Today is **National Ice Cream Sandwich Day.** I have not had a *Klondike* ice cream bar in years.

In 1776 the Continental Congress declared freedom from Great Britain when delegate Richard Henry Lee of Virginia declared, *"That these United Colonies are, and of right ought to be, free and independent States."* In 1790 the first United States Census was conducted. In 1870 the first underground tube railway in the world, the Tower Subway, opened in London, England, running beneath the River Thames. In 1964 U.S. President Lyndon Johnson signed into law the historic *Civil Rights Act* in a nationally televised ceremony at the White House.

Birthdays include Jack Warner (1892), Canadian American film executive of Warner Brothers Studios in California. James Baldwin (1924) was an African American writer and Civil Rights activist who garnered acclaim for his essays, novels, plays, and poems. *Go Tell It on the Mountain* is ranked by *TIME* magazine as one of the top 100 English-language novels. Alysa Stanton (1963) is an American Reform Rabbi and first African American female Rabbi in a small majority-white synagogue in Greenville, NC. John Carroll O'Connor (1924) found widespread fame as Archie Bunker in the CBS television sitcom *All in the Family* and *Archie Bunker's Place*.

**August 3, 2024**

Good morning, all 296. 'Tis **National Jamaican Patty Day and National Watermelon Day.** The first time I bit into a beef patty was when Ed and I visited Jamaica and were invited to a home for dinner. The food was too hot and the rum cake too strong for this teetotaler's taste. I enjoy my Jamaican patties mild.

In 1492 Christopher Columbus set out on his first voyage to the "New World." It may have been "new" to Europeans but not to the Indigenous people living there for centuries. In 1963 the Beatles played their last performance at The Cavern Club in Liverpool.

Birthdays include Elisha Otis (1811), founder of the Otis Elevator Company. In 1853 he invented a safety device that prevents elevators from falling if the hoisting cable fails. I may not always remember his name, but I will bless his memory every time I get into an elevator.

Ernie Pyles (1900) traveled with American soldiers in North Africa, Italy, and France during WW II. His daily columns became so popular that they were published in 400 newspapers nationwide and he received the *Pulitzer Prize* in 1944. Anthony Dominick Benedetto, "Tony Bennett" (1926) was a jazz and pop singer with 20 Grammy Awards, a Lifetime Achievement Award and two Primetime Emmy Awards. He was Ed's and my favorite singer because he sang "our song"— *Because of You.*

**August 4, 2024**

Good morning, all 296. Historical events include that in 1862 the U.S. Government collected its first income tax. In 2007 the launch of Phoenix, weighing 1,477 pounds and positioned on a Delta rocket took place at Cape Canaveral Air Force Station. In 2024 Simone Biles Owens, African American gymnast, had earned 10 Olympic medals and 30 World Championship medals, make her the most decorated gymnast in history and one of the greatest gymnasts ever.

Birthdays include John Venn (1834), noted for Venn diagrams. I mentioned once that I feel like I am in the middle of a Venn diagram with all of you friends and family members. You know me and some of you know each other. 'Tis beautiful to me. Louis Armstrong (1901), nicknamed "Satchmo," was an African American trumpeter and vocalist, among the most influential figures in jazz. His career spanned five decades, and he was a favorite of my Ed's, who proudly played the *Star-Spangled Banner* on his trumpet in high school. Raoul Wallenberg (1912) saved thousands of Jews in German-occupied Hungary during the Holocaust in the later stages of World War II. Barack Hussein Obama II (1961) was our 44th President from 2009 to 2017. He was the first African American President in U.S. history.

### August 5, 2024

Good morning, all 296. Tis **National Underwear Day and National Work Like a Dog Day.** The first underwear dates back to prehistoric times when humans wore loincloths. Men wore linen shorts or "braies" during the Middle Ages when women wore "shifts" under their dresses next to their skin. Slips later replaced shifts.

Although the origins of "work like a dog" are not known, it likely refers to actual working dogs like Sheepdogs and Sled-dogs. I once saw sheep dogs at work in Scotland, where the dogs would drive the sheep into small cages to be sheared. Even after the advent of the airplane, dog teams in Alaska were used for transportation, particularly in Native villages. When I was in Alaska on a cruise, we stopped by the home of Libby Riddles, the first woman winner of the Iditarod.

In 1620 the Mayflower departed from Southampton, England, on its first attempt to reach North America. In 1861 President Lincoln imposed the first federal income tax by signing the Revenue Act. Strapped for cash to pay for the Civil War, Lincoln and Congress imposed a 3 percent tax on annual incomes over $800. In 1966, NYC broke ground on the World Trade Centers.

### August 6, 2024

Good morning, all 296. 'Tis **National Night Out,** and **National Scuba Day.** Being a diver, my son will be interested in **Scuba Day**. When he was in high school, he asked for parental permission to take lessons at the YMCA in Montclair and then go to a nearby quarry to take a scuba diving test in a wet suit. He passed and was certified. I cannot swim but made sure my children learned when they were young. I can't dance, either! One of my favorite treats is a root beer float. I hope to have one when I am on vacation next week.

In 1945 an American B-29 Superfortress dropped the world's first atomic bomb on Hiroshima, Japan. 80,000 people were killed, one of whom was the mother of a Japanese student who studied at *Bennett College* in the late 50s and wrote her autobiography called *One Sunny Day*. In 1962 Jamaica became independent after 300 years of British rule.

Birthdays include Alfred Tennyson (1809), awarded the Chancellor's Gold Medal at Cambridge for *Timbuktu*. I read *Charge of the Light Brigade* in high school. Lucille Ball Arnez (1911) was recognized by *TIME* magazine in 2020 as one of the most influential women of the 20th Century and first to appear on television pregnant in 1952. Andy Warhol (1928) was a leading figure in the Pop Art Movement. Leslie Odom Jr. (1981) is an African American actor, singer and songwriter who gained recognition for his portrayal of Aaron Burr in the musical *Hamilton*.

**August 7, 2024**

Good morning, all 296. This is **Purple Heart Day** and **National Opportunity Day.**

In 1606 the first performance of Shakespeare's *Macbeth* was performed in Hampton Court Palace for Kings James I. I read it in a high school English class, and we had to memorize passages like Lady MacBeth's sorrowful soliloquy. George Washington (1782) ordered the creation of the first Badge of Military Merit (Purple Heart).

Birthdays included Louis Leakey (1903), Kenyan British paleoanthropologist and archaeologist who, along with wife Mary, showed that humans evolved in Africa. Ralph Bunche (1904) was an African American who received the 1950 Nobel Peace Prize for his 1940s mediation in Israel.

**August 19, 2024**

Good morning, all 296. Today is **World Photography Day,** and **World Humanitarian Day.** I have returned to Alexandra. Thanks to you who have been waiting for my musing concerning my trip to Virginia Beach with family and friends. I had my special treat of *Kohr's* frozen custard swirl of orange and white in a waffle cone, and a lox and bagel breakfast at the Pocohontas restaurant.

My first knowledge of a camera was a *Kodak Brownie* that cost one dollar. The Brownie put black and white photography into the hands of amateurs like my Great Uncle Pete. The Polaroid camera during the 1960s took instant photos in color, but it disappeared due to bankruptcy. Sadly, many of my Polaroid photos have faded, but not completely, thankfully. Uncle Pete's wife, my Aunt Rosie, was thrifty. *Hitchner's* cookie factory was near her home, and she would give me a brown paper bag and 25 cents to take there to be filled with broken cookies

Important events included Benjamin Banneker (1791) writing to President Thomas Jefferson urging for justice for African Americans like himself. He was a mathematician, astronomer, almanac author assisting with the initial survey for constructing Washington, D.C.

I wonder how many of you know about the geographic line that separated Pennsylvania from Delaware and Maryland. Surveyor Jeremiah Dixon and Astronomer Charles Mason identified the dividing line between the slave states south of it and the free-soil states north of it. The next time you travel north by car, look for the *Mason-Dixon Line*, part of our American history. Finally, President Franklin Roosevelt (1939) issued a proclamation designating Orville Wright's birthday as a National Aviation Day.

Birthdays include Orville Wright (1871), who, with his brother Wilbur, built and flew the world's first successful airplane on December 17, 1903, at Kitty Hawk, N.C. Gabrielle Bonheur "Coco" Chanel (1883) was founder of the *Chanel* brand. William "Bill" Clinton (1946) was the 42nd President of the U. S. from 1993 to 2001. He was twice Governor of Arkansas before that.

**August 21, 2024**

Good morning, all 296. 'Tis **Child Vision Awareness Month** and **National Senior Citizens' Day.** I remember a past musing about wearing my first pair of glasses at age 10. Praying for blessings on all Seniors on my list, including me. I was concerned about my forgetfulness, but I passed my cognitive tests. Just getting old was my doctor's evaluation.

In 1619 in Jamestown, Virginia, twenty Africans aboard a Dutch ship were the first Blacks to be settled as involuntary laborers in the North American British Colonies. In 1896 the dial telephone was patented. In 1911 a dispatcher in the *New York Times* office sent a telegram around the world via commercial service. In 1971 the *National Aeronautics and Space Administration (NASA)* sent into space aboard the unmanned spacecraft *Voyager II* a phonograph record containing information about Earth and extraterrestrial beings. In 1912 the *Plant Quarantine Act* authorized the *U.S. Department of Agriculture (USDA)* to inspect agricultural products for restricting the entry into our country infested agricultural goods, as well as to organize border quarantines.

Birthdays include William "Count" Basie (1904), African American jazz pianist, organist, composer, and bandleader who formed the "Count Basie Orchestra" in 1935. In 1936 he took it to Chicago for a long engagement and a first recording. Wilton "Wilt" Chamberlain (1906) was a 7ft. African American professional basketball player who played in the National Basketball Association for 14 seasons. I wanted to know the greatest heights of basketball players and discovered that Victor Wembanyama of France, Zach Edey of Canada, and Boban Marjanovic of Serbia are NBA players, each 7ft. 4in. tall.

**August 22, 2024**

Good morning, all 298. 'Tis **World Plant Milk Day.** By celebrating plant milks that are better for our bodies and the planet, **World Plant Milk Day** is a step on the way toward health and sustainability. When I visited my Great Aunt Florence's farm, I would get a pail full of raw milk which was not pasteurized. I don't know the method she used to separate cream from whey so she could churn her butter, but I remember watching her make butter in her churn. There are 17 different plant milks, including coconut, oat, soy and almond milk, which I enjoy the most.

Birthdays include Claude Debussy (1802), whose most famous work, *Clair De Lune,* was what many of us who took piano lessons had to learn. It is one of my favorite classics; also Dr. Denton Cooley (1920), who performed the first successful artificial human heart transplant in the U. S. in 1968. I remember how excited people were when that happened.

**August 24, 2024**

Good morning, all 298. 'Tis **National Waffle Day** and **St. Bartholomew History Day.** I turned to my *Bible* to read about Bartholomew, one of the Apostles.

In 1814 during the *War of 1812*, British troops led by Major General Robert Ross burned down the White House, the Capitol, the Library of Congress, and other government buildings in Washington, D.C. In 1869 the waffle iron was patented by Cornelius Swarthout, a Dutch American inventor. I enjoy waffles covered with strawberries and real whipped cream. At The Palisades Park in NJ, I tasted my first Belgian waffle with strawberries and whipped cream. The term "palisades" refers to the landscape along the western side of the Hudson River. It's a high cliff near the river. In 1759 William Wilberforce was a leader of the abolishment of the slave trade. Named for him, Wilberforce, Ohio was a hub on the Underground Railroad during the Civil War. *Wilberforce University* is an HBCU affiliated with the African Methodist Episcopal Church, and the first college to be owned and operated by African Americans.

Ava Marie Duvernay (1972) is an African American filmmaker and recipient of two Primetime Emmy Awards, two NAACP Image Awards, a BAFTA Film Award, and a BAFTA TV Award, as well as a nominee for an Academy Award and Golden Globe.

**August 25, 2024**

Good morning, all 298. In 1910 the Yellow Cab was founded. I use it here in Alexandria. In 1916 the U.S. Department of Interior formed the National Park Service under President Woodrow Wilson. In 1944 Paris was liberated by the French 2nd Armored Division and the U.S. 4th Infantry Division after more than four years of Nazi occupation during World War II.

Birthdays include Sir Sean Connery (1930), who was first to portray the fictional British secret agent James Bond and starred in seven Bond films between 1962 and 1983. Blair Underwood (1964) is an African American actor who starred in the NBC series *L.A. Law* from 1987 to 1994.

## August 26, 2024

Good morning, all 300! I have been busy working on my manuscript, and now that I reached 300 friends and family members, I have sufficient musings for my 10th book titled *Good Morning All: Musings of a Nonagenarian.* In it will be my memories over 93 years, as well as historical events, fun facts, birthdays, and spirituality that I have been sharing with you for the past 2 1/2 years. I hope some of you will be inspired to record your positive thoughts, too. Everybody has stories that need to be told, especially about our ancestors. Muse and write about them!

'Tis **National Webmistress Day.** My webmistress is a lovely woman and member of my church. Please check my website at www.journeyfromthepast.com, featuring the monument dedication in Edenton, N.C., for my great grandfather Crowder and his brother Thomas, both of whom served in the Union Army during the Civil War. My family knew nothing of Thomas until I discovered his name on the wall surrounding the monument at the *African American Civil War Museum* in Washington. Who was that Patience soldier whose name is inscribed there? I had to find out and eventually discovered that he was my great grandfather's brother. What joy it has been to discover a number of his descendants! Some are on this list.

In 1907 Eri Weisz "Harry Houdini" escaped from chains underwater in 57 seconds at Aquatic Park in San Francisco, CA. In 1920, the Nineteenth Amendment to the U.S. Constitution gave us women the right to vote. In 1945 Japanese diplomats boarded the USS Missouri to receive instructions on Japan's surrender at the end of WWII. I was thirteen years old.

Birthdays include Mary Teresa Bojaxhiu, "Mother Teresa," (1910), an Albanian Indian Catholic nun who was founder of the Missionaries of Charity and a Nobel Prize recipient; Katherine Johnson (1918), who was an African American mathematician whose calculations of orbital mechanics as a NASA employee were critical to the success of the first U.S. crewed spaceflights. She was the "brain" in the movie *Hidden Figures.* Geraldine Ferraro (1935) became the first female vice-presidential nominee; finally, Branford Marsalis (1960) is an African American saxophonist, composer and bandleader of the *Branford Marsalis Quartet.*

## August 27, 2024

Good morning, all 300. It would be my Daddy's 118$^{th}$ birthday. Charles Edgar Patience was the fourth son of Harry and Elsie Miller Patience, and their six sons were called the "Patience Boys."

In 1883 in Java, Indonesia, the *Krakatau Volcano* erupted, killing 36,417. In 1940 Nestle registered the trademark for *Toll House* to market Ruth Wakefield's new chocolate chip cookies. These are my favorite "made from scratch" cookies with walnuts. In 1964 Disney's *Mary Poppins* was released at Grauman's Chinese Theater on the Hollywood Walk of Fame in Los Angeles. I loved it because when I was a kid, I had read the book.

A notable birthday was Lyndon Johnson (1908), who served as the 36th U. S. President from 1963 to 1969, after the assassination of President John F. Kennedy.

Thank you, Lord, for blessing me with so many friends and family members.

## August 28, 2024

Good morning, all 300. First, thank you to those who send me responses or make corrections to my musings. You are the first editors of the book I will publish in 2025!

In 1963 Dr. Martin Luther King Jr. delivered his "I Have a Dream" speech before 200,000 people who marched on Washington, D.C. It was just before I returned to work after a maternity leave. One of my White colleagues asked, *"Don't you think you should earn it?"* I was astounded and told her that her ancestors had still been in Europe when my ancestors were "earning it" here, and it has been paid in full! In 2024 there are STILL great inequities. Will Dr. King's dream ever be fulfilled?

*"This is the day that the Lord hath made. I will rejoice and be glad in it"* Psalm 118:24.

## August 29, 2024

Good morning, all 300. Today I am sharing a response with you from yesterday's musing. *"The original 1963 March on Washington was held on a Wednesday! I had the good fortune of being able to attend. Did not get close to any well-known people but could hear their voices booming over the 'loudspeakers.' At the time, I didn't realize the impact that August 28, 1963, would have on the world. I discarded my pennants and other little souvenirs. It was an exciting day, yet calm, peaceful and beautiful. The crowd was well dressed...some looked like they were going to church."*

Someone else sent me this response. *"Just a thought: Perhaps expound on the March on Washington to include the WHOLE name – 'March on Washington for Jobs and Freedom'."* 'Tis **National Lemon Juice Day,** and **According to Hoyle Day.** I may have mentioned before that I squeeze lemon juice and put it in ice trays to keep in my freezer for future use. **According to Hoyle Day** interests me because I did not know its origin. It honors adhering to the rules and regulations, and it pays tribute to Edmond Hoyle, English expert on card games. There are so many different talents among us humans.

In 1825 Portugal recognized the independence of Brazil. In 1873 the United Kingdom legislated the abolition of slavery in its empire. In 1959 The U.S. Air Force Academy opened in Colorado Springs, CO. In 1966 the Beatle's last performance was in Candlestick Park in San Francisco, CA. In 2005 *Hurricane Katrina* hit most of the U.S. Gulf Coast, causing great devastation and loss of life.

Birthdays included Ingrid Bergman (1915), who starred in *Casablanca* and *Gaslight*, two of my favorite movies. I recommend them to you when they are on *Turner Classics*. Also, John McCain (1936) who was a Vietnamese prisoner for five years before he was released. He became a U. S. Senator from Arizona from 1987 until his death in 2018. Michael Jackson (1958) was an African American dancer, songwriter, singer, dubbed "King of Pop." He was the first artist in music history to have Top 10 singles in five different decades on the Billboard Hot 100.

## August 31, 2024

Good morning, all 300. 'Tis **National Matchmaker Day,** which interests me because I am curious about matchmaking in different cultures. It may have begun when I read Pearl Buck's books about families in China where matchmaking was expected. Then in the play and movie *Dolly,* and *Fiddler on the Roof* in the Orthodox Jewish culture. Lastly, on Netflix there have been several shows about matchmaking among African and Indian families. I knew an Italian neighbor whose father had come from Italy and was married to the young girl chosen for him in America.

A notable birthday is Richard Gere (1949), actor who starred in *An Officer and a Gentleman*, *Pretty Woman,* and *Runaway*. Ed and I enjoyed him in all three movies.

## September 1, 2024

Good morning, all 300. 'Tis **National Forgiveness Day, National Little Black Dress Day,** and **Papaya Month.** I tasted papaya for the first time in Hawaii, and I loved it. The little black dress brings back memories of women's attire before wearing trousers was acceptable. All ladies had a "little" black dress in their wardrobe for funerals and other solemn occasions. On the other hand, a scarf or shawl could jazz it up when women did not have extensive wardrobes. I have a black dress and a black suit for when I need black clothes. I prefer to wear purple nowadays to funerals. To remain solemn and respectful, some people will wear navy blue or gray.

In 1952 *LIFE* magazine published Ernest Hemingway's *Old Man and the Sea*. In 1954 *Rear Window* opened in theaters, directed by Alfred Hitchcock and starred Grace Kelly and James Stewart. I remember seeing it. I was a Hitchcock fan.

Birthdays included Gloria Estefan (1957), who is an eight-time Grammy winner, Presidential Medal of Freedom recipient and rated one of the Top 100 greatest artists of all time by *Billboard*. Thanking God for another Sabbath on which to serve Him.

**September 2, 2024**

Good morning, all 300. 'Tis **Labor Day** and **West Indian Parade Day. Labor Day** was always important in my life until 1992 when I retired. It was the end of schools' summer vacation and back to work again. I think it is horrible that Virginia kids are already back. The **West Indian Day Parade** interests me. It is held annually in Brooklyn, NY. When I was growing up in Wyoming Valley, PA, some Black people living there were called "West Indians." Mrs. Anduze, a friend of my great aunts and a proud usher at my church, came from St. Johns. When I began cruising, I visited several of the islands from which West Indians had migrated to the U.S. I have learned that the West Indians in today's parade may have ancestry from any of the Caribbean islands. I would love to attend for the camaraderie, lively music and delectable food.

In 1882 the first Labor Day observance was held in New York City when 10,000 workers took unpaid leave and marched through the streets to demonstrate the strength of the trade and labor organizations. In 1898 *McCall* magazine was first published. In 1901 Vice President Theodore Roosevelt advised *"Speak softly & carry a big stick."* In 1945 on V-J Day, the formal surrender of Japan aboard USS Missouri marked the end of World War II. In 1985 Jerry Lewis' 20th *Muscular Dystrophy Telethon* raised $33.1 million. In 2021 *Hurricane Ida* hit the Northeast with record flooding in New York and New Jersey. A state of emergency was declared.

An important birthday is Keaunu Reeves (1964). In 2022 *TIME* magazine named him one of the 100 most influential people in the world. Have a fun-filled Labor Day, hopefully with some friends and family members. I am alone, but not lonely. I am blessed to have all of you.

**September 3, 2024**

Good morning, all 300. 'Tis **Skyscraper Day** and **U.S. Bowling League Day.** Skyscrapers have only been around for 129 years. The world's first skyscraper was completed in 1885 in Chicago, standing 138 feet with 10 stories. When I lived in New Jersey, there is a mountain called Eagle Rock, which partially blocks the New York City skyline. For a quarter, we could use binoculars to identify the Empire State Building, Chrysler Building, and the Twin Towers. We all remember how the New York skyline was tragically changed on September 11, 2001. Back in the day, there were Easter sunrise services at Eagle Rock Park, and I attended and enjoyed the Salvation Army Band.

As for bowling, I have tried, but my left-handed self could not do it. I had a bowling physical education teacher at *Bennett College*. Her advice was to watch her and do the opposite. Didn't work. My balls always landed in the gutter.

In 1609 the English navigator Henry Hudson sailed into the harbor of present-day New York City and then up the river named after him. In 1777 an American flag was flown in battle for the first time during a Revolutionary War battle at Cooch's Bridge, Delaware. In 1783 the Treaty of Paris was signed between Great Britain and the American colonies, bringing the Revolutionary War to its conclusion. In 1838 African American Frederick Douglass escaped from slavery at age 20 and would become an abolitionist, author, human rights advocate, and U.S. Ambassador to

Haiti. In 1894 Labor Day was celebrated for the first time as a legal holiday in the U.S. In 1976 NASA's robotic spacecraft, Viking 2, landed on Mars and relayed information about the planet's atmosphere, soil, and rocky surface.

**September 4, 2024**

Good morning, all 300. 'Tis **National Wildlife Day** and **National Legacy Day. National Wildlife Day** is important to me as a biology teacher for 33 years. It focuses on endangered animals and the ongoing efforts to conserve them. Once they are gone, they are gone forever, like the Mammoth, Sloth, Dodo bird, Auk, California grizzly bear, ivory-billed woodpecker, and passenger pigeons of North America. Wildlife also includes plants. To maintain the proper balance in nature, they need to be available to herbivores. In turn, herbivores are eaten by carnivores, and that's how God created it. He gave Adam the mandate to take care of the earth. Humans are not doing a great job nowadays. Yesterday's *Washington Post* SPORTS section had a photo of the 2nd tallest man in the world at 8 feet and .85 inches tall.

In 1807 Robert Fulton began operating scheduled passenger service on his steamboat between New York and Albany. In 1888 the Eastman Kodak Company was founded by inventor George Eastman. In 1893 English author Beatrix Potter wrote the story of "Peter Rabbit" for a 5-year-old boy.

In 1957 nine African American students integrated *Central High School* in Little Rock, Arkansas. They had to make their way through a dangerous crowd shouting obscenities and throwing objects. The National Guard prevented the crowd from entering the school or harming the students. Only three of the nine graduated from that high school, opening the door to integration in the South. In 1998 Google was founded. In 2002 Kelly Clarkson was the first American Idol winner.

Birthdays include Mitzi Gaynor (1931), whose most notable film was *South Pacific* for which she was nominated for the *Golden Globe Award* for Best Actress. It is one of my favorite films. Beyoncé Knowles (1981) is an African American singer-songwriter and actress, lead singer of the R&B group Destiny's Child before launching a hugely successful solo career.

**September 5, 2024**

Good morning, all 300. Tis **National Cheese Pizza Day,** and **National Be Late For Something Day. National Cheese Pizza Day** is one of my favorites, having grown up surrounded by many Italian friends, several of whom are on this list. They are among my "golden friends." The first time I tasted pizza was at the annual block party at *Immaculate Conception Church* near where I lived. In high school, Friday was pizza night for my "gang" and me. We'd go to *Fetch's Restaurant* and order two squares each. All my "gang" is with the Lord now: Ruthie, Jean, Joan, Lucille, and Marguerite. Thank you, God, for the good memories of good friends. I try not to be late for anything, so **National Be Late For Something Day** does not catch my fancy.

In 1698 Russia's Peter the Great imposed a tax on beards. He wanted to bring Russian society in line with Western European models. The Tsar empowered police to forcibly shave those who refused to pay the tax. In 1882 some 10,000 workers assembled in New York City to participate in America's first Labor Day parade. In 1939 the United States declared neutrality in World War II, until the Japanese bombed Pearl Harbor on December 7, 1941. I was nine years old.

**September 8, 2024**

Good morning, all 300. 'Tis **National Grandparents' Day,** and I will celebrate today, being the grandmother of six— four girls and two boys.

In 1504 Michelangelo unveiled his famous sculpture *David* in Florence. In 1664 the Dutch surrendered New Amsterdam to the British, who renamed it "New York." In 1974 President Gerald Ford pardoned his disgraced predecessor, Richard Nixon, for crimes committed while in office. Peter Sellers (1925) was famous for starring in *Pink Panther.* Patsy Cline (1932), my contemporary, was considered one of the most influential vocalists of the 20th Century and among the first country music artists to cross over into pop music. At age 30, she was killed in an airplane crash. She was one of my favorite country and western singers. I love her rendition of *Crazy.* Bernie Sanders (1941) is the senior United States Senator from Vermont. For 10 seasons and 106 episodes, Dr. Henry Louis Gates Jr. has been helping people explore their family history. *Finding Your Roots With Henry Louis Gates Jr.*, is the PBS series that delved into the family trees of almost 250 people. Congratulations to Dr. Gates.

**September 9. 2024**

Good morning, all 300. Today's celebrations are **International Day to Protect Education from Attack,** and **Teddy Bear Day. Teddy Bear Day** reminds me of my trips to California where my granddaughter, who is on this list, and I would visit the Teddy Bear Factory to purchase cute outfits for her teddy bears. She had several and they were all very well dressed. A surprise arrived one Christmas from her. It was a "Granny" Teddy Bear. She wears red shoes and a fancy red hat and spectacles. She looks like the "Red Hat" lady which I was once upon a time, and a *Delta* Soror which I am forever. Thanks for your thoughtfulness, Granddaughter.

In 1850 California became the 31st State. In 1908 Orville Wright made the first one-hour airplane flight in Ft. Myers, Virginia. That was two years after my father was born. I wonder what Grandfather Harry thought about that amazing feat. In 1926 the National Broadcasting Company was created. In 1956 Elvis Presley appeared on the popular *Ed Sullivan Show.* Ed and I were faithful viewers on Sunday nights. In 2000 African American Venus Williams won her first U.S. tennis title. In 2015 Apple unveiled the iPad Pro and iPhone 6s in San Francisco, California.

Colonel Harland Sanders (1890) was founder of the Kentucky Fried Chicken chain and later acted as the company's brand ambassador and symbol. Otis Redding, Jr. (1941) is regarded as one of the greatest singer-songwriters in the history of American popular music and a seminal artist in soul music and rhythm and blues. Someone living in St. Augustine, Florida, sent me three photos of the celebration of its founding in 1565. Thanks.

**September 10, 2024**

Good morning, all 300. 'Tis **World Suicide Prevention Day,** and **National TV Dinner Day.** I remember how exciting TV dinners were back in the day. Each person could have their choice of a meal which we ate on TV tables. That was before microwaves. They were heated in ovens, I presume. Gone was sitting at the dinner table together as a family. I still have a single TV table in my basement. They were all the rage after televisions were placed in living rooms.

In 1608 John Smith was elected to lead Jamestown. Pocahontas married John Rolfe, who took her to England where she died young. In 1846 Elias Howe took out a U.S. patent for a lockstitch sewing machine. I remember the first sewing machines in school when I was in the 7$^{th}$ grade. They were treadle machines that we had to use our feet to power. Later came electric ones. I did a lot of sewing when I would create many of my own outfits, since we were not allowed to wear trousers to work. I made my daughter's clothes until she was in the 7$^{th}$ grade and asked me to stop. I decorated with rickrack which she hated but I loved. The next time I made her anything was to create maternity clothes when she was expecting her first child in the summertime. No rickrack on them. I will give my sewing machine it to anyone who would like to have it.

In 1913 the Lincoln Highway was the first paved road for automobiles to cross the United States. It started in Times Square in New York City and ended in Lincoln Park in San Francisco, California. Over the years, the highway has become just a memory, with just a few reminders along the way. The few segments of U.S. 30 that still carry the memory are known as "Lincoln Way." After the Interstate Highway System was formed in the 1950s, Route 80 became the primary coast-to-coast route from New York City to San Francisco.

**September 11, 2024**

Good morning, all 300. 'Tis **National Hot Cross Bun Day,** and **Librarians Remembrance Day,** and **Patriot Day.** I remember Miss Hazel Poe, librarian at the *West Pittston Public Library* when I was a kid. When I was in $2^{nd}$ grade, Miss Hewitt walked our class to the library, and we got our own library cards. Miss Poe said we could read any of the books on the right side of the library. In $7^{th}$ grade, we could go to the left side. By the fifth grade, I had read all the books on the children's side and Miss Poe let me pick out "A Lantern in Her Hand" by Bess Streeter Aldrich. She told me that I should read all the books by that author, and that became my habit. I was the first one in my class to ask to go on the adult side of the library.

In 1941 construction began on the Pentagon. In 1967 the *Carol Burnett* became a Saturday night staple. Ed and I enjoyed watching her show. In 2011 Americans watched in horror as terrorist attacks left nearly 3,000 people dead in New York City, Washington, D.C. and Shanksville, Pennsylvania. One was a member of my church, Ada Mason and another was Leo Snyder. I remember their names as they are being called in New York City this morning on the $23^{rd}$ anniversary of that sad day. That day, I was talking on the telephone with someone who had invited me to lunch when suddenly, she asked, *"Do you have your television on?"* I turned it on to see the second plane hit the Twin Towers, and our safe world was suddenly shattered. At 8:46 a.m. on this **Patriot Day**, I am watching the 9/11commemoration on CNN.

Jeh Charles Johnson (1951) is an African American lawyer and former U. S. Secretary of Homeland Security from 2013 to 2017. Taraji Penda Henson (1970) is an African American actress who received a Golden Globe Award and nominations for an Academy Award and a Tony Award.

I love the *Washington Post's* description of James Earl Jones, who passed away on September $9^{th}$ at age 93. "He was an African American actor whose thundering Old Testament voice and commanding presence established him as one of his generations most indelible performers, whether in Shakespeare tragedies, the *Star Wars* franchise or a Disney animated classic." He was one of my favorite actors, especially as the iconic voice in *Lion King* which I love.

**September 12, 2024**

Good morning, all 300. 'Tis **National Video Game Day, Gym Day,** and **National Hump Day.** I have never played a video game, but my son did. It never caught my fancy. Neither does going to a gym to exercise. I've bought memberships but am not disciplined enough to go to classes. I do enjoy walking with a buddy, though, along the Potomac River.

Some time ago a Delta Soror on this list informed me that Wednesday is called "Hump Day." I had never heard that before but thought it was catchy, and so I will use it now each week. Yesterday, another friend on this list sent me the following information about it. *"Wednesday first came to be known as hump day since the 1950s. The expression figures Wednesday, the middle of the workweek, as the hump people get over to coast into the weekend."*

I just read that Angela Bassett won her first *Grammy Award* for outstanding narration on *National Geographic's Nature* documentary called *Queens*. She is one of my favorite African

American actresses. In 1992 Mae Jemison became the first African American woman to travel in space.

Birthdays included Jesse Owens (1911), who was an African American track and field athlete who won four gold medals at the 1936 Olympics in Germany where he stunned Adolph Hitler. Linda Gray (1940) is best known for her role on the CBS television drama *Dallas*. I was addicted to it on Friday nights. Barry White (1944) was an African American singer and songwriter, two-time Grammy Award winner.

**September 13, 2024**

Good morning, all 300. 'Tis **Yom Kippur** and **National Peanut Day.** I try to be a positive thinker and have no superstitions. How about you? I'd like some chocolate covered peanuts today.

In 1814 the British bombarded Fort McHenry in Baltimore Harbor for 25 hours during the War of 1812. During this time, the *Star-Spangled Banner* was written by Francis Scott Key. In 1965 the *Today Show's* first totally colored program was broadcasted. Tyler Perry (1969) is an African American actor, filmmaker and playwright, among the country's billionaires!

**September 15, 2024**

Good morning, all 300. **Hispanic Heritage Month** begins today. *Hola amigos y amigas* who are on this list. 'Tis also **Indoor Plant Week.** I have several lovely plants in my living room and kitchen that put oxygen into the atmosphere for us to breathe. Remember photosynthesis? Do you have some plants in your house? If not, you should. In 1821 several Latin American countries declared their independence from Spain. In 1978 African American boxer Muhammad Ali won the world heavyweight championship for the third time with his victory over Leon Spinks.

William Howard Taft (1857) was the 27th U. S. President from 1909 to 1913, and the 10th U.S. Chief Justice from 1921 to 1930, the only person to have held both offices.

**September 16, 2024**

Good morning, all 295. 'Tis **International Cinnamon Raisin Bread Day, Stay Away From Seattle Day,** and **Trail of Tears Commemoration Day.** My mother lived in Seattle for years. I enjoy a slice of cinnamon raisin bread slathered with Philadelphia cream cheese. Makes a delicious and healthy snack.

In 1620 the Mayflower set sail from Plymouth, England. Half of the Mayflower's 102 travelers died during the first year. Survivors were two of my maternal ancestors, Priscilla Mullins and John Aldin, who married and had eleven children, one of whom was my mother's father's ancestor. She was Ruth Alden Bass which I learned from a genealogist on this list. In 1940 the first peacetime draft in the history of the United States was imposed for men ages 21 and 36. There were 20 million eligible young men, but 50 percent were rejected the first year for health reasons or illiteracy. My father's youngest brother was drafted at age 30. He was wounded at the Anzio Beachhead in Italy where most of his comrades were killed. My father was rejected because he had a heart murmur from rheumatic fever when he was a child.

Betty Joan Perske, "Lauren Bacall" (1924) was named the 20th greatest female star of classic Hollywood cinema by the American Film Institute. She married Humphrey Bogart. Riley "B.B." King (1925) was an African American blues guitarist, singer, songwriter, and record producer. He introduced shimmering vibrato and staccato picking that influenced blues electric guitar players.

Stuffed green peppers where I grew up were called "mangoes. Originally, English people had settled there but had a favorite food back in England that was stuffed into a mango. Since they could not get mangoes in Pennsylvania, they began stuffing green peppers and called them mangoes. And so, the custom has continued. A West Pittstonian on my list tells me so.

**September 17, 2024**

Good morning, all 300. This is **National Pet Bird Day** and **National Apple Dumpling Day.** Pet birds in homes were popular in my younger days. My son had one. Do any of you have a bird? I enjoy a warm apple dumpling with a dollop of vanilla ice-cream. Yummy.

In 1683 Dutch scientist Anton van Leeuwenhoek was first to report the existence of bacteria, and he was known as the "Father of Microbiology." In 1978, negotiated by President Jimmy Carter, the Camp David Accords led to a peace treaty between Egypt and Israel. I have visited Egypt. I was supposed to travel to Israel on the same trip, but a war had broken out in Israel weeks before. I never got to walk where Jesus walked, but people from my church did, and several were baptized in the Jordan River. I was baptized was in Bermuda in the Atlantic Ocean. I had always wanted to be immersed and so I stood **by a visiting pastor who was conducting a revival at a local church. I was in my bathing suit. No white robe, as is customary. It was one of my "mountain-top" experiences.**

**September 18, 2024**

Good morning, all 300. **Chiropractic Founders Day** commemorates the day Daniel David Palmer performed the first chiropractic adjustment in 1895 for Harvey Lillard, who had lost most of his hearing 17 years earlier. After the adjustment, Lillard's hearing returned. I have been going to a chiropractor for 60 years now. I began when I kept getting bursitis in my shoulders and hips. I highly recommend the young chiropractor I see here in Alexandria. He keeps me agile. Happy Founder's Day, Dr. B. Thanks for being on my musing list.

I sent a birthday card to a former student whose mother and I have been good friends for years. She was one of a small number of Black students at Bloomfield High School in 1958, and I was the first Black teacher, so we bonded. She is on my musing list. Her daughter is a world traveler. In 1789 the first loan was made to pay the salaries of the President and Congress. In 1793 President George Washington laid the cornerstone of the Capitol Building in Washington, D.C.

Samuel Johnson's (1709) conceived the **"Dictionary," not as** a schoolroom prop, but as a literary work. Frankie Avalon (1940) is an American **singer and former teen** idol. James Gandolfini Jr. (1961) was best known for his portrayal of Tony Soprano in HBO's television series *The Sopranos*. He won three Emmy Awards, five Screen Actors Guild Awards and one Golden Globe Award.

Someone on my list, wrote to me about her Italian heritage. I had interviewed her mother for my first book *Created to Be Free* 25 years ago. She and the mother of one of my classmates told me how they had been discriminated against by some of their teachers after immigrating from Italy. Where I grew up, there were 25 different dialects spoken in the anthracite coal mines. Men and their families had migrated from Europe for work. When anthracite coal was discovered in northeastern Pennsylvania, the Welsh came because they were experienced coal miners. Then the Irish arrived with their brogue and Catholic religion. Then the Italians, the Polish, and others. All were discriminated against, but the second generation were children who met in school. There were parochial schools, too, attached to Catholic churches. My best friend in high school had attended her Czechoslovakian elementary school in Pittston.

At first inter-marriages were forbidden, but I knew of one between an Italian girl and a Polish boy. The word "immigrant" was invented in the U.S. in the early 19th Century when Noah Webster added it to his "Dictionary." Before that people who moved from one place to another were called "migrants."

**September 19, 2024**

Good morning, all 300. I have no prejudice against anyone, having made friends of many ethnicities, a number of whom are on my musing list. During one of the last years of my teaching in 1992, I had in the same class a Buddhist from China, a Jew from Russia and a Muslim from Egypt. And I was a Black Christian. I loved them and they loved me. Recent *Washington Post* headlines remind me of this verse from the Bible: *"If a man says, I love God, and hatest his brother, he's a liar; for he that loveth not his brother whom he hath seen, how can he love God, whom he hath not seen? And this commandment have we from Him, that he who loveth God love his brother also"* 1 John 4:20-21.

**September 20, 2024**

Good morning, all 300. Today is **National Queso Day** and **Fried Rice Day**. "Queso" is a Spanish word that translates to "cheese" in English. We are talking about a melted cheese dip that is a snack or appetizer, which I enjoy. I also enjoy Chinese fried rice with shrimp. I had it for the first time when a Chinese restaurant opened in Scranton, PA, in the early 50s.

In **1893** New Zealand became the first country to grant women the right to vote. In 1973 Billie Jean King won the "battle of the sexes" against Bobbie Riggs who was a Wimbledon champion. She won! In 1984 the *Cosby Show* aired for the first time. In 2011 the official U.S. military policy of "don't ask, don't tell" ended, allowing gay, lesbian and bisexual service members to serve their country. Sophia Loren (1934) is one of the last surviving stars from the Golden Age of Hollywood Cinema, making over 100 films. Ed and I were avid movie-goers.

**September 22, 2024**

Good morning, all 300. 'Tis **National Singles Day.** I guess I am among the singles today, but it is not by choice. My Ed has been gone for ten years. My chiropractor has suggested an apple a day for energy after my 3-4 o'clock nap. Also, since 1982, the ringing of the Peace Bell at the United Nations in New York honors the **International Day of Peace**.

In 1780 American General Benedict Arnold committed treason against America during the American Revolution. In 2008 the final baseball game was played at the historic Yankee Stadium. Nicole Richie (1981) was adopted by Lionel Richie when she was nine years old, and she became a media personality, fashion designer and actress.

**"LET THERE BE PEACE ON EARTH"**
**Written by Jill Jackson-Miller and Sy Miller in 1955.**
*"Let there be peace on earth and let it begin with me.*
*Let there be peace on earth.*
*The peace that was meant to be.*
*With God as our father*
*Brothers all are we.*
*Let me walk with my brother in perfect harmony....."*

**September 22, 2024**

Good morning, all 300. 'Tis **Elephant Appreciation Day.** I appreciate the elephant, which is the mascot of *Delta Sigma Theta, Inc.*, the sorority to which I belong. We all wear elephant jewelry, especially earrings and pins, and we also have pachyderm collections in our homes.

In 1862 President Abraham Lincoln issued a preliminary Emancipation Proclamation to free all enslaved people in the states in rebellion, if those states did not return to the Union by January 1, 1863. They did not. North Carolina was one of them. My paternal great grandfather, his parents and his brother were enslaved at that time in Edenton, N.C. The two young brothers absconded from slavery to join the Union Army in 1864 after the Yankees had penetrated the South.

In 1961 the Interstate Commerce Commission (ICC) outlawed discriminatory seating on interstate buses after six months of protests by the Freedom Riders. Someone on my list was a Freedom Rider when she was a college student. I was in a segregated bus terminal in 1960 when I rode from Greensboro to Charlotte, N.C., on the back of a bus with my five-year-old daughter. We flew back home to N.J. from an unsegregated airline terminal in Charlotte, NC.

Andrea Bocelli (1958) is a magnificent tenor who became blind at age twelve after suffering a brain hemorrhage as the result of a soccer accident. In 1998 he was named one of *People* magazine's 50 Most Beautiful People. I can sit for hours listening to his wonderful voice. Debbie Boone (1946) was best known for her 1977 hit, *You Light Up My Life*. I loved her rendition of the song. Her father is Pat Boone, an American actor, singer, composer, and television personality. Her mother is the daughter of Red Foley, who made a major contribution to the growth of country music. I enjoyed watching his show on Sunday evenings, especially the talented young cloggers.

**SONG: "YOU LIGHT UP MY LIFE"** (6 verses sung by Debbie Boone)
*"So many nights I'd sit by my window*
*Waiting for someone to sing me his song*
*So many dreams I kept deep inside me*
*Alone in the dark but now you've come along*
*And you light up my life*
*You give me hope to carry on*
*You light up my days and fill my nights with song....."*

Thanking you all for lighting up my life. A friend on my list recently sent me a subscription to the *Daily Word*. I also receive the *Guidepost,* a gift from a young cousin on my list. Thank you.

**September 23, 2024**

Good morning, all 300. 'Tis **National Snack Stick Day** and **Redheaded Appreciation Day.** I have never had a snack on a stick. Looks too salty. As for redheads, I've known several who were very freckled. The country with the most redheads is Ireland, while Scotland is the second.

In 1889 Nintendo was founded by Fusajiro Yamauchi in Japan to produce handmade hanafuda playing cards, which led to a toy business and ultimately the video game industry. The company entered the electronic gaming industry in the 1970s. In 1909 the *Phantom of the Opera* was first published as a serial and then was released in volume form in late March 1910. In 1932, the year I was born, the Kingdom of Saudi Arabia was founded from four distinct regions.

"Ray Charles" Robinson Sr. (1930) lost his sight when he was seven years old. He was an African American singer, songwriter, musician, and composer, regarded as one of the most iconic musicians in history and referred to as "The Genius." One of his most famous songs is *Georgia on My Mind*. He is one of my favorite singers. John Coltrane (1926) was an African American jazz saxophonist, bandleader and composer who is among the most acclaimed figures in the history of jazz and 20th-Century music. Bruce Springsteen (1949) is a rock singer, songwriter and guitarist, nicknamed "The Boss." He released 21 studio albums during a career spanning six decades and is most famous for the song *Born in the U.S.A.* Bob Marley (1945) was a reggae singer, guitarist and songwriter. One of his best-known songs is *One Love*.

Someone on my list shared the following prayer with me yesterday:

> *"What's the best way to motivate ourselves?*
> *My first mother-in-law taught me a prayer.*
> *She said, 'Lord, lead me today to those I need and those that need me."*
> *I said, 'Man, what a way to approach a day.*
> *Lead me to those I need and those that need me.'"*

I need all of you. I hope the feeling is mutual.

**September 24, 2024**

Good morning, all 300. 'Tis **World Rivers Day.** I grew up a block from the *Susquehanna River*. Now I reside a mile from the *Potomac River* on which Washington, D.C. sits. The longest river I was ever on was the *Nile* in Egypt. I learned about the *Niagara River* flowing north when my family was visiting Fort Niagara. I was aways Ed's navigator before the GPS was invented. On my map I looked at the names of towns as we passed them while travelling along the *Niagara River*. Interestingly, the *Hudson River* that I had to cross when I lived in New Jersey to get to New York City flows both ways. I have no idea how that is possible.

In 1789 the U.S. Congress passed the Judiciary Act, which created the federal judiciary system, the office of the Attorney General, and the Supreme Court. In 1853 Cornelius Vanderbilt embarked on the first-ever round-the-world trip by yacht. In 1952 KFC opened its first franchise in Salt Lake City, Utah. In 1957 President Dwight D. Eisenhower sent federal troops to Little Rock, Arkansas, to enforce the right of nine Black students to attend *Central High School*, an all-white high school. In 1968 *60 Minutes* premiered on CBS-TV.

Francis Scott Key Fitzgerald (1896) was a writer best known for *The Great Gatsby* in 1925. Jim Henson (1936) was a puppeteer who was the creator of the famous *Muppets.*

**September 25, 2024**

Good morning, all 300. 'Tis **National Comic Book Day, National One Hit Wonder Day, and National Lobster Day.** Debbie Boone fits into the **One Hit Wonder Day** with *You Light Up My Life*. In 1896 Richard Felton drew a comic-book featuring The Yellow Kid in a sequence titled "McFadden's Row of Flats." In 1933 a comic book, "Famous Funnies," was published. Many believe the work to be the first *real* comic book. I enjoyed *Batman, Superman, Wonder Woman,* and *Archie*. We kids used to exchange comic books. Some adults thought they would keep us from reading real books. They did not keep me from doing so. I love lobster tail dipped in butter and lemon. It is really the lobster's abdomen. Former biology students on my list may remember dissecting crayfish, where you learned that fact. The bodies of the two animals are identically formed. I will not order a whole lobster nowadays because it is too much work for me to break the claws to get what's inside.

In 1919 President Woodrow Wilson suffered a severe stroke that left him incapacitated until the end of his presidency in 1921. It became one of the great crises in presidential succession. In 1934 baseball legend Lou Gehrig played his 1,500th consecutive game. In 1981 Sandra Day O'Connor, the first female U.S. Supreme Court Justice, was sworn in.

Barbara Walters (1929) originated *The View*. Michael Douglas (1944) is the son of actor Kirk Douglas and husband of Catherine Zeta-Jones. He is an actor and film producer who has received two Academy Awards, five Golden Globe Awards, a Primetime Emmy Award, the Cecil B. DeMille Award, and the AFI Life Achievement Award. Will Smith II (1968) is an African American actor, rapper and film producer who has received an Academy Award, a Golden Globe Award, a BAFTA Award and four Grammy Awards. Catherine Zeta-Jones (1969) is a Welsh American actress who has received Academy and Tony Awards. For her film and humanitarian work, she was appointed Commander of the Order of the British Empire in 2010. She and husband, Michael Douglas, share birthdays and often celebrate together with a large cake that has two candles in the shape of the number 25 to represent their age gap.

**September 27, 2024**

Good morning, all 300. People are being devastated by Hurricane Helene. One of you is living in the area but is safe. 'Tis **World Tourist Day, National Chocolate Milk Day,** and **National Corned Beef Hash Day.** Canned corn beef was a favorite of Ed's. I would place eggs in hollows of hash in a frying pan and cover them while cooking. I haven't had any in years. Scrapple was another favorite of Ed's, as is my son's. I don't eat any of those salty foods anymore. I eat oatmeal every day with various toppings. As a child, chocolate milk was a special treat. Tastes change, as do circumstances like cooking for one, which I do not enjoy.

In 1908 Henry Ford's first Ford Model T automobile left the Piquette Plant in Detroit, Michigan. In 1919 the Democratic National Committee voted to allow female members. In 1920 New York became the first state to enact comprehensive housing reforms. In 1954 the *Tonight Show* premiered, hosted by Steve Allen. Ed and I went to see it one night. In 1979 the United States Congress approved the Department of Education. In 1986 the Beatles' 1963 hit *Twist and Shout* re-entered the U.S. singles chart after its first appearance 23 years earlier. Samuel Adams (1722) was a Founding Father of the United States who signed the Declaration of Independence.

**September 29, 2024**

Good morning, all 300. Today Catholics celebrate **Michaelmas** or **The Feast of Michael and All Angels**, which signifies the end of the harvest and the beginning of shorter days. 'Tis also **National VFW Day** and **Gold Star Mother's Day and Family Day.** My memory of gold stars goes back to World War II. I took piano lessons at the Immaculate Conception School from Sister Mercia. I walked there and passed a particular house that had in its front window a small flag with three gold stars which meant three sons had died in the war. I did not know the family, but my heart was suffering for the parents. My Uncle Harold, my father's youngest brother, served during that war.

In 1789, the United States Congress passed the Act for the Establishment of Troops, legalizing the existing army. In 2005 John G. Roberts Jr. was sworn in as the 17th Chief Justice of the U. S.

Gene Autry (1907) nicknamed the "Singing Cowboy," gained fame starting in the 30s by singing on radio, in films, and on television for more than three decades. I enjoyed his music when I was young. Jerry Lee Lewis (1935) was described as "rock 'n' roll's first great wild man." Bryant Gumbel (1948) is an African American sportscaster best known for his 15 years as co-host of NBC's *Today*. Gwen Ifill (1955) became the first African American woman to host a nationally televised U.S. public affairs program with *Washington Week in Review* in 1999. She died young from cancer.

**September 30, 2024**

Good morning, all 300. This is **Positive Aging Week** which applies to me and some of you. I remember thinking people 65 should stop driving. One of my Sorors is still driving all over Alexandria at age 94. I am still driving, but only where I know I am going, like to church. 'Tis also **National Chewing Gum Day.** Mayans chewed chicle, a substance from the sapodilla tree, as early as 200 A.D. to freshen breath and remove maize from their teeth. "Chiclets" is an American brand of candy-coated chewing gum manufactured by Perfetti Van Melle.

In 1927 Babe Ruth became the first player to hit 60 home runs in a single season. In 1954 The USS Nautilus, the world's first nuclear-powered submarine, was commissioned in Groton, Connecticut. In 1962 James H. Meredith was escorted into the University of Mississippi by U.S. Marshals to integrate the University of Mississippi. He is noted for reading the 1966 "March Against

Fear" from Memphis to Jackson in protest of the physical violence that African Americans faced while exercising their right to vote.

Birthdays included Deborah Kerr (1921), who was the first person from Scotland to be nominated for an Oscar. Her best-known movies were *An Affair to Remember* and *From Here to Eternity,* both of which I enjoyed very much and like to watch on *Turner Classics*. Cissy Houston (1933) is an African American gospel and soul singer who was backup singer for Elvis Presley, Mahalia Jackson and Aretha Franklin. She is cousin to Dionne Warwick and mother to the late Whitney Houston. When Whitney was a teenager in a choir at the New Hope Baptist Church in Newark, N.J., I took my teenage choir there just to hear that talented girl sing. Johnny Mathis (1935) was an African American singer whose albums achieved gold or platinum status and 73 made the Billboard charts. *Chances Are* was one of his popular songs when I was a young woman.

A *Washington Post* article called *A Sought-after Florida beach town digs out after Hurricane Helene*. It is about St. Petersburg, Florida, where I spent a number of winters. Ed and I might have purchased a winter home there. *Helene* is exactly what he feared.

**October 1, 2024**

Good morning, all 300. 'Tis **Homemade Cookies Day.** If I were making cookies, they would be my favorite Toll House chocolate chip cookies with walnuts.

I will be away from October 8th until the end of the month traveling with my daughter to CT, PA and NYC, after which my granddaughter from California will be visiting me. I will be attending my 74th high school reunion in Pennsylvania. It is an All-Classes reunion, so I might not be the oldest one in attendance. I know of four others who will be there from my 1950 class. All are in good health right now. We are blessed.

In 331 B.C. Alexander the Great of Macedonia defeated Darius III of Persia in the Battle of Gaugamela, which ended the Persian Empire. Persia is present-day Iran. There has always been warfare. History is filled with it. Humankind is cruel, always wanting what someone else has. In 1868 *Little Women*, by Louisa May Alcott, was published by Roberts Brothers in Boston. It was one of my favorite teenage books. In 1885 special delivery mail service began in the U.S. In 1903 the first baseball World Series game was played. In 1949 the People's Republic of China was founded.

Walter Matthau (1921) starred in ten films with his friend Jack Lemmon, including *The Odd Couple*. Ed and I enjoyed their movies. Jimmy Carter (1924) is the longest living President at 100 years old. Dame Julie Andrews (1935) had a career of eight decades, during which she garnered an Academy Award, a BAFTA Award, 2 Emmy Awards, 3 Grammy Awards, 6 Golden Globe Awards, and nominations for 3 Tony Awards. My daughter and I loved her in *Sound of Music*.

**October 2, 2024**

Good morning, all 300. It is **Walk to School Day,** and **National Custodial Worker's Recognition Day**. Thanks for the following response from yesterday:

*"I went skiing years ago, probably in the '70's and stayed at the Trapp Lodge in Stowe. One of the Trapp's greeted you at the door at dinner each night and instruments were played throughout dinner. I always loved the* Sound of Music *movie too, so it is a great memory to be able to say I met one of the Trapps. My cross-country skiing there was wonderful, too. The peace of the woods, untouched snow, and deer roaming was just magical."*

I remember Mr. Francis, custodian at the *Washington Street School* where I spent grades one and two, who would stand in the middle of Exeter Avenue so we little kids could cross it safely. Of course, we had to wait for his permission. Thanks to Mr. Francis for watching out for us.

As far as walking to school, I did so every day for twelve years, whether it was in rain, shine, sleet, or snow. Fathers who owned cars probably had driven to work before our school hours, and mothers did not drive when I was little. Imagine that!

I love fried scallops. Surprising that my Ed did not like them, since he could slurp down raw oysters with lemon juice and tabasco sauce, which I cannot do.

In 1789 George Washington sent the *Bill of Rights* to the States for ratification. In 1836 Charles Darwin returned to England after a five-year journey on the *HMS Beagle*. His observations and collected specimens from this journey led to his theory of evolution by natural selection.

The WMO (World Meteorological Organization) has been responsible for naming hurricanes and tropical storms since the 1950s. However, the history of naming hurricanes dates back to the 1800s when hurricanes might be identified by the places they hit or the year they occurred. In 1928 Alexander Fleming, a bacteriologist at St. Mary's Hospital in London, discovered penicillin by accident. He found mold growing on a Petri dish of staphylococcus bacteria that he had accidentally contaminated. He isolated the mold, naming it penicillin which became the first antibiotic. In 1967 Thurgood Marshall became the first African American Supreme Court Justice, appointed by President Lyndon B. Johnson. He had been a leading civil rights lawyer, the head of the NAACP's legal staff and the solicitor general before becoming a Supreme Court Justice.

Nat Turner (1800) was an enslaved African American carpenter and preacher who led a four-day rebellion of both enslaved and free Blacks in August 1831. His rebellion resulted in the death of approximately sixty White men, women and children before he was captured and hanged after a trial in November. Before his execution, he told his story to attorney Thomas Ruffin Grey, who published *The Confessions of Nat Turner* in November 1831.

Mahatma Gandhi (1869) preached non-violence. "Gandhi Jayanti" is an annual celebration to commemorate his birth. This day is also known as the **International Day of Non-Violence** when Gandhi's teachings and his role in India's independence movement are honored. Johnnie Cochran (1937) was an African American attorney, best known for leading the so-called "Dream Team" during O.J. Simpson's murder trial.

For our Jewish friends, one who is on this list, **Rosh Hashanah** begins at sundown today.

**October 3, 2024**

Good afternoon, all 300. One of yesterday's responses is about *Smartie's* candy, especially popular for Halloween. Another reminded me that Johnnie Cochran owned his namesake nationwide law firm.

'Tis **National No Sugar Day**, promoting a healthier lifestyle and **National Poetry Day**, celebrating the art of poetry, and **Bring Your Bible to School Day.** Also, 'tis **National Wide Awakes Day** that is held every October 3. It celebrates the Wide Awakes, a youth and paramilitary organization of the Republican Party during the presidential election in 1860. It was an open-source network of people who believed in the emancipation of all, abolition and workers' rights.

Concerning **Bring Your Bible to School Day**, when I was a teenager, students would be released early on Mondays to attend Bible studies at churches in town. I carried my Bible to school. There was a time when many women carried a small Bible in their purses and men one in a pocket. They were too small to read comfortably. Now we have Bibles on telephones. I thank my grandson for putting it on mine. Now with it on screens and telephones, fewer people are carrying their Bibles to church.

In 1778 Captain James Cook anchored in Alaska. He was famous for his three voyages between 1768 and 1779, particularly to Australia and New Zealand. In 1789, George Washington issued his Thanksgiving proclamation, designating for *"the People of the United States a day of public thanksgiving"* to be held on *"Thursday, the 26th day of November"* of that year. In 1904 Mary McLeod Bethune opened the Daytona Normal & Industrial School which became *Bethune-Cookman University*. She founded the National Council of Negro Women in 1935 which still exists and presided for a myriad of African American women's organizations. She was the sole African American woman officially part of the U.S. delegation that created the United Nations Charter on June 26, 1945. After working on the presidential campaign for Franklin Roosevelt in 1932, the year in which I was born, she was appointed a national advisor. She was also a personal friend of the First Lady, Eleanor Roosevelt. Mary McLeod Bethune was called the "First Lady of Negro America" by *Ebony* magazine in April 1949.

Birthdays included Karen Bass (1953), elected to California's 47th Assembly district in 2004 and the first African American woman serving in the state legislature. She was reelected in 2006 and 2008 and served as the 43rd mayor of Los Angeles. Alfred Sharpton Jr. (1954) is an African American social justice and civil rights activist and Baptist minister, having preached his first sermon at age four. Presently, he hosts a weekday radio talk show, *Keepin' It Real*, which is nationally syndicated. Also, he is a political analyst and weekend host for MSNBC. Gwen Stefani (1964) is an American singer-songwriter and co-founder, lead vocalist and the primary songwriter of the band *No Doubt*.

## October 4, 2024

Good morning, all 300. 'Tis **World Habitat Day, World Animal Day, National Golf Lovers Day,** and **National Truckers Day.** Happy **Golfers Day** to you on my list who love the sport.

Today is the **Feast Day for Giovanni di Pietro di Bernardone**, known as Francis of Assisi. Canonized by Pope Gregory IX on July 16, 1228, he is commonly portrayed wearing a brown habit with a rope tied around his waist with three knots symbolizing the three Franciscan vows of chastity, poverty and obedience. St. Francis is associated with patronage of the environment and of animals. It is customary for some Catholic churches to hold ceremonies to bless animals on his feast day now being called **World Animal Day.**

In 1535 the *Coverdale Bible*, the first complete Bible to be published in English, was printed in Antwerp, Belgium, with translations by William Tyndale and Miles Coverdale. In 1648 Peter Stuyvesant, Governor of New York, established America's 1st volunteer firemen. He appointed a group of four fire wardens to inspect chimneys of the thatched-roof houses and to levy a fine of three guilders for each un-swept chimney. The money was used for hooks, leather buckets and ladders which were then given to citizens to protect their communities from fires. In 1824 Mexico became a republic. In 1883 the Orient Express departed on its first official journey from Paris to Istanbul, Turkey. In 1957 the Space Age began when the Russians launched the first satellite into orbit.

Birthdays included Rutherford Hayes (1822), who was the 19th President of the U.S. Charlton Heston (1923) starred in *The Ten Commandments* and *Ben-Hur*. Ed and I enjoyed him in both films.

## October 6, 2024

Good morning, all 300. Today is **National World Communion Sunday**, bringing together all Christians.

In 1683 thirteen Mennonite families from Germany founded Germantown in Philadelphia, Pennsylvania. Today they are considered Protestant and are found all over the world. The only Mennonite I have met ran a "bed and breakfast" in Milton, Pennsylvania, where I had been invited to give a presentation on one of my books. The owner wore a distinctive cap on her head to designate her religion. In 1871 the Fisk Jubilee Singers, an African American a cappella ensemble from Nashville's Fisk University, began its 1st national tour of U.S. in Cincinnati, Ohio. In 1876 the American Library Association organized in Philadelphia.

In 1927 *The Jazz Singer* premiered at the Warner Theatre in New York starring Al Jolson. It was the first film with synchronized speech, music and sound effects, marking the end of the silent-film era. The movie was remade many years later with Neil Diamond. Ed and I enjoyed it. In 1935 the Market Street Railway in San Francisco began using trackless trolley coaches. San Francisco is one of my favorite cites, where at the Fisherman's Wharf I can purchase clam chowder served in a bowl made out of delicious sourdough bread.

Fannie Lou Hamer (1917) was an African American women's rights and voting activist and vice-chair of the Freedom Democratic Party at the Democratic National Convention in 1964. Anthony Dungy (1955)) served as an NFL head coach for 13 seasons with the Tampa Bay Buccaneers and Indianapolis Colts. Leading the Colts to victory in Super Bowl XLI in 2006, he became the first African American head coach to win the Super Bowl.

**October 7, 2024**

Good morning, all 300. I will be away from my computer while I am in CT, PA and NYC. 'Tis **National Bathtub Day** and **National Frappe Day.** When I was little, we had no bathtub in our house. On Saturday nights everyone took a bath in a tin tub in the kitchen near the coal stove. We had to get ready for church the next day. We sponge-bathed during the week. Later, we had a bathtub with claw feet, which was a large and deep tub, wonderful for taking long leisurely bubble baths. When my present townhouse was being built, I requested a whirlpool which I enjoyed for years. I have not used it lately because I no longer can pull myself up and out of the tub. Now it is the walk-in shower.

I have never had a frappe, which is a Greek iced coffee drink made from spray-dried instant coffee, water, sugar, and milk. I like my coffee very hot, not too strong and black.

In 1765 the Stamp Act Congress convened in New York City to devise a unified protest against new British taxation. In 1806 carbon paper was patented in London by inventor Ralph Wedgwood. It was very important at one time to make copies of a document. The carbon would get all over our hands, though. Some people wore gloves when working with it. In 1952 the first *Bandstand* broadcast was in Philadelphia on WFIL-TV. In 1955 Dick Clark joined as a substitute-host. The show's popularity helped him become a media mogul and inspired other long-running music programs, such as *Soul Train.* Teenagers loved his shows. In 1982 the musical *Cats* opened at the Winter Garden Theater on Broadway, NYC. It ran for 18 years and won seven Tonys and one Grammy Award. Even though I lived across the Hudson River, I never got to see it. When tickets were $25.00, we thought that price was too high. Some Broadway tickets now go for $200 and higher.

Birthdays included Desmond Tutu (1931), South African theologian and human rights and anti-apartheid activist. He was the first Black African Bishop of Johannesburg from 1985 to 1986 and Archbishop of Cape Town from 1986 to 1996. Josephine Occhiuto "Joy Behar" (1942) is an American comedian and television co-host of *The View* since the beginning of the series in 1997.

**November 19, 2024**

Good morning, all 300. 'Tis **Equal Opportunity Day, Discovery of Puerto Rico Day, National Play Monopoly Day,** and **National Entrepreneur's Day.** I remember summer days when my cousins and I played Monopoly for hours in a shaded sitting room. Congratulations to several entrepreneurs on my list. I have tried being one at different times in my life when selling World Book, Shaklee vitamins and Primerica insurance. However, I do not have the soul of an entrepreneur who has to be a hustler. I had a friend who put 7 kids through college while she was selling the insurance.

I am thinking about my two *Bennett College* friends who hailed from Puerto Rico. Rosa could not speak any English when she left home in 1950, but Carmen helped Rosa become a successful student. Rosa and I celebrated our 70$^{th}$ college reunion at Bennett in May. We had "Tea" with the president of *Bennett College*.

In 1493 Christopher Columbus reached Puerto Rico in 1493 during his second voyage to the Caribbean. In 1620 the Mayflower reached Cape Cod and afterwards explored the coast. In 1805 the Lewis and Clark expedition reached the Pacific Ocean, becoming the first European Americans to cross the West. It was with the help of Sacagawea, a young Native American woman. In 1863 President Abraham Lincoln delivered his Gettysburg address. In 1965 Kellogg's Pop Tarts pastries were created. My kids loved them, but I was not particular about them. In 1977 Egyptian President Anwar Sadat became the first Arabic president to visit Israel.

Birthdays included African American Baseball Hall of Fame catcher Roy Campanella (1921), and American fashion designer Calvin Klein (1942).

**November 20, 2024**

Good morning, all 300. A man recently wrote a letter to me from Toronto, Canada, whose mother was a contemporary of my father's and left a journal that he wants to publish. The Patiences mentioned in the man's letter were my father's first cousins whom I knew.

'Tis **Name Your PC Day** and **National Peanut Butter Fudge Day.** I think I would enjoy the peanut butter fudge candy today since I like the ingredients. As for naming my computer, it is simply "She." My blue van is called "Blue Belle" after my *Bennett College* sisters who are called "Belles" and whose colors are blue and white. My husband always called his automobiles "Bessie" like cows. I have no idea why he did. I guess I never thought to ask him the reason.

In 1789 New Jersey was the first state to ratify the Bill of Rights. In 1866 the first national convention of the Grand Army of the Republic (G.A.R.) was held. My great grandfather was a member. I have a photo of him in the GAR (Grand Army of the Republic) standing with his comrades. He was the only Black veteran in the group. In 1866 Howard University was founded in Washington, D.C. for "Colored" students. According to my computer, the Pantene company has identified 110 different skin tones in *Homo sapiens.* In 1923 African American Garrett Morgan patented his traffic signal design, adding a "caution" between "stop and go." In 1925 Salvador Dali gave his first one-man show in Barcelona, Spain. I enjoyed visiting the Salvador Dali Museum in St. Petersburg, Florida. In 1947 Nobel Laureate Edwin Land demonstrated the first instant camera, the Polaroid Land camera. I took many photos with mine; however, through the years, sadly, many have faded.

Joseph Biden (1942), was the 46th President of the U.S.

**November 21, 2024**

Good morning, all 300.

One week 'til turkey day and all of its fixings. How wonderful if you will be with your family. Thank you much, My Dear Ed, for you are dearly missed.

In 1865 Shaw University was founded for Blacks in Raleigh, N.C. It was originally called the *Raleigh Theological Institute* by the American Baptist Home Missionary Society, becoming the first HBCU (Historically Black Colleges and Universities) in the South, later named "Shaw" after its benefactor Elijah Shaw. In 1964 Verrazano-Narrows suspension bridge was the world's longest connecting New York City with Staten Island and Brooklyn. In 1968 the Supremes and Temptations released *I'm Gonna Make You Love Me.* In 1980 the television show *Dallas* episode "Who Done It?" revealed who shot J. R. That episode garnered 83 million viewers. In 1989 President George H.W. Bush signed legislature for no smoking allowed on domestic flights. I was so glad.

Marlo Thomas (1937) was producer, activist, and daughter of actor Danny Thomas, St. Jude's supporter, and wife of Phil Donahue. African American Michael Stranahan (1971) was a former professional football player and current broadcaster.

Throw away any potatoes that are sprouting. They may be forming solanine poison that makes you ill. Store them in a cool, dark place.

**November 23, 2024**
     Good morning, all 300. 'Tis **Eat a Cranberry Day** and **National Cashew Day.** My favorite cranberry relish is made with *Ocean Spray* whole berries. I don't suppose many of you know about the Japanese American connection with *Ocean Spray*. During World War II property was taken from many Japanese who lived in California and whole families were interred in camps in western states. Some Japanese were sent to Seabrook, New Jersey, to work for *Ocean Spray* and many remained there after the war. Another blight on our democracy. Later, Congress appropriated $38 million to settle 23,000 claims totaling $131 million. The final claim was adjudicated in 1965.
     My favorite nut is a cashew. Native to Brazil and Venezuela, it was cultivated by Portuguese explorers who exported the nuts to other lands. India is a top producer today.
     In 1783 Annapolis, Maryland, became the U.S. Capitol until 1784 when Philadelphia was followed by New York and then Washington, D.C. in 1790. In 1897 the portable pencil sharpener was patented by an African American inventor named John Lee Love, called "The Love Sharpener." In 1897 African American inventor Andrew Jackson Beard invented the "jerry coupler" to connect railroad cars. Born a slave in Woodland, Alabama, after emancipation he became a farmer, carpenter, blacksmith, railroad worker, businessman, and inventor. In 2006 he was inducted into the National Inventors Hall of Fame in Akron, Ohio. In 1923 Cecil B. De Mille's first version of the film *The Ten Commandments* premiered in the U.S. When I was a teenager, on Monday nights a program called *Lux Presents Hollywood* was broadcasted on the radio with host Cecil B. De Mille. Lux was a brand of soap.
     In 1937 John Steinbeck's *Of Mice and Men* premiered in New York City. I remember having to read it in a high school English class, but I don't remember in which grade it was. In 1939 the Nazi Governor of Poland required Jewish Poles over the age of eleven to wear a blue star of David. In 1942 U.S. Coast Guard Women's Auxiliary (SPARS) was authorized.
     In 1945 most wartime rationing of food ended. I can remember standing in line with my Great Aunt Lillie with our green ration coupon books in hand to purchase certain foods, including sugar, coffee, butter, chocolate, cooking oils, processed foods, canned fish, cheese, and canned milk. Mothers had to be very creative with their meal planning, like dyeing white margarine yellow to look like butter. In 1960 Tinseltown was dedicated in the Walk of Fame at Hollywood Blvd. and Vine St.
     In 2021 Egypt reopened its 3000-year-old Avenue of the Sphinxes in Luxor with a grand ceremony. The promenade connects a temple in Luxor to one in Karnak. I visited both places while in Egypt in 1988. Sphinxes and rams were part of the religion of ancient Egypt when Ra, the sun god, was worshipped.
     Birthdays included Miley Cyrus (1992), singer, songwriter, and daughter of Bill Ray Cyrus. African American Tom Joyner (1949) is a philanthropist and host of *The Tom Joyner Morning Show*. African American Robin Roberts (1960), daughter of a Tuskegee airman during World War II, was the first woman to co-host NFL Primetime. She was inducted into the Women's Basketball Hall of Fame in 2012. Presently, she is a co-anchor on *Good Morning America* and is also an author.

**November 24, 2024**
     Good morning, all 300. 'Tis **Celebrate Your Unique Talent Day, Christ the King Feast Day,** and **Buy Nothing Day.** I'd love for you to share your unique talent with me. I mastered dissecting earthworms and frogs. Three of my former students are on my list. How do they rate me?
     I play the piano some. I have sewed, drawn, painted, creweled, needlepointed, caned chair seats, and written books at different times in my life. When my father and father-in-law were living, I enjoyed making different kinds of pretty Christmas cookies for them. Presently, I am a muser. When

my husband was alive, I prepared whatever he liked, and he was content. He liked meat loaf, but I have not made one since he passed away ten years ago.

My kids chuckle together about the quick meals I prepared for them. *Rice-a-Roni*, TV dinners and *Hamburger Helper*. We all survived, even my husband with his high blood pressure. He did not die from it. Sadly, he developed Parkinson's.

**Christ the King Feast Day** emphasizes the true kingship of Christ with the idea of the kingdom being where Christ sits at the right hand of God the Father. It is recent to the liturgical calendar of the Catholic Church, having been added in 1925 by Pope Pius XI. Lutheran, Anglican, Episcopal, Congregational, Moravian, Methodist, Presbyterian, Nazarene, Reformed, United Church of Christ, United Protestant, and Orthodox churches also believe it. Baptists are not on the list because your churches are autonomous, meaning self-governing.

In 1897 English author Ann Sewell sold her manuscript *Black Beauty* for 40 pounds. Written to induce kindness, sympathy and understanding for horses in an era before automobiles, it was the first major story in children's literature. Black Beauty, a handsome, well-born and well-bred horse, narrates the story. In 1903 African American Clyde Coleman patented the automobile electric starter.

In 1932 the General Pulaski Skyway, named for the Polish military leader who fought for the U.S. during the Revolutionary War, was once called the Newark-Jersey City Viaduct. It can be seen when driving the New Jersey Turnpike to New York City. In 1933 Fred Astaire's first film *Dancing Lady* was released. He starred in nine films with dancer Ginger Rogers. They were very popular, and I enjoyed them very much. In 1950 *Guys and Dolls* ran for 1200 performances, winning five Tony awards. It was the first Broadway play I ever saw. It was during my honeymoon in 1952 in New York City when two front seat tickets had been given to us for a wedding gift by someone from the Jewish Community Center in Wilkes-Barre where Ed worked.

Birthdays included Zachary Taylor (1784), the 12th U.S. President, was a career officer in the U.S. Army, rising to the rank of Major General. His was the shortest presidency, dying after 16 months from a stomach disease. African American Scott Joplin (1868) was a composer and pianist. Dubbed the King of Ragtime, he composed more than 40 ragtime pieces, one ragtime ballet and two operas.

**November 25, 2024**

Good morning, all 300. 'Tis **National Secret Santa Day, Native American Heritage Month.** Several of us on my musing list claim indigenous ancestry. Someone on my list became a dear friend after I gave her a Secret Santa gift years ago at a *Delta Sigma Theta, Inc.* Christmas party. Thanking her for continuous love and help with my editing. My daughter will be here in Virginia to accompany me to our church's Christmas extravaganza with Yolande Adams featured. I'd like once again to attend the *Messiah* rendered by an outstanding choir.

In 1792 African American Benjamin Banneker, mathematician and astronomer, first published his *Farmer's Almanac*. In 1834 *Delmonico's*, one of NY City's finest restaurants, provided a meal of soup, steak, coffee, and half a pie for 12 cents. In 1841 thirty-five survivors of the mutiny on the slave ship *Amistad* returned to Africa. In 1897 Spain granted Puerto Rico autonomy. In 1905 Telimeo made the 1st advertisement for a radio set costing $8.50. In 1920 the first Gimbel's Thanksgiving Parade was held in Philadelphia. In 1937 the World's Fair of Paris closed after 31.2 million visitors. In 1950 the United Nations gave Eritrea to Ethiopia. In 2000 the *New York Times* named its 25 greatest actors of the 21st Century with African American Denzel Washington as No 1.

Birthdays included Mexican American Ricardo Montaban (1920), best-known as Mr. Roake on *Fantasy Island*. I was a fan. John F. Kennedy Jr. (1960) was born in Washington, D. C. Less than three weeks earlier, his father had been elected the 35th President of the U.S. Joe Di Maggio (1914) became an American baseball center fielder who played his entire 13-year career in Major League Baseball for the NY Yankees.

In 1844 Karl Benz was born in Germany. He was an engine designer and automotive engineer. His Benz Patent in 1885 was for the first practical modern automobile. Franz Xaver Gruble (1787) was a primary school teacher, church organist and composer who wrote *Silent Night* in 1816.

**November 26, 2024**

Good morning, all 300. A cousin asked me yesterday what crewel is. It is creating a picture by using a needle and thread. I have several of my creations hanging on walls in my home. One is a Van Gogh sunflower, and another is one of beautiful pansies, a favorite flower. 'Tis **National Tree Day.** In 1913 Joyce Kilmer wrote a poem called *Trees*. I had to memorize that poem in school and was in a choir that sang it.

*"I think that I shall never see*
*A poem as lovely as a tree....."*

In 1842 Notre Dame was established. In 1863 President Abraham Lincoln declared the final Thursday of November as Thanksgiving Day. In 1922 English Egyptologist Howard Carter entered the Tomb of King Tut. I had the pleasure of entering the empty tomb in 1988. King Tut's body is in the Museum of Cairo, along with his famous mask. In 1942 *Casablanca* starring Humphrey Bogart and Ingrid Bergman premiered, becoming one of the most iconic films.

Birthdays included Charles Schulz (1922), who introduced the world to Charlie Brown and Snoopy. Anna Mae Bullock, "Tina Turner" (1939) was an African American singer, songwriter and actress.

**November 27, 2024**

Good morning, all 300. When I was teaching in N.J., we had half day today on the day before the holiday. There would be two pep rallies held in the Bloomfield and Montclair High School gyms. They were Turkey-day rivals in football. Soon after my son's graduation in 1991, the Thanksgiving Day rivalry ended. 'Tis a shame because it was always a big homecoming time for alumni, particularly those who had come home from college. I loved greeting my former students at the stadiums.

'Tis **1$^{st}$ Macy's Thanksgiving Day Parade** and **National Jukebox Day.** The history of the jukebox dates back to the late 19$^{th}$ Century when the first coin-operated music machines were invented. Originally called "nickelodeon," the term "jukebox" was not used until the 1930s. I love them, especially in some Greek diners where one still may be found at each booth.

In 2013 Walt Disney's *Frozen* was released in American movie theaters. I have a great-great niece who loved it. I gave her a book about it for one of her birthdays. She's a young lady now. In 2019 the 400$^{th}$ anniversary of the end of the Transatlantic Slave Trade was celebrated with the Year of Return in Ghana.

Birthdays included Lee Jun -fan "Bruce Lee" (1940), a Hong-Kong-American martial artist and actor. African American Jimi Hendrix (1942) was considered the greatest guitarist in the history of popular music. Caroline Kennedy (1957), daughter of President John Kennedy, is an author, diplomat, attorney, and Ambassador to Australia.

**November 28, 2024**

Good morning, all 300. I remember the Thanksgivings of my youth when I attended the football games with friends. We'd wear our green and white ribbons and sit right next to the band as a cheering body. I can remember the trombones playing *Hold That Tiger*. We always drank a cup of hot chocolate and enjoyed a hot dog with mustard. The only kind of boots "back in the day" were the rain ones called "arctics," or heavy work boots called "clod hoppers." When snow boots were later invented, thankfully, they were lined for warmth. When I got home, I would smell the roasting turkey. I did not participate in cooking, but I washed the dishes and scoured the pots and pans. Afterwards, the good China, crystal and silverware would be put away until Christmas dinner. Another chore of mine was to polish the silverware with a special kind of cream. I inherited Great Aunt Lillie's beautiful silverware which is stored in a special cloth that prevents tarnishing.

In 1520 the Portuguese navigator Ferdinand Magellan began crossing the Pacific Ocean. In 1821 Panama declared independence from Spain. In 1843 the Kingdom of Hawaii was officially recognized by the United Kingdom and France as an independent country. That lasted until America stole it, for in 1898 American businessmen pushed for annexation to gain full control over Hawaii. They were successful and Queen Liliuokalani was forced to give up her throne.

In 1909 Sergi Rachmaninoff's *Piano Concerto No. 3,* one of the most difficult genres, premiered at the New Theatre in NYC with the composer as soloist. In 1929 Richard E. Byrd made his first South Pole flight. In 1984 over 250 years after their deaths, British born William Penn and his wife were made honorary citizens of the U.S. Having grown up in Pennsylvania and taking a course in Pennsylvania history at Wilkes College, I am very familiar with William Penn after whom the state was named following a war with the Yankees living in Connecticut. In 2016 Merriam-Webster's word of the year was "gas-lighting." It was the title of the movie *Gaslight,* one of my favorite black and white films. It has superb acting.

African American Berry Gordy (1929) is a songwriter, producer and founder of *Motown Records.*

**November 29. 2024**

Good evening, all 300. In 1947 the United Nations approved the resolution for the partitioning of Palestine. Birthdays included Winston Churchill (1874), British statesman, military officer and Prime Minister of the United Kingdom during World War II; African American Adam Clayton Powell II (1908), Pastor at Abyssinian Baptist Church in Harlem and a politician; African American Billy Strayhorn (1915) was a member of the Duke Ellington Orchestra; African American Chadwick Boseman (1976) was the star in *Black Panther.*

**November 30, 2024**

Good morning, all 300. I received my first Christmas card yesterday. It reminds me of my Great Aunt Mabel who always mailed her cards so they would arrive on the day after Thanksgiving. The cost of a stamp is 73 cents nowadays, compared to the 3 cents it was when I was a kid.

'Tis **National Gratitude Month**. I am so thankful for all of you friends and family. You help me keep my mind sharp. I enjoy researching tidbits that may be of interest to some of you. Today is **St. Andrew's Day** which is a Scottish holiday when haggis is eaten. I tasted that ethnic food when I was in Scotland. It is an acquired taste, just like poi is in Hawaii. I visited the Highlands to see the lovely heather on the moors in late summer. The Highlands are so far north and so high that no trees can grow there. Only the low growing purple/pink heather survives there, which is a beautiful sight. Highlanders are known for woolen articles woven from their sheep. I saw sheep being sheared and the sheep dogs that herded them. Sheep really are unintelligent, but those dogs are geniuses. I also visited the Castle at Edinburgh where my stepmother and I attended a "Tattoo" that consisted of bag pipe bands marching while playing. We enjoyed it.

'Tis also **National Stay at Home Because You're Well Day**. When I was teaching, I called them "mental health" days. I never took my sick days off and so had a lot accumulated when I retired for which I got some extra money.

'Tis also **National Mason Jar Day.** Mason jars were used by women to can food for over the winter. Oh, how unbearably hot the kitchens became, even with open doors and windows!

In 1753 Benjamin Franklin received the Godfrey Copley medal "on account of his curious experiments and observations on electricity." In 1803 Spain ceded her claims to the Louisiana Territory to France which later sold it to the U.S. In 1896 the first successful electric power plant opened in Buffalo, N.Y. In 1900 a German engineer patented the front-wheel drive for automobiles. In 1960 Barbados gained independence from Great Britain.

Birthdays included Samuel Clemens "Mark Twain" (1835), writer and essayist who was praised as the greatest humorist the U.S. has produced. He's known for *The Adventures of Tom Sawyer* and *Huckleberry Finn*. I visited Twain's spacious home in Hartford, Connecticut, now the Mark Twain Home and Museum, a Natural History Landmark. His next-door neighbor in 1874 was Harriet Beecher Stowe, schoolteacher, abolitionist and author of *Uncle Tom's Cabin*. I also visited her home which is quite modest compared to Twain's.

**Mark Twain's famous sayings:**

*"The fear of death follows from the fear of life. A person who lives fully is prepared to die at any time."*

*"The two most important days in your life are the day you are born and the day you find out why."*

*"Wrinkles should merely indicate where smiles have been."*

### December 1, 2024

Good morning, all 300. 'Tis time to get my Christmas decorations out with wreaths placed on my front door and porch railings. My beautiful Christmas cactus is in bloom. I purchased a red cyclamen which is beautiful, too.

In 1887 Sherlock Holmes first appeared in print in *Study in Scarlet* by Arthur Conan Doyle. In 1913 the 1st drive-in gasoline station opened in Pittsburgh, Pennsylvania. In 1913 Ford Motor Company instituted the world's first moving assembly line for the Model T Ford. In 1918 Iceland was granted independence by the Danish Parliament. In 1929 the game *Bingo* was invented by an American toy salesman named Edwin Lowe. In 1941 Japanese Emperor Hirohito signed the Declaration of War with the U.S. In 1955 African American Rosa Parks was arrested for refusing to go to the back of a bus in Montgomery, Alabama.

In 1965 the airlift of refugees from Cuba began. One was a student of mine. I attended a conference about him with his mother. She described to me how her family got out of Cuba with nothing but the clothes on their backs. Her family had been very wealthy in Cuba. My student was having a hard time adjusting to his new life. In 2024, five years after a catastrophic fire reduced Notre Dame Cathedral in Paris to a smoldering shell, journalists got a first glimpse of the Gothic masterpiece's fully restored breathtaking interior.

Birthdays included Bette Midler (1945), actor and singer best known for *Wind Beneath My Wings;* Mary Martin (1913), actress who starred in *Peter Pan*, *South Pacific* and *Sound of Music*. She is the mother of Larry Hageman who played J. R. in the weekly soap opera *Dallas*. African American Richard Pryor (1940) was an award-winning comedian.

### December 2, 2024

Good morning, all 301. 'Tis **National Build Joy Day.** *"Joy to the World, the Lord is come....."*

In 1806 James Madison was re-elected President of the U.S. In 1840 William Henry Harrison was elected President of the U.S. In 1859 abolitionist John Brown was hanged for murder, treason and encouraging slaves to revolt. In 1888 "The Great White Hurricane" was a monster snowstorm that buckled D.C. and expanded north to Maine. The storm prompted Boston to create the first subway line. In 1927 the first Model A Ford sold for $385.00.

**December 3, 2024**

Good morning, all 301. 'Tis **National Day of Giving** and **Advent Begins. Advent** is a seasonal observance celebrated by most Christians. It is four weeks of remembering Jesus' birth at Christmas and His coming back to earth at His second coming. Many churches light candles in commemoration. Mine does.

In 1586 Sir Thomas Herriot introduced potatoes to England from Columbia, South America. In 1828 Andrew Jackson was elected the 7th President of the U.S. In 1847 the African American abolitionist and orator Frederick Douglass published his newspaper called the *North Star*. In 1911 Willis Carrier introduced his invention for air-conditioning. In 1967 the first human heart transplant was performed in South Africa by Dr. Christiaan Bernard.

**December 4, 2024**

Good morning, all 301. 'Tis **National Pie Day** and **International Cheetah Day.** Cherry, blueberry, lemon meringue, sweet potato, and apple are all my favorite pies. I find the spotted African cheetah to be a beautiful animal. It is biologically classified as a cat. However, it has some dog characteristics similar to the greyhound, with its very long legs and big feet. No other animal is built so. Its long legs allow it to run extremely fast. All cats have retractable claws which fold inward. Cheetahs do not, just like dogs, and so they can always be seen. A most unusual cat.

In 1816 James Monroe was elected 5th President of the U.S. In 1864 James Knox Polk was elected 11th U.S. President. In 1906 Alpha Phi Alpha, the first Black Greek Letter Fraternity, was formed at *Cornell University*, now open to all men. In 1927 African American Duke Ellington opened at the famous *Cotton Club* in Harlem, NYC. Blacks were not allowed to be patrons back then, even though many Black entertainers performed there. In June 1935 Blacks were finally allowed to become patrons. In 1930 the Vatican approved the *rhythm method* for birth control. Paul Revere had 16 children. In 1945 the Senate approved U.S. participation in the United Nations. In 1954 the first Burger King opened in Miami, Florida. In 1978 Dianne Feinstein was named San Francisco's first female and Jewish mayor.

Birthdays included Suzanne Malveaux (1966), TV journalist and cousin to Dr. Julianne Malveaux, a former President of *Bennett College*; and Jay-Z (1969), African American rapper and record producer.

**December 5, 2024**

Good morning, all 301. 'Tis **International Volunteer Day.**

In 1492 Christopher Columbus was the first European to sight Hispaniola, which is modern Dominica Republic and Haiti. In 1792 George Washington was re-elected President. In 1804 Thomas Jefferson was re-elected President. In 1832 Andrew Jackson was reelected as President. In 1935 the *National Council of Negro Women* was formed by Dr. Mary McLeod Bethune. In 1941 Elizabeth Kenny's new treatment for polio was approved. In 1946 U.S. President Harry Truman created a committee on Civil Rights. In 1955 the historic bus boycott began in Montgomery, Alabama, led by Rosa Parks and others.

Birthdays included Robert Louis Stevenson (1850), novelist, essayist, poet, and travel writer known for *Treasure Island* and *Dr. Jekyll and Mr. Hyde;* African American William Grant Still (1878), composer of nearly 200 musical works including symphonies, ballets, operas, and choral works. He was the first African American to conduct a major symphony orchestra. African American poet Gwendolyn Brooks (1917) wrote her first poem, *Eventide*, at age 13. By age 16, she had written and published 75 poems.

**December 6, 2024**

Good morning, all 301. On this day I am 92 7/12 years old with three friends who are 104. One is on this list and the other two do not use a computer. I would not have learned how to use one if it had not been for transcribing my stepmother's autobiography in 1998. Since that time, I have owned three computers and written nine books.

'Tis **National Miner's Day.** My young life was full of anthracite coal miners living in northeast Pennsylvania. When my grandfather, Harry, was a young boy, he wanted to go into the mines like many immigrant boys did as young as six and seven. They were boys who would never have the opportunity to go to school. Their large families needed their wages. Harry's father, a former slave, insisted that all eight of his children get an 8$^{th}$ grade education. He was the second child and not allowed to go to the mines until he was 13. When he did, in his spare time he began whittling objects out of shiny pieces of coal. He whittled beautiful hearts to be worn on a chain or ribbon. His friends liked them so much that he began to sell them. When he was 17, he injured his arm on a conveyor belt at the Exeter Mine. His parents encouraged him to start a business of his own, which began on their back porch. That led to a successful business, first with his three younger brothers and later with his sons, my father included. He continued carving coal until his death from pneumonia in 1972 at age 65. My father loved his work.

In 963 Leo VIII was elected Pope. To date there have been 266 Popes. In 1790 the U.S. Congress moved from New York to Philadelphia. In 1849 African American Harriet Tubman escaped from slavery for the second and last time. In Maryland an interesting museum has been dedicated to her, which I visited once. In 1865 the 13$^{th}$ Amendment of the U.S. Constitution was ratified to abolish slavery. In 1877 for the first time, Thomas Edison introduced his phonograph. In 1884 the aluminum capstone set atop the Washington Monument made it the tallest human-built structure in the world. In 1923 the first U.S. Presidential address on the radio was given by President Calvin Coolidge.

Birthdays included Joyce Kilmer (1886), the writer of the poem *Trees*; Ira Gershwin (1896), lyricist famous for *Embraceable You* and *I got Rhyth;* Joseph Lamb (1887), the only White ragtime pianist and admirer of African American ragtime pianist Scott Joplin.

**December 9, 2024**

Good morning, all 301. 'Tis **National Pastry Day, Christmas Card Day,** and **Weary Willie Day.** My favorite pastry is an apple turnover drizzled with white icing. "Weary Willie," the most well-known clown, was Emmett Leo Kelly who worked in circuses and carnivals as a trapeze artist but later developed the clown character.

Many of you are mailing Christmas cards. I always receive some very beautiful homemade ones which I save in a treasure box to look at year after year. Others will be e-mailing greetings like I am.

In 1854 Alfred Tennyson penned the *Charge of the Light Brigade*. I remember reading the poem in a high school English class. In 1941 Adolf Hitler ordered for U.S. ships to be torpedoed three days before he declared war on the U.S. In 2015 Germany Chancellor Angela Merkel was named *TIME Magazine's* "Person of the Year."

Birthdays included John Milton (1608), English poet and author of *Paradise Lost*; Clarence Birdseye (1886), founder of the modern frozen food industry; Emmett Leo Kelly (1898), "Weary Willie." As bad as World War II was, the formerly jobless young men became soldiers, sailors and marines. After the war, the *G.I. Bill of Rights* gave many the opportunity to get lucrative positions.

Kirk Douglas (1916) was one of my favorite actors. Stacy Abrams (1973) is an African American politician, lawyer and voting rights activist.

**December 21, 2024**

Good morning, all 303. I am wondering how many of you know why we Christians celebrate Christ's birth on December 25th when we don't know exactly when He was born. Most likely it was in the spring when sheep were roaming the hills for food. In the times of the Roman Empire, various gods were worshipped, one being Saturn during the month of December. It was a weeklong celebration with the giving of gifts. However, after Emperor Constantine's conversion to Christianity in 312 A.D., he instituted the celebration of Christ's birthday on Dec. 25th in 336 A.D. Not until 1870 did Christmas become a federal holiday in the United States, proclaimed by President Ulysses Grant.

Last evening I watched on Netflix a movie called *The Six Triple Eight*. I am particularly interested because my stepmother, Alice Patterson, was a WAC whose unit did not go overseas. Alice joined the WAACs (Women's Auxiliary Army Corps) soon after she graduated from *Bennett College*. The WAACs was formed on May 15, 1942. It was a time when all units of the Army were segregated, which did not change until 1949 by President Harry S. Truman. In her autobiography, *Bittersweet Memories of Home*, Alice tells of the discrimination she and other Black WACs suffered in the South. The WACs disbanded on October 20, 1978, when it was integrated with male units. The Senate passed legislation last year for the 6888th Central Postal Directory Battalion to receive Congressional Gold Medals. President Joe Biden signed the bipartisan bill in March. There are only two women still living to receive one.

**December 24, 2024**

Good morning, all 303. I am sending this message from my daughter's home in Connecticut.

**January 1, 2025**

Good morning, all 303. Sadly, we are mourning the death of President Jimmy Carter, a great man in every way. I am also mourning the death of a high school classmate who has recently passed. I saw her last in October at our 74th class reunion. Jasmine will be missed by the few classmates still living in West Pittston, Pennsylvania.

I had a lovely "Selah" last month and am "back in the saddle' again. I spent several days with my daughter and her family in Connecticut where snow was covering the ground. When driving back to Virginia with my grandson, I wanted to see where the snow had begun. It was only from New Jersey north. My lucky snow-bird friends on this musing list have returned to the warmth of Florida. In my mind's eye I see the lovely gray-green palm tree in the front yard of my friend in Naples. I am so looking forward to spring.

I have begun organizing my manuscript for the book I want to publish of my two and a half years of musing. Thanks to you who tell me that you enjoy my musings. I do enjoy sharing them with you.

'Tis **New Year's Day, Rose Bowl Game Day,** and **World Day of Peace**. Many of you will watch the 111th Rosebowl Day parade today and the game between Ohio and Oregon later. Our family went to a Rose Bowl Parade in Pasadena when my kids were young. What I remember most was that it was a very cold morning. I believe Ohio State was playing then, too. Some of you will be eating ethnic foods that others will know nothing about. Enjoy! Many Black people enjoy hoppin' John on New Year's Day. It is a dish made from black-eyed peas and rice and served with greens, usually collards. The beans are for wishing for gold and the greens for cash in the new year.

In 1677 the first medical publication in America was in Boston. It was concerning smallpox. In 1801 The Act of Union between Great Britain and Scotland along with Ireland created the United Kingdom of Great Britain and Ireland. In 1921 Agatha Christie published her first novel, *A Mysterious Affair at Styles*. In 1942 Count Basie recorded the music single jazz standard *One O'clock Jump*. In 1977 President Jimmy Carter pardoned almost all Vietnam War draft evaders. In 1985 Jessye Norman, an African American opera singer, sang *Simple Gifts* at the second inauguration of Ronald Reagan. In 1988 U.S. accepted the immigration of 30,000 Vietnamese children. One was my student. In 1987 B. B. King, African American musician, donated his 7,000-record collection to the University of Mississippi.

Birthdays included Captain John Smith (1580), explorer, soldier, author, and Under Governor of the Jamestown Colony of Virginia; Paul Revere (1735) was a military officer and industrialist who engaged in the midnight ride in 1750. I read *The Midnight Ride of Paul Revere,* by Henry Wadsworth Longfellow, in high school. Betsy Ross (1752) was credited as having made the 2nd official U.S. flag, although that was refuted by others. African American George Washington Carver (1864) was an agricultural scientist and inventor who promoted crop rotation between cotton and peanuts, soybeans and sweet potatoes. He found hundreds of uses for peanuts that put nitrogen back in the soil that was depleted by tobacco and cotton.

**January 2, 2025**

Good morning, all 303. 'Tis **Ancestry Day** and **National Buffet Day. Ancestry Day** interests me most, being my family's "griot" or storyteller. I took the *ancestry.com* DNA test and earned that my genes are from seven different ethnicities. I also learned the names of my great-great grandparents, Thomas and Hester Lawrence, who were slaves in Edenton, N.C. before and during the *Civil War*. How delighted I am to have found many new cousins via *ancestry.com* and *23 and me* which describe how the Lawrence and Patience cousins found each other in 2018. "Curious Georges" may like to read my book *Deeply Rooted in North Carolina*. www.journeyfromthepast.com

The best buffet I ever had was at the Hotel Piccadilly in New York City years ago. I used to take my students on field trips to the Bronx Zoo and then to the hotel for the smorgasbord.

In 1788 Georgia was the 4th state to ratify the Constitution. In 1839 the first photo of the moon was taken by French photographer Louis Daguerre. In 1890 Alice Sanger became the first woman White House staffer. In 1903 U.S. President Theodore Roosevelt shut down the Post Office in Indianola, Mississippi, for refusing to accept its approved postmistress because she was Black. In 1906 Willis Carrier received a U.S. patent for the world's first air conditioner. In 1929 U.S. and Canada agreed to preserve the Niagara Falls. In 1938 book publisher Simon and Schuster was founded. In 1965 African American Rev. Dr. Martin Luther King began a drive to register Black voters. In 1969 African American Dr. Benjamin Mays was named the President of the Atlanta Board of Education. He was also President of Morehouse College. In 1974 the 55 MPH speed limit was imposed by President Richard Nixon.

Birthdays included African American actor Cuba Gooding Jr. (1968); Dr. John Hope Franklin (1915) was an African American historian who in 1995 was awarded the *Presidential Medal of Freedom* by President Barack Obama.

### January 3, 2024

Good morning, all 303. 'Tis **National Bean day.** I will make some chili for dinner with kidney beans from my pantry shelf.

In 1521 Martin Luther was excommunicated from the Roman Catholic Church. Thus began the Protestant Reformation. In 1852 the first Chinese arrived in Hawaii to work in the pineapple fields. James Mitchner's "Hawaii" tells their story. In 1853 Solomon Northrop, author of *Twelve Years A Slave*, was freed after being held illegally in slavery. In 1959 Alaska was admitted as the 49th state. African American Adam Clayton Powell Jr. (1961) was elected chairman of the U.S. House Education and Labor Committee. In 1961 U.SS. broke diplomatic relations with Cuba. In 1962 Pope John XXIII excommunicated Fidel Castro. African American Leontyne Price (1985) made her final operatic appearance in a televised performance of *Aida* at the Metropolitan Opera, N.Y. African American Aretha Franklin (1942) was the first female artist to be inducted into the Rock and Roll Hall of Fame in 1987.

### January 6, 2024

Good morning, all 303. Just to let you know that I will not be sending a daily musing any longer. Just one every now and then to you dear friends and family members. Not to worry. My daughter will always know if I "am up and at it," and my grandson lives 20 minutes away. I have begun to work on the manuscript for my 10th book, *Good Morning All: Musings of a Nonagenarian*. I have 2 ½ years of musings. I must eliminate duplications and there are many. It is tedious work, but I will let you know when it is finished.

I will appreciate hearing from you from time to time and I will respond back. Thanks for being my friend.

I will continue to trust in the Lord.

I will continue to PUSH (Pray Until Something Happens).

I will continue to pray for each of you.

**Post Script:**

Very recently, **"Carrie" Edwards Williams**, born in 1866, a Black Appalachian educator, was introduced to me. A mural painted of her is found in Thomas, WV, on the site of the school she taught in the Coketon Coal camp.

I learned about her through the painter, herself, Ari Printz, since my father, which was unbeknownst to me, is considered an Appalachian artist since he was born and reared in the Wyoming Valley of Pennsylvania that is surrounded by Appalachian Mountains that travel over 2,000 miles in the eastern U.S. from Maine to Georgia while passing through 14 states.

Ari Printz was researching my father's unique anthracite coal art when she discovered me. A Curatorial Fellow at the Smithsonian American Art Museum in Washington, D.C., she is interested in placing some of my father's art in the museum. I have several pieces to donate for safe keeping.

I find Carrie Williams interesting to add to my book because in 1898 she fought and won a significant civil rights case, Collins vs Board of Education of Fairfax District, which upheld West Virginia's law requiring equal school terms and established equal pay for teachers regardless of their race. That was half a century before Brown vs Board of Education in 1954 with Thurgood Marshall.

**Edenton Statue**

The last anecdote in my 10th book concerns the statue of a Confederate soldier that stood for decades in the center of the beautiful town of Edenton, N.C. Many readers will remember that my first known Black paternal ancestors were slaves on the Briols plantation in Edenton, and so seeing this statue always sent negative vibes through me when I visited.

You also will recall that on April 22, 2023, the Lawrence/Patience family erected a joint tombstone in the Providence Missionary Baptist Church Burial Grounds in Edenton to honor their two Civil War ancestors, Crowder Patience (103rd PA Infantry) and Thomas Patience/ Lawrence (5th MA Cavalry). Many friends and family members from across the country were present to share our joy.

On August 31, 2025, the statue of the Confederate soldier was removed to be replaced by a 25 M waterfront business for the town. The Confederate soldier is to be relocated for viewing in the Veterans Memorial Park behind the Chowan County Courthouse.

Hopefully, one day, I will get to see the new Edenton waterfront. Perhaps, my Cousin Joseph Lawrence, born and bred in Edenton, will drive me back home to where my first known ancestors, Thomas and Hester Lawrence, are buried. I am "deeply rooted in North Carolina" which is the name of my 9th book in which I describe how the Lawrence and Patience families happily discovered each other via 23andme in 2018 after not knowing each other for 154 years.

**FINIS**

**2025**

Please continue to pray for me until the Lord calls me home one of these days.

**Griot Juanita Bernice Patience Moss**
**Dr. J**

**www.journeyfromthepast.com**

**703-780-7882**

www.ingramcontent.com/pod-product-compliance
Lightning Source LLC
Chambersburg PA
CBHW080434230426
43662CB00015B/2266